The Proud Peoples

The Heritage and Culture
of Spanish-Speaking Peoples
in the United States

Harold J. Alford

The Proud Peoples

The Heritage and Culture
of Spanish-Speaking Peoples
in the United States

DAVID McKAY COMPANY, INC.
New York

THE PROUD PEOPLES

LIBRARY OF CONGRESS CATALOG CARD NUMBER: 73–188265

MANUFACTURED IN THE UNITED STATES OF AMERICA

Contents

PART IV: THE MIGRANTS

PART V: THE MILITANTS

Introduction

The first wheels that rutted the land that would become the United States were Spanish.

The first horses ridden by man across the Great Plains—the first cattle, sheep, goats, pigs, domestic poultry—were Spanish.

Also Spanish were the first oranges, lemons, limes, peaches, pears, apples, and apricots grown in the New World.

The first European plows and gardening tools in North America were Spanish.

In fact, the first European feet to touch the shores of what is now the Southern United States were Spanish. From that moment—probably less than 20 years after Christopher Columbus set sail from Spain on his first voyage—until the discovery of gold in California more than three centuries later, the dominant European influence across the vast territory from ocean to ocean, up into the heartland from the Carolinas through Missouri and Kansas to the Southwest and north along the Coast to Nootka Sound on Vancouver Island, was Hispanic.

Evidence of this influence still abounds. And people of Hispanic heritage—Spanish-Americans, Mexican-Americans, Latin Americans, Puerto Ricans, Cubans, and others—are the second largest minority in the United States today.

With the onslaught of Anglo expansion westward from New England in the late 1800s, Spanish-speaking people became strangers in their own land, shouldered aside, but clinging to their culture in proud but impoverished enclaves that survived in the Southwest and then in the early twentieth century were infused with new numbers from Mexico, Puerto Rico, Cuba, and other Central and South American countries. Often demeaned, discriminated against, they grew steadily in number, becoming always more restless.

Then, in the 1950s and 1960s, a new breed of militant leadership—Chicanos César Chávez and Corky Gonzales—and elected officials—Puerto Rican Herman Badillo and Mexican-American Henry Gonzales—together with angry young men from the *barrios* of Los Angeles, Denver, Chicago, and New York re-kindled the sense of pride in Hispanic-Mexican-Indian heritage. Refugee Cubans building successful new careers, Puerto Ricans and Mexican-Americans surviving the Anglo-oriented school systems and achieving stature in the professions, and educators initiating bilingual programs for children—these all served notice in the 1970s that the proud peoples of Hispanic heritage were a vital and irresistible force. They would demand the role of partner, not second-class citizen, in the shaping of the future.

This book is simply a restatement of the history of these peoples in the territory that is now the United States. Gleaned from many sources, it is designed to dramatize the chronology, the contributions, the difficult status, the desperate needs, and the dynamic potential of the people of Spanish descent who live and work in every part of the land where their forebears first trod.

For assistance in searching out and shaping the narrative, I am indebted to many people: Lee Schryver, whose idea it was; Ann Elmo, who thought of me; and especially my research associate at Kansas State University, Mrs. Helen Gross, whose insatiable curiosity, boundless energy, and intense concern for people, provided the knowledge and resources necessary for the substance of the story.

To Professor George I. Sánchez of the University of Texas I owe a deep debt of gratitude for his counsel on the Mexican-American aspects of the book, including his willingness to read a rough first draft of the manuscript and make corrections when I erred in my interpretation of sources.

To Clarence Senior, now of Rio Grande, Puerto Rico, and to Luis Quero Chiesa, Chairman of New York City's Board of Higher Education, I owe a similar debt for pointing out shortcomings in the interpretation of the Puerto Rican experience.

To Dr. José Rolando Espinosa Carballo, President of the Cuban Teachers in Exile and Professor of the Cuban Culture Program at the University of Miami, I acknowledge my debt for insights concerning the Cuban people, and to Professor George Nossa, of Manhattan Community College, New York City, I offer my thanks for his insights as a U.S. educator born in Colombia, South America.

My wife, Winifred, not only read and commented on the manuscript and provided a congenial writing environment during more than two years of book preparation, but also involved herself directly by developing the index. Mrs. Betty Dey, my Administrative Assistant, organized other aspects of my work and helped with the manuscript in many ways.

At least one hundred others willingly supplied information and assistance. Whatever faults this book may have—including omissions of some of that information and the failure to acknowledge all that went into it—are attributable to the author alone and in no way to his advisors or assistants.

My hope is that *The Proud Peoples* will serve as an accurate, readable, and constructive contribution to the growing but still lamentably limited body of contemporary literature on the highly significant Hispanic heritage of the United States.

Harold J. Alford
Princeton, New Jersey

Part 1

The Explorers

Chapter 1

ℱirst ℱeet

ℬoldly, the four men moved toward a small rise of ground, their moccasined feet making only a whispering sound on the sandy soil and their deerskin-clad bodies blending into the terrain, so that from a distance only their movements made them visible. Behind them—a respectful interval between—their escort was strung out in a long line, meandering among the giant cacti, which dominated the plain.

Then they were where the land fell away, and they could see the campground, and, beyond it, the sea.

For long minutes, none of the four spoke. It was as they had been told it would be: the sea rising to the horizon as no inland river or lake could do; the campground between them and the shore peopled by men and animals at once familiar and alien—familiar because the camp people were like a vision of themselves out of the past; alien because in costume and equipment the camp people were unlike any of the many tribes the four had visited in their long years of wandering.

Suddenly, their leader was on his feet, across the crest and running swiftly down the sandy bank, a cry of exultation ringing in the air as he ran. And behind him, the other three leaped into action, charging down the slope and toward the camp, as if their tiny band could overwhelm the panoplied force before them by the sheer clamor of their charge.

The reaction in the camp was startled but swift. Armored men leaped to silvered saddles; foot soldiers rushed for loaded muskets. But before a shot was fired or a sword unsheathed, the shouts of the advancing men ceased somehow to be just shouts and became words of a liquid language, a language all the men in the camp recognized, a language that stopped the action of the riders and musketeers, who stared, transfixed, at the four approaching runners.

Boldly though they had moved, the four were close to exhaustion when they reached the camp outposts. Heavy dark beards clearly identified them as of a race different from the other natives of the area; yet their lined, weather-browned faces and lean, sinewy bodies were not dissimilar in color to those of the native tribesmen now lining the crest of the ridge overlooking the campground. That is, except for one: one of the gaunt, bearded four, now almost in the center of the camp and surrounded by armored, bearded men, was black.

The year was 1536, less than 50 years since Christopher Columbus had set sail from Spain on his first voyage of discovery.

The place was a point near the mouth of the Rio Yaqui where it emptied into what is now called the Gulf of California.

The event was the completion of the first transcontinental trek by Europeans across the broad reaches of what was later to become the southern face of the United States of America, from the Atlantic Ocean to the Pacific.

The four bearded, savage-appearing individuals who had rushed the camp on the shores of the Gulf of California were the sole remaining survivors of a company of 600 colonists who had sailed from Spain in June 1527, and who—

their numbers already reduced to 400—had landed on the Florida coast at Tampa Bay on Good Friday, 1528. In the ensuing eight years, the four, separately and together, had endured storm, shipwreck, slavery, solitude, and starvation as they ever moved toward the setting sun and eventually came to the shore of the Great South Sea, and to contact with a Spanish foraging party up from San Blas Compostela, principal town of New Galicia, northernmost 16th century settlement in Spanish Mexico.

This union successfuly concluded what is certainly one of the epic journeys of mankind and one of the crucial chapters in the history of the Spanish-speaking people in the area that is now the United States.

Leader of the four who made the fabulous pilgrimage from Florida, across what we now call Louisiana and Texas to the Pecos, up into New Mexico, across the Rio Grande and the Continental Divide and down out of the Sierra Madre to the west coast of Mexico, was Alvaro Núñez Cabeza de Vaca. His companions were Alonso del Castillo Maldonado, Andrés Dorantes, and the black Moor, Esteban, who was Dorantes's slave.

Probably it was Juan Ponce de León, a member of the initial permanent colony in the New World, established at La Española (Hayti) by Columbus on his second voyage in 1493, who led the first Spanish expedition actually to set foot on future United States territory.

In April 1513, Ponce de León landed at the mouth of a large river (now the St. Johns), near the present site of Jacksonville, and took formal possession of what he assumed was an island, naming it "La Florida" because of its lush vegetation and in honor of the Easter season.

Twenty years later, a mutinous pilot, Fortun Jiménez, became the first European to set foot in the Californias. Jiménez and a small crew on an expedition authorized by Hernan Cortéz, conqueror of Mexico, having killed their captain, put ashore at the Bay of La Paz in Baja California, in 1533.

However, until the eight-year trip of Núñez Cabeza de Vaca and his three compatriots, exploration of the land that was to be the United States was marked by just a few footprints in the coastal sands, coagulated by drops of blood shed during brief but brutal chance encounters between natives and Spaniards.

Of course, some of the footprints were deep.

After his first trip to Florida, Ponce de León returned in 1521 with two ships, 200 men, 50 horses, a number of other domestic animals, and farm implements to cultivate the soil. He landed on the west coast, near Charlotte Harbor, just south of present-day Sarasota, where he set about founding what he hoped would be the first permanent Spanish settlement on "La Florida."

However, in the eight years between Ponce de León's first landing in Florida and his first attempted settlement, other explorers had made forays into the low-lying Florida swampland. They had not been searching for Bimini, site of the fabled fountain of youth, which—in addition to the discovery of new lands, the location of a northern passage to India, and, of course, gold and silver and jewels—had been the object of Ponce de León's explorations. They had come ashore for the certain wealth that lay in the capture of natives to use as slaves in the already thriving agriculture and commerce of the West Indies.

As a result, when Ponce de León arrived for the second time, natives did not wait to see if he came in peace. They immediately and furiously attacked and drove the colonists into the sea. An arrow in Ponce de León's side caused his eventual death, when he and the remnants of his party arrived back in Cuba in their one remaining boat.

Almost the same thing happened in 1526 to a company of 500 men and women, 89 horses, and other equipment on six ships—a force larger than that with which Cortés had conquered Mexico—outfitted by Lucas Vásquez de Ayllón, who made the mistake of trying to establish a settlement on the same site that slave hunters in his own employ had plundered in 1521.

Although Vásquez de Ayllón had been instructed by Charles V of Spain not to use the Indians this time as slaves or indentured servants, the natives again did not wait to ask questions. As a consequence, Vásquez de Ayllón quickly retreated south from the original site he had chosen—Cape Fear, an island off the coast of North Carolina—to a site at the mouth of the Pedee River, which he named San Miguel de Guadalupe (now Georgetown, South Carolina). Here an exceptionally cold winter, lack of food, mutiny, and a revolt by black slaves—brought with the group from the West Indies—preceded attacks by the Indians, which resulted in the death of Vásquez de Ayllón and the return of fewer than 150 of the remaining sick and dying settlers to Santo Domingo.

Thus, despite attempts at colonization and the fact that pilots such as Alonso de Piñeda, agent of the Governor of Jamaica, and Esteban Gómez, a deserter from Magellan, had sailed the entire eastern American shoreline from Cape Breton on the tip of Nova Scotia, around the Florida Keys, and up to discover the mouth of the Mississippi River and to map the coast of Texas, all by 1525, no European had survived for long ashore on the mainland north of Mexico. Then, in June 1527, Pánfilo de Narváez sailed from Spain in command of the expedition for which Alvaro Núñez Cabeza de Vaca was the treasurer, and among whose company were Alonso del Castillo Maldonado, Andrés Dorantes, and Esteban, the Moor.

The journey of Núñez Cabeza de Vaca and his three companions, which was to end eight years later on the shores of the Gulf of California, actually started at what is now Tampa Bay on the west coast of Florida, midway up the cape.

De Narváez, already down to 400 of the 600 personnel with whom he had left Spain, and minus two of his ships,

which had been wrecked in a hurricane near Trinidad, was
told by the natives that there was a land to the north named
Appalachen, teeming with gold. Although Núñez Cabeza de
Vaca advised him against it, de Narváez decided to send the
fleet up the coast to find a good harbor while he and the rest
of the company pressed inland to search out Appalachen.
Once out of sight, the ships, with the women of the company, turned back to Cuba. The 300 men who were left
struggled northward across the Withlacooche and the Suwanee Rivers, through dense forests, and eventually
reached Appalachen, which turned out to be 40 clay huts,
near the present site of Tallahassee, Florida.

Their food stocks gone and constantly plagued by attack-
ing bands of roving Indians, they turned south to the sea
again. When the ships failed to appear, they were forced to
kill their horses for food. From the horsehides and their own
weapons, the company managed to construct five boats, and
the remaining 242 men—48 having died from disease, hunger, or Indian arrows—put out from shore, hoping to sail
westward to Mexico, which they thought was nearby.

More than a month later, they reached the mouth of the
Mississippi River. Swept far out to sea by its current, the
boats were separated in a violent November storm, and
Núñez Cabeza de Vaca's frail craft was smashed on the
shore of Galveston Island, off Texas.

Emaciated and ill, battered and exhausted from the
buffeting of wind and waves, Núñez Cabeza de Vaca lay on
the shore and waited for the gray dawn to provide enough
light for him to search out other survivors. The strongest of
the small band, one Lope de Oviedo, climbed a tree and
spotted an Indian village. The Indians helped the suffering
Spaniards to the village, where they warmed and fed them.
The next day they located further survivors, among them
Dorantes, del Castillo and Esteban, and brought them to the
village.

Although the Indians continued hospitable, heavy storms
prevented fishing and food gathering of all kinds, and by

spring, of the 80 expeditioneers who had survived storm and
shipwreck, only 15 remained. When a plague also deci-
mated the ranks of the Indians, many of the tribe felt that
the Spaniards had caused the deaths by magic. The chief
suggested that if they could kill, they could also cure, and,
while he prevented his tribesmen from destroying the Spaniards on the spot, he indicated that if they did not go about
healing the sick Indians, they would not eat.

Núñez Cabeza de Vaca decided that there was no point
in simply waiting around to starve to death, so he copied the
actions of the Indian medicine men by blowing upon the ill
and passing his hands over them. In addition, he said a Pater
Noster, an Ave Maria, and a heartfelt prayer of his own for
God to heal the sick and thereby save him and his small
company. The method, for whatever reason, was efficacious.
Núñez Cabeza de Vaca's patients prospered and the Spanish band survived.

However, food remained scarce, and relationships between Spaniards and Indians delicate, so 12 of the group
who were strong enough to travel bribed one of the Indians
to guide them westward along the mainland coast. The
three who were left, at this point too ill and weak even to
attempt the journey, were Núñez Cabeza de Vaca, de
Oviedo, and a man known as Alaniz, who died shortly afterward.

Gradually, the Indians' stance changed from that of host
to that of captor. While continuing to exploit Núñez Cabeza
de Vaca's prowess as a medicine man, they treated him and
de Oviedo otherwise as slaves, setting them to digging edi-
ble roots from below the surface of the water and among
the cane until the skin was torn from their fingers and the
bloody appendages could no longer clasp the roots and
stems.

Naked and barefoot, they somehow survived; their bodies
adapted to the weather, disease, and hunger; pain, priva-
tion, and fatigue no longer threatened to destroy them. In
addition, Núñez Cabeza de Vaca began to learn the lan-

guage of his captors and the dialects of the tribesmen with
whom he came in contact on food-foraging expeditions. He
learned to make weapons like the Indians' and to hunt. He
became an intermediary between tribes, whose warring prevented them from trading with one another. He became almost an itinerant peddler, carrying from the coast seashells,
which the interior Indians could use as tools, and bartering
with them for skins and flints and coloring materials, which
were not available to the coastal Indians. He was the first
European to see and to describe the buffalo. On his own, he
would have tried to escape and make his way westward to
Mexico, but de Oviedo was reluctant to leave the security of
slavery and Núñez Cabeza de Vaca was reluctant to leave
de Oviedo.

Eventually, however, de Oviedo agreed to attempt an escape, and Núñez Cabeza de Vaca transported him from
island to mainland, since de Oviedo could not swim. Southward, at the mouth of the Colorado River, another tribe
sought to take them captive, and de Oviedo decided he
could not go on. Leaving Núñez Cabeza de Vaca, he turned
back to servitude.

Now alone, Núñez Cabeza de Vaca headed inland, along
the Colorado River, where eventually he stumbled into the
midst of two Indian tribes gathering pecans for their
winter's food store. A huge, cross-eyed Indian seized him
and dragged him off as a slave. Flung down beside another
slave, Núñez Cabeza de Vaca cried out in surprise and joy:
it was Andrés Dorantes. Also captive were Esteban, Dorantes's Moorish slave, and Alonso del Castillo Maldonado. The
four, as far as they knew, were the only survivors of de Narváez's great expedition of 600 soldiers and settlers.

Through the winter, the captives planned their escape for
the next summer, when the tribes would go farther west to
gather prickly pears. But before they could make their escape, the two tribes quarreled, and one group left, taking
del Castillo with them. Unwilling to go on without del Castillo, the other three spent an additional year in slavery, and

then, when the tribes gathered once again on the prickly pear plains, the four were reunited and managed to escape at last.

Westward, they came upon another tribe who had heard of Núñez Cabeza de Vaca's magic as a medicine man. When a sick Indian whom he had treated recovered, the tribe responded with meat and fruit for the Spaniards. With winter coming on again, the four stayed on as welcome guests, and then they moved southward to the great sand belt between the Nueces and the Rio Grande. There they scraped and softened animal hides for the natives, in order to be able to eat the scraps of meat that still adhered to the undersides of the skins. Finally, they bartered for two dogs, which gave them more meat than they had had for many months.

Another spring came, and they crossed the Rio Grande into Mexico, recrossed west of the Pecos, came on the great river again near the mouth of the Conchos, and followed it to the vicinity of what is now El Paso. Everywhere the Indians had heard of Núñez Cabeza de Vaca's healing powers. After he had performed an operation with a conch shell knife, cutting a flint arrowhead from a man's shoulder, the trek became almost a triumphal tour.

Across the arid plains of Chihuahua, over the Continental Divide, and down the Rio Yaqui to the meeting with the first of the Europeans they had seen in eight years, Núñez Cabeza de Vaca and his companions were escorted from tribe to tribe and to the end of their transcontinental journey.

Although the sheer survival of Núñez Cabeza de Vaca and his three friends was notable enough, their saga has importance in the history of Spanish-speaking people in the area that is now the United States for a number of other reasons.

First of all, they made the transition from conquistador to peon and finally to respected personages, a transition that, many generations later, Spanish-speaking peoples are still in the process of trying to make.

Second, they survived because, while retaining their ethnic identity, they adapted to the culture in which they found themselves, and adding strength to strength, created for themselves a role unique and singularly powerful.

Third, in their travels, they were told tales by all the tribesmen, recurring themes being the Seven Cities of Cibola, and the golden land of Quivira; these tales, which Núñez Cabeza de Vaca merely reported, not attesting to their truth but only to the fact that the Indians clearly believed them, were the stories that caused Cortéz to renew his efforts to explore north from Mexico City, and later led Francisco Vásquez de Coronado to make his great foray into the areas of Arizona, New Mexico, Texas, and Kansas.

But the joyous union of the Núñez Cabeza de Vaca party and the Spaniards encamped on the shores of the Gulf of California was soon turned to bitter dissension, for the encampment was that of a slave-hunting expedition, and despite the pleas of Núñez Cabeza de Vaca, the Spaniards set on the Indians who had accompanied him on the last stage of his journey, killing or capturing most of them. Similar events were to characterize the relation of Spaniard and Indian through the troubled years of quest and conquest that followed.

Chapter *2*

Conquistadores

In Mexico City, in the fall of 1536, Antonio de Mendoza, recently arrived first Viceroy of New Spain, listened to the tales of Núñez Cabeza de Vaca and his companions with mounting excitement. "Rest, recuperate, and then return to the North to seek out the Seven Cities of Cibola," he urged.

But Núñez Cabeza de Vaca, del Castillo, and Dorantes were only then beginning to relearn how to endure the wearing of clothing and sleeping in soft beds and were in no way ready to engage again the unknown waste, despite promises of gold and glory. For his part, Esteban, the Moor, was still the slave of Dorantes, and could not blaze his own trail.

Núñez Cabeza de Vaca leisurely returned to Spain to put into writing a narrative of his travels. There, Hernando de Soto—Knight of the Order of Santiago; brother-in-law to Balboa, discoverer of the Pacific; captain to Pizarro in the conquest of Perú; and recently appointed by the Emperor as Governor of Cuba and Adelantado of Florida—urged Núñez Cabeza de Vaca to return with him to seek out the wealth in the lands he had traversed on foot. But Núñez Cabeza de Vaca, by this time, was unwilling to undertake an expedition except as Commander-in-Chief, and so de Soto mustered his own force of 600 and set out for the New World.

In the spring of 1539, three separate expeditions set foot on soil that was later to become the United States.

In the far West, Francisco de Ulloa, operating under orders from Cortéz sailed up the Gulf of California to the mouth of the Colorado River, from where he viewed the mountain peaks of Alta California.

More centrally, Esteban, purchased from Dorantes by the Viceroy Mendoza, moved up the Sonora Valley and crossed into what is now New Mexico as a guide for Fray Marcos de Niza, a Franciscan friar who had served with Pizarro in Perú. Fray Marcos was assigned by the Viceroy and by Francisco Vásquez de Coronado, recently appointed Governor of New Galicia, to search out a route that Vásquez de Coronado, himself, could follow later to claim the Seven Cities of Cibola for the Emperor of Spain.

And in the East, on May 30, 1539, Hernando de Soto landed near Tampa Bay in Florida at almost precisely the same spot as Núñez Cabeza de Vaca and his companions had landed with the de Narváez expedition on Good Friday, 1528.

Thus, the Spanish explorations proceeded simultaneously, thrusting up in the East from the West Indies, which Columbus had discovered, and in the center and West from Mexico, which Cortés had subjugated. But East or West, the goals were the same: gold, glory, and power for self, for Spain, and for the spirit of God.

De Ulloa, the sailor, having viewed the mountain peaks of California, returned to his home base.

Esteban, however, picked up where Núñez Cabeza de Vaca had left off. Now, like a Moorish prince, he who had been a slave moved out in command of some 300 Indians. Some of them were the remnants of those who had followed the wanderers and been taken into captivity but who were now given the opportunity to return to their homeland as interpreters to the expedition. The rest were Mexicans who were seizing this opportunity to share in the search for riches to the north.

Wearing plumes of brilliantly colored feathers, with bells and rattles dangling from his arms and legs, and carrying a "magical" gourd marked by one white and one scarlet feather and the sound of jingling bells, Esteban moved magnificently back up the Yaqui Valley, turned northwest along the San Pedro in what is now Arizona, and then veered northeast to reach the Gila. Adopting Núñez Cabeza de Vaca's role of medicine man and healer, Esteban gathered about him a growing retinue of Indians who told him that he was but 30 days' journey from the turquoise doors of the Seven Cities of Cibola, beyond which were other provinces even richer and more fabulous.

Fray Marcos had asked Esteban to send back a small cross if he found a land that was affluent and populous. Esteban sent back a cross that stood as tall as a man.

Fray Marcos hastened to follow through the rugged country between the Sierra Mogoyon and the Sierra Blanca ranges. In every village where Esteban had paused to prepare the way, Fray Marcos was received as the invulnerable man of God, whose symbol of the cross reflected the special protection of the morning and the evening star.

By mid-May 1539, while Hernando de Soto was still completing his preparations for sailing from Havana to Florida, Fray Marcos had reached the Apache plains, and, in triumph, stood on a high mesa from which, through the clear, rarified air, he could see the first of the fabled cities, the intense, brilliant late afternoon sunlight striking golden beams from the walls that rose high against the face of the Zuni Mountains.

It was a moment of great joy and promise that was shattered by the sudden appearance of a straggle of bloody and beaten survivors of Esteban's entourage; for in the Zuni city of Hawikuh, the pueblo whose walls glinted golden in the spring sunlight, Esteban's triumphal tour had terminated in a sudden shower of arrows.

Fray Marcos gathered a small pile of stones and planted in it a scraggly wooden cross. In the name of the Emperor of Spain, he took possession of the golden city of his vision and of all cities that might lie beyond, calling them the New Kingdom of San Francisco. Then, the myth of his invulnerability pierced by the arrows that had pierced the body of Esteban, he retraced his steps through the mountains and across the plains, no longer surrounded by Indians seeking to touch the hem of his cassock, no longer housed in habitations strewn with garlands. Starving and in constant peril, he made his way back to New Galicia.

Across the continent, at almost the same moment that Zuni arrows were stabbing into the unprotected body of Esteban, other arrows were striking sparks from the armored bodies of the Spanish horsemen, vanguard of de Soto's troops who were landing on the shores of Tampa Bay in Florida. The Spanish horsemen charged the native archers, killing two and sending the others fleeing through wood and swamp, where the pursuing horses floundered and bogged down.

On the dusty floor of an abandoned hut in a deserted village, de Soto found his first evidence of the wealth of the New World: a scattered handful of pearls, crudely burned through for stringing as beads.

And a foraging party brought back one more human remnant of the de Narváez expedition: Juan Ortiz, who had stayed with the boats and returned to Cuba as de Narváez struck out on foot across the waste. Sent back by de Narváez's wife to search for her husband, Ortiz had been immediately captured by Indians, but, like Núñez Cabeza de Vaca, had survived as a slave, as a fugitive, and as a go-between, keeping alive as he was traded from tribe to tribe by learning the languages and adapting to the customs of his captors. Although in his 11 years' wanderings, he had seen no gold nor jewels, Ortiz did report the stories of rich lands just beyond the horizon, which he had heard from the Indians.

De Soto sent back to Cuba for more supplies, established a permanent settlement on Tampa Bay—garrisoned with 50 men and 30 horses—and on August 1, 1539, with Ortiz as guide and interpreter, moved out on his journey to those lands beyond the horizon.

Ortiz guided as best he could, but the heavy armor of men and horses, the weight of forge and hammer to keep the army in repair, and the humid heat in the insect-infested slime and slither of the swamps slowed movement and sapped strength. The natives slipped quietly out of sight before de Soto's men, who were greeted only by deserted villages, devoid of either bread or booty, in what had been inhabited spots in the wetlands.

And then, on the shores of the Suwanee River, the Spaniards came to a cluster of palmetto-thatched clay hovels that was different: around it, shining golden in the September sun, were fields of ripened maize. Under Ortiz' tutelage, the 550 lancers, crossbowmen, and arquebusiers, together with the accompanying priests and Dominican friars, settled down to gathering the corn. Then they either alternately soaked and burned the kernels into a sodden, tasteless mass, or ground them in the hollowed logs that natives had abandoned, sifting the crude flour through their mail shirts to provide the makings for a coarse cornbread and other concoctions.

Beyond the Suwanee, the Indians were not as wary, and de Soto was able to make contact with village chiefs, whom he first wooed with gifts and speeches interpreted by Ortiz and then seized as hostages, which he exchanged for food and slaves.

At a village near what is now Tallahassee, however, the Indians decided to fight rather than forfeit. It was a mistake, because the Spaniards, in armor, on horseback, and with superior weaponry, killed or captured almost all the 400 natives, and, with this new complement of slaves and the fields of grain, beans, and pumpkins ready for the October harvest, settled down for the winter.

During the five months' hiatus, de Soto sent out exploring parties in the surrounding area. As the year changed to 1540, one group discovered Pensacola Bay and, in scouting along the Gulf Coast, came upon a beach where heaps of white bones contrasted sharply with the brilliant blue of the water. Here Hernando de Soto was standing on the spot where de Narváez had ordered the slaughter of his horses for the building of the horsehide boats in which he and so many of his company had perished. To many of de Soto's men, the bleak skulls of the horses seemed symbolic of what would happen to them if they did not turn back; but de Soto, though he still had found no treasure, was determined to press on.

As de Soto returned to Tallahassee to prepare for new excursions, the Viceroy in faraway Mexico City, on January 6, 1540, ordered Francisco Vásquez de Coronado, Governor of New Galicia, to advance without delay to the Seven Cities of Cibola. Riding beside Vásquez de Coronado on this expedition would be Fray Marcos, who, on his return to Mexico City, had told of his vision of the golden walls and, in the telling, had reconvinced himself of the treasure and triumph that lay to the north.

On February 23, 1540, the great expedition gathered at Compostela, where the supply ships commanded by Hernando de Alarcón rode at anchor in the edge of the Pacific, and the Viceroy rode his horse in review of the 300 soldiers, 700 Indians, 1,000 horses, long lines of pack mules, and droves of cattle, sheep, goats, and swine that were to insure this magnificent menage of food and transport whatever terrain and travail they might encounter.

With the sunlight sparkling from the silver saddles, from the polished mail, and from the serene sea, the columns of men and animals and the three supply ships set their parallel courses to the north.

On March 3, 1540, as Vásquez de Coronado's columns

crawled toward Culiacán, their next rendezvous point, still in Mexico, Hernando de Soto broke his winter camp in Florida and also moved out to the north, traversing what is now the state of Georgia and arriving at the end of April on the banks of the Savannah River just below the present site of Augusta, Georgia.

As de Soto's men lined one shore, an armada of canoes filled with Indians put out from the other side and advanced toward the Spaniards.

But this was not an attack. In the lead canoe stood a stately woman clothed in furs and feathers and wearing necklaces of pearls. Ashore, she folded her arms and silently surveyed the Spanish soldiers, in their less than shining armor, and their horses—strange, fearsome animals, indeed.

Stepping forward, de Soto moved deliberately straight toward her. She held her ground, head high, eyes haughty.

A few feet in front of her, he stopped.

At that, she stepped forward, taking one of the strings of pearls from her shoulders as she did so and placing the necklace around de Soto's neck.

Through interpreters, de Soto found that she was the chieftainess of a tribe called the Cufitachiqui.

She, seeing how pleased he was with the pearls, told him that burial mounds on the other side of the river contained enough of the softly iridescent gems to load all of his horses.

Transported across the river in the Cufitachiqui canoes, his men also given gifts of food and furs, de Soto—standing on the soil of what is now South Carolina—could well believe he had finally come to the frontier of the fabulous lands of wealth he had heard about.

From the graves, his company secured 350 pounds of pearls and pearl sculptures of babies and birds. Here the men who had been so ready to give up the expedition when they encountered the bones of de Narváez's horses were now ready to found a permanent settlement.

In Culiacán, at the same time, April 22, 1540, Vásquez de

Coronado was dividing his land forces so that he and Fray
Marcos and a small advance party could lead out ahead of
the slow-moving main body.

To Melchior Díaz, one of the ablest of the scouts, he assigned the task of striking out to the northwest to link up
with Hernando de Alarcón and the supply ships. De Alarcón, in the meantime, had sailed to the head of the Gulf of
California, and, taking to a number of small boats, was sailing up the Colorado River.

In South Carolina, de Soto was not satisfied with one haul
of pearls and furs. Taking the chieftainess of the Cufitachiqui captive, he marched farther north and crossed into what
is now North Carolina. On the march, his captive chieftainess escaped, and with her went a huge cane box full of
the finest of the unbored pearls that de Soto's men had so laboriously dug out of the burial mounds.

De Soto, however, was in search of greater gain. He
pushed on up the slopes of the Smoky Mountains and over
into present-day Tennessee. There, after resting and gorging
on fat, succulent opossum, he decided to turn back from the
beautiful but unpromising hills, to a place called Coosa,
near what is now Birmingham, Alabama, where, he had
been told, lived the greatest prince of all.

Thus, in June 1540, Hernando de Soto reached the northernmost point of his expedition—and, as it turned out, of
any Spanish expedition—into the area that was to become
southeastern United States.

In the West, June was well past the rendezvous time for
Hernando de Alarcón and his supply ships to link up with
land forces of Vásquez de Coronado. So de Alarcón, having
ascended the great Colorado River for a number of miles,
sailed back to the coast in his small boats, raised anchor on
the supply ships, and returned to Compostela.

Melchor Díaz, marching overland to meet de Alarcón,
came to the Colorado River many miles above its mouth.
Following it downstream, he discovered that he had missed
de Alarcón by only a few days. Accidentally wounded by

one of his own men, Díaz, leader of the first land expedition to come in view of Alta California, died in that month of June 1540, and his command returned to Sonora.

In June, too, Vásquez de Coronado came to Cibola.

Pushing ahead with 25 foot soldiers, 80 horses, some Indians and some Negroes, he moved northeast over the divide into the San Pedro Valley, worked eastward along the edge of the Santa Catalina Mountains, swung north across the Gila River, followed up the Zuni watercourse, and came to the high mesa that had been the farthest reach of Fray Marcos.

The excitement and tension as Vásquez de Coronado's company approached the view was almost too much to bear. This time, too, as Fray Marcos pointed out, the sun was high overhead so that they would get a clear view of the city and not have to squint into the slanting rays of the setting sun.

And, indeed, they did get a clear view. But what they saw was not the sight they had been led to expect—not the scene of shining splendor, of fabulous wealth and glory. What they saw was just a crumbling cluster of colorless mud structures huddled forlornly against the towering, threatening Zuni cliffs! Cibola, city of golden dreams, was an empty myth. Reality was Hawikuh, a crowded, cruel city of disillusionment and doubt.

The hot June sun beat down on the silent, stunned group. Doubt, dismay, and disbelief turned to frustration and fury. The impact of the shattering of their hopes swept like an earth shock through the ranks of horsemen and foot soldiers; they turned away from the unpleasant prospect before them to seek out Fray Marcos and to destroy him as their visions of plunder had been destroyed.

Only the quick action of the other monks, who formed a protective screen around him, and the strong command of Vásquez de Coronado, who, sword drawn, spurred his horse between the monks and the menacing troops, ordering the angry soldiers to halt, saved Fray Marcos's life.

"He lied! He's an agent of the devil! He deserves to die!" the soldiers shouted.

"He was lied to!" Vásquez de Coronado told them. "He was wrong, but he meant no harm."

"No harm?" a bearded trooper snorted. "He led us to this God-forsaken spot where we'll probably all die of thirst and starvation, and you say he meant no harm?"

"I say let's go on to Hawikuh," Vásquez de Coronado persuaded. "I say let's get our food and drink from the fortress!"

And so the company moved out, Vásquez de Coronado, himself, in the lead, to attack Hawikuh—Cibola—the pitiful pueblo of an impoverished people.

But it was not to be an easy conquest.

As the advance party approached the walls of the town, the Zuni warriors—who had killed Esteban and his retinue —hurled stones down at the Spaniards, striking Vásquez de Coronado to the ground and resisting mightily the charge of the horsemen, which, nonetheless, finally broke the defenses and brought Hawikuh under Spanish control.

Vásquez de Coronado was dragged to safety, and his small band set about finding food and preparing to defend the town until the main party should arrive. Meager stocks of dwarf corn and shallow cisterns of warm, brackish water constituted the wealth of the Zuni stronghold. Vásquez de Coronado, recovering slowly, dispatched messengers back to Mexico and sent Fray Marcos with them to make certain the disgruntled and discouraged soldiers did not destroy the frightened friar after all.

That summer, Hernando de Soto continued to wax fat on the wild fruit and game of Alabama, and he found that Coosa was, indeed, a wealthy land—in maize and furs and natural resources. But de Soto saw no gold in Coosa, and he moved back south along the Coosa-Alabama River to the Gulf in the vicinity of what is now Mobile. There he was ambushed, and, although his company slaughtered the belligerent natives, he lost all his baggage and supplies, together with the remaining captured pearls and all the religious accouterments of the accompanying priests.

Through the fall of 1540, the wounded, shattered fragments of de Soto's command rested and recuperated while de Soto, himself severely wounded, sought the strength to rekindle their hope and enthusiasm for the search.

Vásquez de Coronado, also slowly recovering from his battle scars during that same long summer and fall, dispatched several small parties to search for some fragment of the fabled riches of the area, and they ranged widely over the territory that is now Arizona and New Mexico.

García López de Cárdenas led the group that first came on the Grand Canyon of the Colorado.

Hernando de Alvarado and Fray Juan de Padilla, with 20 men, ventured in the other direction. After long days of trudging across the wastes, they saw in the distance what appeared to be ivory towers rising to great heights against the precipitous flank of a massive escarpment jutting up at the edge of the plain. Cautiously riding out alone in front of his group of adventurers, de Alvarado was met by an equally cautious delegation from the vertical city, whose walls, on closer inspection, were no more ivory than the walls of Hawikuh had been golden.

"Acoma, Acoma," the leader of the delegation repeated, gesturing toward the amazing clay structure in which living unit piled on living unit from the valley floor to a height of more than 350 feet up the cliff.

Following their peaceful encounter, de Alvarado and his company journeyed on and eventually came to the Rio Grande and, beyond, the upper reaches of the Pecos at the foot of the Santa Fe Mountains.

As winter set in, Vásquez de Coronado had moved his force to the vicinity of Albuquerque, where an Indian whom they called "El Turco" told them stories of a new El Dorado named Quivira, where, he said, fish as big as horses sported themselves, and huge canoes with 20 rowers on a side and with high carved golden prows thrusting up among their white sails, floated on the surface of a river two leagues wide, like water lilies on a pond.

While Vásquez de Coronado was wintered-in by the cold winds blowing from the mountains of New Mexico, de Soto moved to the present state of Mississippi and settled down in the land of the Chicashaws. Then, in April 1541, both de Soto and Vásquez de Coronado—recovered from their battle wounds and losses during their peaceful winter encampments—were on the move again. Vásquez de Coronado headed east into Texas territory, and de Soto headed west to where, during the first week of May 1541, he stood on the bank of the Mississippi River.

While de Soto's men set about felling trees and constructing barges to cross the great river, Vásquez de Coronado hunted buffalo in the huge herds that roamed the vast plains. Castañeda, the expedition's historian, described them by saying, "A thousand horses and five hundred of our cows and more than five thousand rams and ewes, and more than fifteen hundred friendly Indians and servants, in traveling over these plains, would leave no more trace where they had passed than if nothing had been there—nothing—so that it was necessary to make piles of bones and cow dung now and then so that the rear guard could follow the army."

In June, de Soto crossed the Mississippi River into Arkansas; Vásquez de Coronado, deep in Texas, ordered his main body, under Don Tristán de Luna y Arellano, back to Tiguex, in New Mexico, while he took 36 men and headed north, following "El Turco" and his tales of Quivira.

In July, units of de Soto's small remaining band pushed diagonally across Missouri, past the Osage, to the Kansas River; de Soto, himself, moved westward across northern Arkansas to the Neosho River in Oklahoma.

Only a few miles west, in that month of July, Vásquez de Coronado and his small party were making their hot, dusty way still farther north through Oklahoma and on to the vicinity of what is now Great Bend, in central Kansas. "El Turco," still babbling of sparkling sailboats floating on the clear surface of an immeasurable stream, became more and more nervous as the weary miles dragged by.

"Where's this new El Dorado, this treasure trove of beauty and wealth?" Vásquez de Coronado demanded.

"Just beyond the place where earth meets sky," "El Turco" assured him. "Just another sunrise to sunset."

And, sure enough, shortly after the next midday, the golden sheen of domes, low on the horizon, pulsated through the heat waves rising visibly from the flat land.

Rousing his horse from its shambling walk to a dispirited, jarring trot, Vásquez de Coronado, in sight, at last, of his fabled Quivira, urged his small band on toward the glorious conclusion of their journey. Eyes only for the domed roofs shimmering in the distance, neither Vásquez de Coronado nor his men noticed that "El Turco" did not share their haste and excitement. Lagging behind, he soon disappeared in a fold of the terrain.

For "El Turco" had lied!

When the great conquistador and his company came close to the village, they found no river, no boats, no jewels. The golden domes were the brown thatched roofs of squat mud huts in whose entrances huddled lank-haired natives. The only water was in the clay pitchers carried laboriously from a single well, on the shoulders of the native women.

This time it was Vásquez de Coronado, himself, who turned from the evidence of the end of his quest.

" 'El Turco!' " he cried. "Bring me 'El Turco!' "

And the men of his expedition turned, too, with a shout, and scoured the land for "El Turco"--and found him!

"You lied!" Vásquez de Coronado rasped. "You're an agent of the devil! You deserve to die!"

Vásquez de Coronado had him garroted, and then he set up a cross on the spot, with the inscription burned deep in the wood: "Francisco Vásquez de Coronado, General of an expedition, reached this place."

Thus, in the summer of 1541, the expeditions of de Soto and Vásquez de Coronado made their deepest penetration into the heartland of what is now the United States, and, finding no gold or silver or glory, turned back, not knowing that they had come within a few hundred miles of each other in this alien place so many thousands of miles from their own homeland.

De Soto wintered on the south bank of the Arkansas River, not far from the present location of Fort Smith. Vásquez de Coronado wintered near Taos in New Mexico.

Don Hernando de Soto, Governor of Cuba and Adelantado of Florida, died of fever on May 21, 1542. Francisco Vásquez de Coronado had fallen from his horse and been seriously injured toward the end of winter, and in April 1542, had started south to face the Viceroy of Mexico—with no riches, no glory, and only a small portion of the hundreds of men with whom he had set out three years before.

Still, in that same summer of 1542, which saw the end of the hopes of de Soto and Vásquez de Coronado, the Viceroy Mendoza sent out yet another expedition, this one by sea, to search for the Strait of Anian, a reputed passage across the north of the New World, which would provide a short cut from Spain to the Orient.

In command of this expedition was Juan Rodríguez Cabrillo, who sailed up the west coast of the peninsula now known as Lower California, and on September 28, 1542, landed at present-day San Diego, thereby being the first European to touch the west coast of what was to become the United States. On this voyage, Rodríguez died in the islands of the Santa Barbara channel, but Bartolomé Ferrelo sailed as far north as the Rogue River in Oregon—a point reached on March 1, 1543—before returning to the port of origin, Navidad, on the west coast of Mexico.

Ferrelo's return—and the return at the same time, down the east coast of Mexico, of the final stragglers from de Soto's grand force—marked the end of a remarkable series of explorations that took place in a scant four-year period between 1539 and 1543, during which time Spanish expeditions had traversed much of the main body of the southern

United States, from the Carolinas on the east to Oregon on the west, viewing such major geographical features as the Mississippi River and the Grand Canyon.

Searching for visible wealth and instant glory, the Spaniards had been frustrated and destroyed by a land that was later to yield up wealth in minerals, oil, fur, and foodstuffs beyond the wildest dreams of those who would wrest the riches from it. And among the ironies was the fact that the precursors of the great herds of cattle and swine, the vast flocks of sheep and goats, and the tens of thousands of horses that would roam this land and contribute in many ways to its profuse oppulence, were the animals in the droves of Vásquez de Coronado and de Soto; for these were all species not native to North America, and the Spanish imports were the first of their kind to tread the lush prairies, the mountain meadows, and the barren wastes of this strange land.

Chapter 3

La Florida

In the mountains of New Mexico, a long-haired, bearded man crouched beside a campfire, slowly turning a jack rabbit on a spit, an unsheathed cutlass lying beside the pelt it had helped strip from the animal.

In a thicket beside a drying stream in Texas, an emaciated, almost naked skeleton of a man dabbed at a slowly healing, six-inches-long slash in his thigh with a river-dampened rag that had once been part of a velvet pantaloon.

The year was 1542, and Francisco Vásquez de Coronado had just limped back to Mexico City, with the living remnants of his glorious command, to report to the Viceroy Mendoza that the fabulous Seven Cities of Cibola were nonexistent and the golden land of Quivira was just a huddle of mud huts. But not all of Vásquez de Coronado's company could be counted among those who had died or had returned with their commander to Mexico. Some had strayed and survived; some, wounded or captured, had succumbed neither to their battle sores nor to their captors. These abandoned casualties and strays were, in fact, the first actual European settlers north of what is now Mexico.

Of most who remained behind when Vásquez de Coronado and de Soto departed, no record remains. However, three missionaries—two Franciscan friars and a lay brother —chose to maintain their missions to the Indians. Fray Juan de la Cruz continued to work among the Pueblos at Tiguex; the lay brother, Fray Luis Descalona, made his headquarters at Pecos; and Fray Juan de Padilla returned to the Indians who hunted the plains at Quivira and beyond.

Fray Juan de la Cruz and Fray Luis Descalona were very old men, yet neither survived to live out their natural lives, each being killed before the end of the year 1542 by members of the tribes to which they were attempting to minister.

Fray de Padilla, accompanied by a Portuguese soldier, Andrés Docampo, and two young oblates, Lucas and Sebastián Donadoes, of Michoacán, Mexico, took leave of Fray Juan de la Cruz at Tiguex and, with Andrés on the single horse leading the way, trudged across the Texas sands to the Pecos River where Descalona built a little hut outside the pueblo and tended a small herd of sheep as well as his mission flock, the Pueblo Indians.

Then Fray de Padilla and his companions turned their plodding feet toward a corner of what is now Colorado, and later moved on across the flat western plains of Kansas to the edge of the rolling bluestem-grass grazing lands of the buffalo and the blue-veined Flint Hills, source of the Indians' buffalo hunting weapons. There, where Vásquez de Coronado had planted his large cross at the Quivira Indian village that had been the site of the death of "El Turco" and the end of Vásquez de Coronado's quest, Fray de Padilla established his mission.

He was accepted and revered; but, not satisfied, he determined to move on to work with other tribes. Only a day after setting out on his new journey, he was attacked and killed by members of one of the tribes he was seeking.

Andrés Docampo and the two Mexican oblates escaped death, and, in an odyssey rivaling that of Núñez Cabeza de Vaca and his group, survived for nine years before finally coming to the Mexican town of Tampico on the Great Gulf, where they told of the Christian martyrdom of Fray Juan de Padilla, Fray Juan de la Cruz and Fray Luis Descalona.

Thus began the period of almost three centuries during which the Spanish missions in the area that was to become the United States were the most persistent single European influence in the territories they penetrated—but not because they succeeded in their Christian endeavor; rather because they blazed new trails of discovery and punctuated the paths with small settlements that provided a sense of security and stability in a hostile and uncertain land.

Unlike the initial explorations of the conquistadores, the missions did not develop simultaneously across the southern face of what was to be the United States. Almost 50 years were to pass before others essayed to enter the lands traversed by Vásquez de Coronado and Fray de Padilla.

But along the Gulf Coast, even before the return of Fray de Padilla's companions from Quivira, two Dominican friars, Fray Gregorio de Beteta and Fray Juan García, aroused by the tales told by remnants of de Soto's entourage, attempted the trek north along the coast of Texas, Louisiana, and Georgia to Florida.

Failing in the first attempt, the two tried again and again between 1544 and 1547, when they joined forces with another Dominican, Fray Luis Cancer, who conceived that the Church alone, unencumbered by hostility-arousing soldiers and armored, plundering conquistadores, could win the American aborigines and save their souls for eternal redemption.

To secure permission to make an unescorted mission journey, Fray Luis sailed to Spain and was able to enlist the support of the King for a Florida penetration in which no landing would be made in any locality where Spaniards had threatened the Indians during previous years, "For," Fray Gregorio pointed out, "all that land is still running with the blood of the Indians."

In 1549, with a ship and supplies, Fray Luis, accompa-

nied by Fray Gregorio and Fray Juan, together with a third
Dominican, Fray Diego de Tolosa, and a Spanish oblate
named Fuentes, sailed from Veracruz to Havana, where
they acquired a native Floridian convert, Magdalena, as interpreter, and proceeded northward to the west coast of
Florida.

Unfortunately, despite careful planning and good inten-
tions, the Dominicans made their first landfall at Tampa
Bay, where the natives were still violently hostile with mem-
ories of de Soto. Within a few days, the Indians had killed
Fray Diego and the oblate Fuentes and had reconverted
Magdalena to the ways of her ancestors. Within a week,
Fray Luis, himself, was dead, and Fray Gregorio and Fray
Juan had returned in terror to Veracruz.

It was ten years before another serious attempt was made
to colonize along the coasts of Florida or the lands lapped
by the Gulf of Mexico to the west and the Atlantic Ocean to
the north.

In 1559, however, the Viceroy Velasco determined to
send out a large party of colonists to make permanent settlements on the Gulf Coast and at Santa Elena on the South
Carolina coast. To select the site on the Gulf Coast, the
Viceroy dispatched Guido de la Bazares with three vessels
and a party of 60 soldiers and sailors. De la Bazares made
land on the eastern side of the delta of the Mississippi River
and, sailing eastward through the shallows, eventually came
to what is now Mobile Bay.

On his return, de la Bazares reported enthusiastically
about the open forests of pine, the different varieties of oak,
the nut trees, cedars, laurel and chinquapin, palm trees, and
vines, stretching from the very edge of the shore far back
into the interior. "Beneath their spreading boughs," de la
Bazares stated, "colonists will find lush grazing for horses
and cattle. Birds wing through the forests so thickly they
can almost be knocked down with sticks. Other game
abounds, and, in the teeming waters, the natives have built
fish ponds and scoop fish up with their bare hands as they

lean from great canoes. Not only that, but the agriculture of
the Indians produces rich yields of maize, beans, and pumpkins. It is a land of plenty, just waiting to provide easy living
and a rich return for those who have the enterprise and courage to make it their home."

So, on June 11, 1559, a fleet of 13 vessels set sail from the
port of Veracruz, after a parting address from the Viceroy,
who had accompanied them on the march from Mexico
City.

Commander of the party was Don Tristán de Luna y
Arellano, who had been Vásquez de Coronado's second in
command on the search for the Seven Cities of Cibola. Six
of Don Tristán's captains had been with de Soto. In the
party, also, there were Coosa women who had followed the
other Spanish expeditions to Mexico, and who were now
homeward bound to Florida. And many of the soldiers had
been recruited from those who had been wrecked upon the
coast in the frequent treasure ship tragedies that had occurred between the first Spanish incursion into the Caro-
lina-Florida coastal areas and the selection of this particular
expedition—soldiers who had been rescued by the Indians,
made slaves, and who had finally escaped to return to Mexico.

The willingness of so many who had previously endured
the hardships and become familiar with the terrain, the
tribes, and the terrors of this still unsettled land testified to
the strength of the mysterious magnetism that lured expedition after expedition to its swamps and forests.

De Luna y Arellano's force consisted of 1,400 persons, including soldiers, women, children, servants, Negro slaves,
and the returning Coosa Indians, together with 240 horses,
cows, and sheep, and food and clothing stores for a full year.
Six Dominican friars constituted the religious contingent
who, with the entire complement of colonists, had been
charged by King Philip II "not to conquer those nations, nor
to do what has been done in the discovery of the Indies, but
to settle, and by good example, with good works and with

presents, to bring them to a knowledge of Our Holy Faith and Catholic Truth."

More than a month was consumed in the voyage from Veracruz to a landfall off the coast of Florida, and another month was occupied in probing westward to Mobile Bay and then back to Pensacola Bay, where, on August 14, 1559, Don Tristán put ashore to colonize and fortify the port, while he sent a galleon back to Mexico with a report on the initial stages of his expedition.

"There is great promise of a fertile and peopled country in the interior," he wrote, "and with more horses and supplies, we will survive well and will not be compelled to obtain food by force from the natives, whose good will I desire to gain."

In addition to the ship dispatched to Mexico, de Luna y Arellano assigned three vessels to sail around the tip of Florida and up the Atlantic coast to Santa Elena, near what later became Port Royal, South Carolina, the other destination selected for colonization by his party.

Another month had gone by in setting up camp on the shores of Pensacola Bay, in dispatching the ship to Mexico, and in getting the expedition to Santa Elena underway. Then, on the night of September 19, "There came from the north a great tempest which lasted for 24 hours with constantly increasing violence. It shattered to pieces five ships, a galleon, and a barque, with great loss of life. It swept the caravel with its cargo into a grove of trees more than an arquebus-shot from the shore, and besides the loss of the vessel carrying most of the provisions for the army, the waters destroyed the greater part of the materials already landed. Indeed, so fierce and terrible was the storm and such the devastation it wrought, that, unable to account for it by natural means, it was attributed to evil spirits, and some of those on shore at the time averred that they had even seen the devils in the air."

Beyond the horizon the three ships destined for Santa Elena were scattered in the storm. When the winds finally subsided and the waters calmed, the captains decided to abandon the Santa Elena enterprise and sail back to Havana.

His camp a shambles, his ships gone, his stores and supplies ruined, de Luna y Arellano desperately sent exploring and foraging parties out in several directions to seek food, shelter, or friendly natives. All except one returned within a few weeks, exhausted, empty-handed and discouraged, and reported that the country was sterile and uninhabited.

The last, a larger party, pushed further inland, finally coming to the shores of the Alabama River and a deserted Indian village of 80 huts. Searching the surrounding forests, they found a few Indians who, under the patient questioning of two monks, Fray Anunciación and Fray Salazar, revealed that the town had been partly destroyed and its inhabitants driven away by the army of de Soto who had wintered in that neighborhood in 1539–40.

Some maize, beans, and other provisions remained in the deserted habitations; so the leader of the party sent word back to de Luna y Arellano, who, leaving a lieutenant with 50 men and Negro slaves in charge of the port at Pensacola Bay, moved out with the remaining 1,000 of his colonists to the town on the shores of the Alabama River. By spring, all of the salvageable stores and the Indian leftovers were gone, and the members of the colony spent most of their time shuffling through the forest, seeking acorns, which they could grind and soak, first in salt water and then in fresh, to eliminate some of the bitterness. Leaves and twigs became luxuries that added variety to the diet.

De Luna y Arellano, on the verge of despair, sent a company of 50 horses and 150 foot soldiers, together with the Dominican friars, Salazar and Anunciación, even farther inland. Day followed day, but instead of food and friendly natives, they found a deserted world in which the vegetation grew sparser and the soil became thinner. Finally they had no food at all—no leaves, no bark, or twigs from trees.

"Turn back, turn back!" the soldiers pleaded. But there

was no point in their turning back because certain famine awaited them in the main camp, and there was always hope —even if dim—ahead; so the friars led out and the others followed, stumbling step after stumbling step.

When the soles of his boots were worn through, Fray Salazar cut a piece from the upper and gnawed on it as he trudged along. Feeling slightly restored, he built a small fire that night and boiled another piece of his boot, which he shared with the men around him. Suddenly leather straps became the source of life. Boiled leather straps from armor or harness, gnawed leather boot bits and the strips from the lining of shields, all contributed the slight sustenance that meant survival.

Finally, in June, emerging from the uninhabited pine barrens and sand hills of southern Alabama, the company came upon a grove of chestnut and walnut trees. Gorging themselves with the nuts, the bootless, almost naked soldiers gathered as much fruit as they could carry and pushed on in better spirits.

After 50 days of almost continuous marching, they reached an Indian town near a large river called by the natives Olibahali. They were now in the modern Coosa County, Alabama, near Hatchet Creek.

For three months the party recuperated and fattened itself on the abundant supplies which the friendly natives shared unstintingly. Fray Anunciación tried to convert some of the Indians but was unsuccessful. However, in his conversations, he learned that two of de Soto's followers, a soldier and a Negro slave, had remained behind and lived a dozen years with these Indians before they had died.

The tribe with whom the Spaniards were camping was in the process of making war on a neighboring tribe to the west, and the Spanish soldiers assisted in a successful attack, which ended with the enemy tribe promising to pay the hosts of the Spaniards a tribute of chestnuts and other fruit three times a year.

While Fray Salazar and Fray Anunciación remained with

most of the group in northern Alabama, a small party of one officer and 12 soldiers retraced their route to the spot on the Alabama River where de Luna y Arellano had made his settlement.

As they neared the town, they fired two volleys from their arquebuses.

There was no response.

Cautiously, they approached the buildings, but there was no sound or movement. Entering the town, their feeling of foreboding intensified, and, as they came around the corner of a building, it changed to a sudden sense of shock! Above a clutter of broken barrels and empty supply cases, the body of a Spaniard hung from a tree, in whose bark was carved the inscription: "Dig below."

Digging, they uncovered a pot in which was a message that told of the sickness and famine that had plagued the colony until, despairing of any hope for the return of the expedition he had sent to the north, de Luna y Arellano had buried the message by the marked tree and headed south, with his entire colony—except for the thief who had tried to steal more than his share of supplies—to the port on Pensacola Bay.

Following the colony, the small group finally came to Pensacola Bay, where they found misery and mutiny.

During the winter, more than 200 of the colonists at Pensacola had died, and most of the survivors were desperate to return to Mexico or the lush, warm islands of the Caribbean. The arrival of the small party from the north, however, intensified de Luna y Arellano's determination to stay in the land and complete his mission of colonization, and he ordered the company to move north to the area of food and friendly Indians. Almost all of his command and the remaining women and children were exhausted and emaciated from their bitter winter of starvation and disease. They refused to obey de Luna y Arellano, and demanded, instead, that he find some way to return them to their homes. In addition, his camp master, sympathetic to those who wished to abandon the enterprise, persuaded two of the soldiers to carry a message back to the northern expedition, ordering their return to Pensacola Bay.

Assuming the order was from de Luna y Arellano, Fray Anunciación and Fray Salazar broke camp and headed back toward the Gulf. The company arrived at Pensacola Bay just as two supply vessels from the Viceroy arrived from Mexico, in response to the optimistic report de Luna y Arellano had sent to Mexico in 1559, before all his troubles began. By that time, however, winter had set in again. The colony, still split by dissension, did not dare take to sea, and was forced to spend more miserable months at the port.

In the spring, Fray Anunciación succeeded in effecting a reconciliation between de Luna y Arellano and the rebellious majority of his company, all of whom he had condemned to death as traitors. But at the very moment of their rapprochement during Holy Week, 1561, a fleet of four vessels appeared in the bay. The fleet was commanded by Angel de Villafane with orders to supersede Don Tristán de Luna y Arellano, who, in the Viceroy's opinion, had failed to carry out his assigned mission by not occupying Santa Elena on the Atlantic coast. With de Villafane was Fray Gregorio de Beteta, one of the survivors of the tragic mission of Fray Luis Cancer.

While de Luna y Arellano returned to Havana, de Villafane set sail for Santa Elena. However, he did not succeed in founding a settlement there, either, since at every landfall along the way, members of his party deserted, and, though he explored the rivers near Santa Elena and other areas up to Cape Hatteras, he was unable to find any bay that he felt was suitable for anchorage or any land that he felt was suitable for colonization. On July 9, he returned to his starting point, and settlement of Florida was officially abandoned by Philip II on September 23, 1561.

Ironically, the first permanent successful settlement by the Spanish in Florida, and, for that matter, in the whole area that was to become the United States, was founded less

than four years later, on August 28, 1565, when Pedro Menéndez de Avilés (see Appendix for biography) dropped anchor in a harbor, on the Atlantic side of Florida, which he
named after St. Augustine.

King Philip's decision to reconsider the settlement of
Florida was based not on any real belief in the future of the
colony but rather on the necessity of getting a landhold to
protect the routes of the Caribbean treasure ships and also
to stop the incursion from the north of the French, who also
were now colonizing along the Atlantic Coast and, by 1565,
were comfortably ensconced in a settlement near the mouth
of St. John's River, only a short distance north of Menéndez's first settlement at St. Augustine.

Philip, therefore, granted Menéndez three years in which
to colonize Florida. He was to take with him 400 hogs, 400
sheep, a few goats, and 500 slaves. He was to erect forts and
settle two or three villages of a hundred residents, each to
contain a monastery, a church, and "king's house," erected
around a large plaza.

To carry out this ambitious charge, Menéndez sailed from
Cádiz, Spain, on July 28, 1565, in command of a 600-ton
vessel, the *San Pelago,* six sloops of 50 tons each, and four
smaller ships for operating in the shallow waters off Florida.
Aboard were 2,646 persons—soldiers, sailors, four Jesuit
priests, four secular clerics (with licenses of confession), 117
craftsmen, locksmiths, silversmiths, tanners, cloth shearers,
millers, and others. There were supplies of arms and ammunition. Each day of the voyage, the soldiers and the
craftsmen all practiced shooting arquebuses on the decks,
and, under the direction of the clerics, repeated the Christian doctrine litanies asking for "victory over the heretics,"
meaning the French Lutherans, or Huguenots, who were
colonizing along the Carolinas.

On August 28—having lost 30 men and three priests, who
deserted in the West Indies, and minus half his ships, which
had been scattered in Atlantic storms—Menéndez arrived

at the place he called St. Augustine after the saint whose day it was when he made port.

The settlement of St. Augustine started with the fortification of a large Indian house. Around the house, Menéndez dug a trench. Against the house, he made a bulwark of logs and earth.

"Maybe it will be the French," he said, "or maybe the natives, but whoever attacks St. Augustine will lose more than they gain." And he immediately set about making more fortifications and extending his outposts to the north and west, making forays against the French before they attacked him, one encounter being so bloody that the site is still known as Las Matanzas (The Massacre).

Within two years, Menéndez had made himself the terror of the coast. He had also established a line of posts between Tampa Bay and Santa Elena in the Carolinas and had even attempted colonization in Virginia. Exploring a large part of the interior of South Carolina and North Carolina, he had blazed trails that were followed and then extended by missionaries who spread out through Florida, Georgia, and the Carolinas, three Jesuits starting their unsuccessful work in the area in 1566, one being killed immediately and the others retreating to the safety of the West Indies for contemplation and recuperation.

In 1568, Menéndez sent out 14 more Jesuits, who found the natives singularly disinterested in the Latin litanies, in the sacraments of baptism, marriage, and Holy Communion, and in attending Mass, expressing their disinterest by eventually killing all of the Jesuits, whose order, as a result, had abandoned the territory by 1573. They were followed by nine Franciscans, who exhibited more patience, more ingenuity, and more longevity than their predecessors. By 1615, the Franciscans had erected more than 20 mission stations, which, like Menéndez's settlements at St. Augustine, Santa Elena, and San Mateo (Fort Caroline), survived and formed the first permanent examples of the Church's work in the area of the United States, an era that was to flourish in Florida first and then to be paralleled by separate mission eras farther westward during the next century.

Although members of Menéndez's initial party, like the members of the expeditions that had preceded them across the whole face of the southern United States, was made up largely of individuals who had not come there to plow and plant, but to find riches, there were also those who realized that in order to survive, they would have to plant roots—not only of foodstuffs, but, indeed, of their very lives—into the soil, and find sustenance from that which was produced by the sweat of their brows and the calluses of their hands.

Menéndez died in Spain in 1574, while he was assisting in the building of a great armada with which Phillip hoped to destroy England as a seapower. It was not until fourteen years after his death, however, that the Great Armada sailed, and, in the English Channel suffered a defeat that contributed to Spain's—not England's—demise as a seapower.

But in Florida, Menéndez's original party was followed by more than a thousand new settlers, who brought more livestock, more artisans, and more dedicated and determined colonists, establishing the Spanish language and Spanish institutions as a permanent part of the physical and social setting of the area.

Part 2

 *The Settlers*

Chapter *4*

 *Nuevo Méjico*

*T*oward the end of the 16th century, as the Spanish farmers began to till the moist tidewater-level soil along the coasts of Florida and the Carolinas; as tradesmen set up shop in scattered settlements serving the farmers with processed foodstuffs and yard goods; as blacksmith and woodworker struck sparks from forge and piled the floor with shavings from logs being worked into boards to manufacture the plow, the wheel, and the harness necessary to the stockman and farmer; and as Franciscan monks pushed inland from the sea to the heartlands of Georgia, seeking to bring word of the one true religion to the agrarian natives of the red-soiled hill country; other Franciscan fathers, up from Mexico, were leading new incursions into the arid Pueblo country of what was to be Arizona, New Mexico, and Texas, after a 40-year hiatus in explorations in that area following Vásquez de Coronado's dejected return to Mexico.

First feet along a new route into what was to become the Great Southwest of the United States were those of Fray Agustín Rodríguez, Fray Francisco López, and Fray Juan de Santa María, who, in 1581, followed the Rio Conchos to its

43

convergence with the Rio Grande and then turned north-west to follow that great river for hundreds of miles deep into the new territory. Because of a Spanish royal decree in 1573, which prohibited military expeditions among the Indians, the Rodríguez party was ostensibly missionary in purpose. However, nine mounted soldier-traders under the command of Francisco Chamuscado, equipped with coats of mail for both horse and rider, were an integral part of the expedition, which also included 19 Indian servants; 90 horses; 600 cattle, sheep, goats, and hogs; together with stocks of merchandise for barter with the natives.

The missionaries and their retinue went far into the territory, along the Santa Fe River, and up to Taos, near what is now the Colorado line, crossing over to the buffalo plains east of the Pecos River and returning beyond the Rio Grande to the Indian towns of Acoma and Zuni, pausing on the way to initiate the carving of names on El Moro Cliff, now known as Inscription Rock.

Three soldiers who had been part of the Vásquez de Coronado party 40 years before were still alive and assimilated into the Zuni culture, but memories of the Spanish military power of Vásquez de Coronado's troops were still alive also, and when Rodríguez and López decided to settle at a spot on the Rio Grande above the present site of Albuquerque, it was, unfortunately, at the same spot where Luis Descalona had chosen to settle when Vásquez de Coronado returned to Mexico. As with Descalona, Rodríguez and López were killed by the Indians, once their soldier escort left them. Fray Juan had been killed earlier, when he set out alone to take messages back south of the Rio Grande.

Two servants, who had fled the mission on the death of Fray López, eventually made their way to Mexico, and a rescue party was organized immediately under the leadership of a merchant-trader, Antonio de Espejo. De Espejo's small party hardly paused on discovering that the mission had, indeed, been totally wiped out. Essentially a miner and businessman, de Espejo left the Franciscan monk, Bernal-

dino Beltrán, to work on the saving of souls, and, with just
four companions, struck out to the west and eventually became the first Spaniard actually to discover the rich ores of
which the Indians had for so long been telling the conquistadores.

Near what is now Prescott, Arizona, de Espejo wrote, "I
found the mines, and with my own hands I extracted ore
from them." The ore, of course, was silver, and the area
mountainous and difficult of access. Despite the fact that de
Espejo asserted, "Where the mines are located, the country
is good, having rivers, marshes and forests; on the banks of
the river are Castilian grapes, walnuts, flax, blackberries,
maguey plants, and prickly pears," the rigors of mining and
the difficulty of transport rendered ineffectual the attempts
to exploit de Espejo's discoveries when he told of them on
his return to Mexico in 1583.

Political wrangling immediately ensued, with de Espejo
seeking to secure a royal commission to develop the territory. While royal favor shifted from one petition to another,
Gaspar Castaño de Sosa became impatient and organized an
expedition of 170 persons, including women and children,
who set off without authority with a wagon train of supplies
to colonize in New Mexico. Arrested after about a year for
his unauthorized entry, de Sosa was returned to Mexico City
in chains.

Other unauthorized expeditions followed, all ending in
disaster.

Finally, in 1595, Don Juan de Oñate (See Appendix for
biography), a wealthy mine owner of Zacatecas, whose father had been with Vásquez de Coronado's company and
whose wife was a descendent of Montezuma, secured a government contract on his offer to equip an expedition at his
own expense. On April 30, 1598, de Oñate took formal possession of New Mexico at a point on the Rio Grande below
El Paso del Norte.

De Oñate's expedition consisted of about 400 soldiers,
300 colonists, many priests, a baggage supply train of 83

wagons, and 7,000 head of stock. Its commissioning in 1595 coincided with the commissioning by the Crown of Sebastián Vizcaíno, to colonize Lower California as a defensive outpost to protect the Philippine trade, initiated as early as 1565. The two expeditions—de Oñate's and Vizcaíno's—were regarded as part of the same enterprise to develop the New World as a permanent Spanish colony after the loss of the seas to England in the defeat of the Spanish Armada.

While Vizcaíno was initially unsuccessful, the people of de Oñate's expedition had clearly come to stay. One of his officers, Captain Luis de Velasco, included among his baggage suits of blue Italian velvet, rose satin, purple Castilian cloth, chestnut-colored cloth, and Chinese flowered silk. He had doublets of Castilian dressed kid and royal lion skin, gold-trimmed. He had green silk stockings with points of gold lace, linen shirts, linen breeches, 40 pairs of boots, shoes, and gaiters, hats trimmed with silver cord and colored feathers; he had four saddles of blue flowered Spanish cloth bound with Cordovan leather, three suits of personal armor and three suits of armor for his horse, plus swords, daggers, and a silken banner; he also carried a bedstead with two mattresses and in his retinue had servants and 30 horses and mules.

De Oñate's formal possession of New Mexico, on April 1, 1598, began with artillery salutes, Mass, a sermon, a presentation of a comedy written by one of his captains, and was followed by a two-day celebration.

On May 4, 1598, de Oñate set out with 60 men "to pacify the land." On July 11, he established the first Spanish capital in New Mexico, at the Tewa village of Yugeuingge, on the west bank of the Rio Grande opposite the present site of San Juan Pueblo in New Mexico. Making peace with the natives of the area, de Oñate began work on the first Spanish irrigation ditch in the New World on August 11, 1598. And then, on September 8, 1598, exactly 33 years after the founding of St. Augustine, Florida, by Menéndez, the second Spanish city in the future territory of the United States was founded by de Oñate in New Mexico. He called it San Francisco de los Españoles.

At a solemn ceremony held in a native *kiva*, or sacred pagan council chamber, the Christian chapel, built in just two weeks, was consecrated. Then there followed a week of festivities and sports, participated in by both Spaniards and Indians, and including the romantic spectacle of a mock battle between Spaniards and Moors, in which the Spaniards, aided by St. James, were victorious.

Although de Oñate originally called the city San Francisco de los Españoles, it was known, from 1598 to 1601, as San Juan Bautista de los Caballeros. Later abandoned because of flooding, it was succeeded by a new capital on the east bank, called San Gabriel del Yunque which, in turn, was supplanted by Santa Fe, a few miles distant, but San Juan Bautista, first settlement in New Mexico, like St. Augustine in Florida, marked the permanent involvement of the Spanish in the territory.

Out on the coast, on the other hand, Sebastián Vizcaíno continued to have his troubles. On May 5, 1602, he sailed from Acapulco and up the outer reach of Lower California. Finally, in November, he dropped anchor in San Miguel Bay, naming the site San Diego, an appellation that remains today. Sailing north, he discovered Monterey Bay on December 16, and by January 12, he had passed—without finding it—the entrance to the Golden Gate, and stood off Cape Mendocino, the northern limit of his exploration, after which he returned past Monterey, and on March 21, 1603, arrived at Acapulco.

Although the Count of Monterey, for whom Vizcaíno had named the most attractive bay he had discovered, immediately planned to occupy the port and make a permanent settlement there, the Count was replaced by a new Viceroy who had no interest in the project, and Vizcaíno, a commoner—although one who had initially become prosperous through his merchant trade—found himself, as had many aristocrats, ruined in health and fortune, and his discoveries remained unexploited for 160 years.

While Vizcaíno was sailing up the Pacific Coast and back —his explorations so quickly fogged in like the Golden Gate, itself, which he had missed—de Oñate had decided to seek out the golden Quivira, which Vásquez de Coronado surely had also missed.

On June 23, 1601, he struck out across the Great Plains with 80 men. Following down the Canadian River, he turned northeast, traversed what is now Oklahoma, and entered the land of the Quivira Indians near the present site of Wichita, Kansas. His only discovery was that Vásquez de Coronado had not been wrong. There was no golden Quivira.

When de Oñate and his company approached San Gabriel once again on November 24, he found the place virtually deserted. No rain had fallen during his five months' absence, and settlers, soldiers, and all but one of the missionaries had scattered in many directions, seeking some way to avoid total starvation.

De Oñate confiscated all the supplies he could find in pueblos around the area and set out at once to force the settlers and soldiers to return. A small part of them did return, together with seven new missionaries, and de Oñate immediately engaged them in capturing buffalo, which he planned to domesticate. While the settlers never did succeed in developing tractable buffalo herds, in the process they did secure meat and thousands of pounds of tallow to supplement the diet from the fields that they now were able to cultivate and harvest through the use of irrigation.

Reestablishing the settlement, initiating stock raising, and insuring adequate agriculture through irrigation, occupied all of Juan de Oñate's time and energy for the next three years. But then, on October 7, 1604, he took 30 soldiers— most of them inexperienced recruits—and two priests, and set out to seek the great South Sea.

Crossing plains ("more inhabited by hares and rabbits than by Indians"), rivers ("with little water but many great fish"), and mountains ("of pine forests which were eight leagues across"), they found deposits of silver, natives weaving clothing from cord made of vines, and crops of maize, beans, and gourds supplemented by plentiful deer and mountain sheep.

Greeted and aided by friendly tribes of Indians, they came to the Gulf of California at the mouth of the Colorado River on January 25, 1605, and spent four days searching for pearls—which they did not find—and in deciding that Lower California must surely be an island.

On the return journey, they found food scarce and the natives even scarcer; so, driven by hunger and the hope that just over the next mountain range or across the next river they would find game or natives willing to share their stock of maize or beans, the company pushed on desperately, finally eating their horses in order to stay alive. They covered in three months the territory they had leisurely passed through in four months on the way out. But despite their hardships—and the initial inexperience of most of de Oñate's men—the company arrived back at San Gabriel on April 25, 1605, "all sound and well, and not a man missing."

In just seven years—between February 7, 1598, when he left Santa Barbara at the beginning of his northern trek, until that April 25, 1605, when he returned from his exploration from the Gulf of California—de Oñate had succeeded in founding the first permanent settlement in the territory that was to become the southwestern United States; he had organized the first mission system among the New Mexico Indians; he had explored the territory east to Kansas and Texas and west through New Mexico and Arizona to California as extensively as all of his predecessors combined; and he had verified both the lack of ready wealth and the store of potential riches that characterized the area.

Yet while he was on his last expedition, blazing the trail to the Gulf of California, personal enemies within his own entourage prepared a devastating secret report against him, his conduct, and the whole exploration of the Southwest, criticizing his frequent harsh treatment of the Indians, as well as his alleged mismanagement of the settlement.

The report was dispatched on March 31, 1605, a scant month before de Oñate himself had returned from the westward expedition. Emaciated and exhausted from his own physical efforts, his great fortune dissipated by the huge expenditures of his seven-year odyssey, de Oñate was served, on June 7, 1606, with an order from King Philip III of Spain that no more explorations be made in New Mexico, that de Oñate go back to Mexico City to be tried for maladministration and crimes against the natives and members of his expedition, and that another governor be appointed in his place. Penniless and discredited, de Oñate resigned on August 24, 1607.

Just a few days more than three months before—on May 14, 1607—a small expedition from England had sailed up the James River on the coast of what was to be Virginia, and on a small island had staked out a settlement, which they called Jamestown, the first permanent English settlement in the New World.

And as the English were taking their first tentative steps toward colonization of the land that was to become the United States, King Philip III of Spain was seriously considering abandoning St. Augustine, Florida, as well as limiting exploration in the area north of his substantial Mexican outposts.

Already the Spanish had withdrawn from Santa Elena; and, in the face of intense native revolts in 1597, St. Augustine had pulled in its outposts and become a tense military garrison, supporting and supported by the troops manning Fort San Marcos, located on the northern edge of the town.

St. Augustine had about 120 shops and houses, together with a church, convent, a six-bed hospital, and a fish market. There were a few administrators, friars, Indians, and Negroes, but most of the residents were soldiers, their wives and children, and shopkeepers, deriving their livelihood from the needs of the military.

St. Augustine, itself, was a sandy bank, surrounded and cut through the fresh- and saltwater marshes, lagoons, and dunelike stretches that couldn't be used for agriculture. Frequent storms and floods harrassed the people and threatened to engulf the whole city. Even San Sebastián, which was only two musket shots away from St. Augustine, had land that was better for farming and less subject to floods than the original Florida settlement.

Nonetheless, Franciscan friars, working ever deeper into the interior of Georgia, and settlers who followed them, brought back glowing tales of the lush productivity of the uplands.

Governor Canzo, one of Menéndez's successors, was determined not to abandon St. Augustine but rather to make the North American mainland of Florida and Georgia a vital part of the Spanish empire instead of a backward, unpopular military and mission outpost with little of the glitter and pomp of the busier imperial centers. To King Philip he extolled the rich hinterland of Georgia. "It abounds," he said, "in minerals, jewels, and fertile soils to support a growing population and sustain St. Augustine. In addition, many native souls are ready for harvest by the Church, and New Mexico is only two hundred leagues distant from Georgia and can be easily reached."

With the center of Georgia at an estimated distance of only 40 leagues from St. Augustine, and New Mexico alleged to be only 200 leagues more, King Philip and the Council of the Indies finally were brought to believe there would be great advantages in maintaining Florida both as an outpost and as an entry into what must surely be a bonanza back-country, despite all of the evidence to the contrary that had been gathered over the years of conquest and exploration.

Stories of vast crops of corn, beans, large green grapes, white plums, cherries, melons, venison, turkeys and innumerable other fowl, together with huge sturgeon and other fish, gave visions of a lush road to fortune.

Samples of the rich brown earth—without statements of how sticky and deep it became when wet, grabbing at feet and wheels and plows—were clear evidence that the prospect was indeed bright.

The whole concept of following a trail of gold and silver mines from Georgia to New Mexico was irresistible.

St. Augustine was not abandoned.

More friars and settlers were dispatched to the territory.

And though none of the grandiose schemes for westward expansion were actually ever undertaken, the Franciscan missions in Florida and Georgia continued to increase, and Spanish customs were implanted in both natives and settlers.

In the west, Pedro de Peralta arrived in San Gabriel early in 1609 as the new Governor of the territory, with instructions to find a better site and move the capital and the colony.

His instructions were explicit. The dimensions of the plaza, the location of the church and public buildings, the number and direction of the streets, the distance between the defense wall and the nearest houses—all were set down carefully. Also detailed were the number, rank, and powers of the governing officials, and a specific minimum number of married men allowed to form the new colony.

The community thus founded by de Peralta was Santa Fe.

The founding of Santa Fe was the final act in the first stage of the Spanish colonization of what was later to become the south central United States.

Chapter 5

Churros and
Churches

*P*edro de Peralta, *Governor of New Mexico, a territory that,* in theory, extended from the Mississippi River to the Pacific Ocean and from Mexico northward indefinitely, had, as his constituency at the time of the founding of Santa Fe in 1610, only 48 Spaniards remaining from the companies of de Espejo, Rodríguez and de Oñate. Nonetheless, 48 there were, and with them were a few horses, a few sheep, a few cattle, a few goats, and a few acres of land turned by the plow and sowed with wheat and corn brought up from Mexico and watered by the irrigation system de Oñate had instituted in the first year of his stay.

More than any other single person, Don Juan de Oñate— that once-rich silver mine owner of Zacatecas, but by 1610 a penniless, discredited, physically beaten individual—was responsible for providing permanent Spanish influence in the territories that he personally traversed.

For it was the seed grains of de Oñate's expedition that sent tendrils of green across the arid New Mexico and Texas landscape, and it was his livestock that dropped offspring along El Camino Real, or The Royal Road, and their offspring, in turn, begat more, in constantly growing herds that spread across the face of the great land.

But one of the important Spanish livestock contributions almost did not make it.

In January 1598, when de Oñate's expedition was moving north from Mexico, the Conchos River, which they had to cross, was a raging torrent, which the mounted soldiers successfully navigated astride their strong swimming horses, and which the cattle—plunging, bellowing, but surging straight ahead—also breasted.

But the first of the 4,000 ugly, bare-bellied, long-legged Churro sheep, which de Oñate had as his flock, were dragged down by their water-soaked fleeces and drowned.

"We can't swim the sheep," de Oñate said. "We must build a bridge."

"But how?"

"Remove the wheels from the wagons," de Oñate said.

While some of the men started to carry out that part of de Oñate's orders, he directed other squads of men to start chopping down the scrub trees growing along the waterway.

De Oñate had the wheels rolled to the river. Secured by ropes tied to trees on the bank, they were then floated out into the torrent, with men on horseback holding them in position while others tugged the line across to the far shore, where the ropes were also secured to trees.

What de Oñate had devised from the wooden wheels of the supply carts were the pontoons of a floating bridge.

The men who had chopped down the scrub trees now stripped the branches and laid the trunks on top of the wheels afloat in the stream. They then covered the logs with the brush they had removed from the trunks. And, finally, a layer of earth on top of the brush and logs provided the finished roadway across which the Churros plodded, docilely and dry shod.

When the last of the sheep were across, de Oñate had his men push the logs and the brush and the earth off the floating wheels and into the swollen Conchos River. Pulling the wheels to dry land on the northern bank of the Conchos, they replaced them on the wagons, and, by twilight, the entire caravan was quietly in camp prepared to push on in the morning.

In many ways, that crossing the Conchos was one of the most significantly dramatic events in the Spanish occupation of the Southwest.

As Winifred Kupper put it in the *Golden Hoof*, "The Churro wore no clashing armor; he carried no flag. But he was to build in these lands an empire that would outlast any disposition of lands under whatsoever flag. Little could the conquistadores have guessed that, while they might claim for Spain the lands they had traversed, and hold them with travail and bloodshed and tragic setbacks, the real conqueror of the Southwest walked placidly along with them, the lowliest in their train."

The Churro hardly looked to be a conqueror. Even in Spain, he was not highly regarded, because he was small, his wool was thin and long and coarse, his horns branched oddly, and he was altogether a miserable looking creature. But the Churro was hardy and his meat was good, and that was why he was loaded into the precious space aboard ships sailing to the New World. And that was why de Oñate, a successful desert farmer, brought 4,000 of the Churro sheep with him when he moved north across the Conchos.

And from that moment, the land, so similar to Spain in topography and climate, belonged to the Churro.

The high, dry, broad mesas, rimmed by even higher mountains and laced by grassy valleys, were ideally suited to the Churro and the Churro to the land.

The Pueblo Indians had long used wild cotton, rabbit fur, and even the long hair of the buffalo for spinning and weaving, but given sheep and taught the use of wool, they forsook use of most other materials, and the Churro became the partner of the Indian.

De Oñate also had in his van more than a thousand head of cattle.

Like the Churros, de Oñate's cattle were not aristocrats. They were black, mean, fighting cattle from Andalusia. Lean, Moorish stock with wide horns, which curved menacingly forward above suspicious, baleful eyes, they were faster, more belligerent, possessed of keener reflexes, and wilder in every way than their native cousins, the lumbering buffalo.

Like the Churros, the Spanish cattle found on the treeless prairie a land that was their own. Their meat was not prized, but their hides and tallow were.

And then there was the horse. Of all the many transactions between the Spanish and the Indians—from mutual massacres to enslavement, intermarriage, and friendly commerce—the most significant and perhaps the most tragic was the introduction of that glorious animal of transport, the horse, by the Spanish into the territory of the foot-migrant Plains Indian.

Horses had already proved themselves capable of survival in the New World north of Mexico, from the swamps of Florida to the high mountains of Colorado and across the arid wastes of Arizona, New Mexico, Texas, Oklahoma, and Kansas, as they stolidly supported the soldiers in Spanish armor and trudged the weary miles, sometimes tugging heavily loaded, wooden-wheeled carts behind them.

But most of the conquistadores' mounts were stallions. They towered over and terrorized the natives and were largely responsible for the total dominance of a few Europeans over hordes of Indians wherever the Europeans sought to dominate, but they did not multiply.

De Oñate introduced 150 mares into the territory, along with 150 colts and 25 additional stallions.

De Oñate's objective was to settle permanently in the territory, to establish stock farms and ranches, and to seek metals and other natural resources for commerce. His stock was breeding stock, and the size of the herd increased. And since the Spanish *rancho* operations were still based on a concept initiated when Columbus' first party had set foot on New World soil—that of utilizing the native population as a work force, with even the lowliest Spanish peon as a privileged overseer—the Indians around the settlements of de Oñate's company were pressed into service, tilling the soil, working the mines, tending the sheep, and caring for the horses; but none of the stock, nor the ores, nor the crops, belonged to the Indians.

The idea of using harness in one form or another to increase the capability of moving heavy loads was not new to the natives; women and dogs had long been harnessed as beasts of burden to transport weighty loads. Now de Oñate and his followers introduced the far stronger and far swifter draft horse.

And the strength of the horse as a puller of loads was something the migrant Indian began to covet. The natives learned to cut off the excess growth of hoof, and nail on an inch of iron to give the animal better footing and increase its capability of movement over uneven ground and rocks. Then the Spanish taught the Indians to ride—bareback, because saddles were scarce and the propagation of horses far outgrew the ability of the saddlemakers to keep up.

The soft back of the animal as a seat, the thrill of its muscles gathering underneath for speed, the responsiveness of its gait and direction to the pressure of knees or the touch of hand, and the rush of the air against his own face as the animal raced across the land was more than the Indian could resist: the horse must be his, not merely to borrow and use while he worked as a servant to the Spanish, but to own as he ranged free after the buffalo and after new hunting grounds beyond the horizon.

And so, at night, he crept into de Oñate's corrals and picked the swiftest of the steeds and rode them into the darkness.

And the Spanish set guards, and occasionally caught the horse thieves, but more often than not, failed to catch them.

And if the horse thieves were caught, they were hanged, as were the first two caught by de Oñate in 1598.

But fear of death could not match the lust for possession. And so the Indian horse herds grew, while the Spanish men dwindled from the original 400 of de Oñate's company to the 48 who remained at the founding of Santa Fe.

With de Oñate's removal from the scene, the drive to colonize was also removed. Those who followed de Oñate to the governorship of the territory were more interested in preserving themselves within the walls of Santa Fe and extracting their livelihood from a tax on the production of the Indians than they were in expanding the settlements.

But a new force—the same one that had shouldered the soldiers and planters into the interior of Georgia from the sandy soil of the Florida beach on which St. Augustine stood—began to work in the territory of New Mexico.

That force was the Franciscan friar, who, in the years that followed, successfully settled along the trails first explored by his missionary brothers in the entourage of Vásquez de Coronado.

In Georgia and Florida, the missionaries had launched out on their journeys of conversion with minimal military and civilian support. Their missions were mostly rude log shelters, and their only companions and protection were the Indians they converted.

By 1615, missionization in the Georgia territory had reached its high-water mark, with 20 missions in the principal Indian villages. The Indians, accustomed to living from the natural fruits of the soil, supplemented by plots of maize, were not envious of the Spanish horses, and although the animals were used by the soldiers and some of the farmers, only an occasional chief had one of his own, usually a gift for some depredation he had not undertaken.

Cattle, too, were confined to the European farms, for the friars were afraid that the cattle would trample the Indian gardens and would cause more trouble than they were worth.

Although conversions were announced by the thousands, the mission work in the East was marked by constant small uprisings of both converted and unconverted natives, and the padres held their ground only through courage, dedication, and not a little bending of the laws of the Church to meet realities of pagan existence.

In the territory of the great Southwest, conversions also took place by the thousands, but the establishment and conduct of the missions was much more formal and complex than along the Eastern seaboard.

From their homeland, the Spanish friars brought a knowledge of great Church architecture, a smattering of European building methods, and a vision of the glories of the Renaissance.

On the plains of the great Southwest, they found a native architecture, based on the effective architectural use of the few raw materials at hand.

Here, already, were the four- and five-story apartment houses. They were rectangular, terraced, massive, with flat roofs characterized by protruding *vigas*, or round, weight-carrying logs, spread over with smaller poles at right angles, layered with long grasses, rushes, small branches or split sticks, and a thick layer of mud. The walls themselves were formed of stone with adobe mortar, or with adobe alone, cast or puddled into place in stratified layers, the interior and exterior surfaces then coated with white gypsum or light-colored clay, frequently decorated with contrasting colors.

Here, also, were the great circular *kivas*, the ceremonial chambers, their cribbed roofs supported by pillars, supplying a meeting place for large groups.

Abandoning the cathedral concept of vaulted ceilings and great arches, the priests, nonetheless, clung to the two basic plans of Christian churches: the coffin-shaped plan, narrowing at the sanctuary; or the cruciform plan, with chambers running off at right angles, and the altar placed at the joining of the cross.

To provide for more rapid construction, the friars devised a method of pre-casting adobe bricks by mixing the mud with straw in standard forms and allowing the sun to dry them into rocklike consistency. To sustain the weight of larger logs needed to provide a greater span for larger congregations, the builders thickened the walls with several tiers of adobe brick. To provide the stability of square, rather than round *vigas,* or beams, they taught the natives the use of the iron adze, which they could also use to split the logs for door frames and windows and for carving on the roof beams, the columns, and the altar.

From the first, the key to Spanish productivity was use of native labor. The horse, the gun, and the wheeled vehicle provided physical power to dominate, and there was absolute authority in the faith that Christianity was the one true religion, which it was the Europeans' duty and destiny to bring all mankind.

Thus the handful of Spanish and their *mestizo*—or half-Spanish, half-Indian—followers from Mexico, not only went to work to convert the natives in large numbers but also to press them into service as laborers and extract from them direct tribute in goods and food.

It was the Indians who dug the irrigation canals, who fashioned the wooden stick plows on the Egyptian model from the sparse growth at hand, and who followed those plows, harnessed to the Spanish draft animals, gouging productive fields from the fertile but thin soil of the valley of the Rio Grande.

It was the Indians who formed bricks from adobe and straw, who raised the bricks into place and carried and hacked the great beams that surmounted them, and who prayed and did penance in the mission churches they thus constructed.

But at the same time, the friars took as their responsibility the education of the natives in the language and the customs and the art of the European culture as well as in the manual skills of construction and crop tending and animal husbandry.

Fray Cristóbal de Quiñones, a member of de Oñate's party, brought with him what was the first organ in the territory that is now the United States. He installed his organ in the monastery at San Felipe Pueblo and trained the Indians to sing Gregorian chants for the church service. Bernardo de Marta, who arrived in New Mexico territory about 1600, took over when Fray Cristóbal died in 1609; and, from the original training of these two teachers, the *Alabado*, a religious ballad form based on the Gregorian chant, was developed and sung by large numbers of Indians and Spaniards during the subsequent centuries.

In the initial absence of a common tongue, friar and Indian resorted to pantomime and mimicry, out of which developed the *autos sacramentales*, plays that became part of the total heritage of the Southwest, starting with the mock battle between the Moors and the Christians that took place when de Oñate claimed the territory for Spain in 1598; others dealt with Adam and Eve, Cain and Abel, and then the pageants of the New Testament, including St. Joseph, the Magi and the shepherds.

By 1608, there were eight padres at work in the territory of the Rio Grande, with at least 8,000 Indians baptized and working on the farms, which were growing up around the missions. By 1617, there were 11 churches, and the missions of New Mexico were elevated to a *Custodia* of the Franciscan order and were given the name of St. Paul. Fray Alonso de Benavides was appointed custodian of New Mexico; and, in 1629, when he was relieved of this post, he wrote an account for the King about the territory. By that time, there were 50 missionaries in the field, ministering to 60,000 converts in 90 pueblos grouped into 25 missions.

Gradually, the Spanish settlements expanded out from Santa Fe until they extended from Taos in the north to

below Isleta on the Rio Grande. But the Spanish, themselves, were spread very thin. Even Santa Fe, the only in-
corporated town, numbered just about 250 Spanish, of
whom but 50 had arms. This small group boasted some 700
servants; corn and cotton cloth, extracted as tributes from
the Indians, constituted the main source of livelihood for
the Spanish.

To supply additional materials for agriculture, for the
continuing search for precious metals, and for trade, a committee representing Church and State met in Mexico City in
1609 to decide upon a definite method of transporting goods
to the new province.

It was determined that every three years a train would be
organized and sent to New Mexico, returning to Chihuahua
with salt, copper, turquoise, blankets, and Indian slaves to
be sold in the mining areas of northern Mexico. The route of
this train would be along El Camino Real, the Royal Road,
which ran from Veracruz on the eastern coast of Mexico to
the vicinity of what is now El Paso, and then along the bank
of the Rio Grande to the present site of Albuquerque; from
that point, it led northward along the flank of the Sandias,
up La Bajada to the mesa, and across the plateau to the
foothills of the Sangre de Cristo at the village of Santa Fe.

As in Florida, Georgia, and the Carolinas, the first half of
the 17th century was characterized by the conversion of Indians, the building of missions, the establishment of basic
agriculture, and the initiation of trade. There was also constant minor unrest among the natives, brought on by forced
labor, destruction of traditional customs and religion, and
the extraction of direct tribute.

In 1640, a group of Indians near Santa Fe rebelled against
the friars who had whipped, imprisoned, and eventually
hanged 40 Indians who would not give up their own religion. Intensifying tensions in the territory was a growing
conflict between Church and State in the Spanish regime,
when the need for servants and goods became acute.

By 1660, the Franciscans of New Mexico were threatening to abandon the entire province, and the Governor was trying to stop the Church's exploitation of the Indians by ordering the friars to cease requiring the Indians to spin and weave cotton *mantas.*

In 1676, an Apache outbreak against the secular forces was countered by the hanging, imprisoning, or selling into slavery of the Apache leaders.

Then, in 1680, both in Florida and in the Southwest, the Indians mounted coordinated revolts that—while relatively minor in Florida—resulted in New Mexico in the killing of virtually every Spanish farmer and friar in the whole Rio Grande area and the expulsion of the few remaining Spaniards from Santa Fe and from the territory.

The victorious Pueblos, under their leader Popé, a Tewa medicine man, destroyed official records, tore down and burned churches, washed baptized Indians with *amole,* or soapweed, in the Santa Fe River to cleanse them of the stain, and annulled Christian marriages.

For more than a decade, Spanish rule ceased to exist in the territory, but Spanish customs, Spanish agricultural methods and Spanish livestock—which had, for more than three quarters of a century been taking root in the sandy soil and in the lives of the natives—could not be totally eradicated, and tenacious vestiges of that Spanish heritage characterized the practices and the products that continued to thrive under Indian cultivation and use.

Chapter 6

Panorama

On *September 14, 1692, Don Diego de Vargas Zapata y Luján Ponce de León,* newly appointed Governor of New Mexico, raised the royal banner of Spain again over Santa Fe after his expedition had successfully re-entered the territory of New Mexico, surprising the natives at the pueblos between El Paso and the capital city, and forcing them to surrender, with hardly a blow struck on either side.

Leaving a small garrison at Santa Fe, de Vargas returned to Mexico, where he recruited 800 settlers and headed back to northern New Mexico in 1693.

This time the natives were ready, and every mile of the journey was marked with blood. For almost two years the Governor and his troops battled the Indians, who—now expert horsemen, well mounted on the animals they had bred from the herds captured in the expulsion of the Spanish in the great revolts of 1680—slashed at the armored riders and slow-moving foot soldiers in swift forays and carefully concealed ambushes that were almost as frustrating in their suddenness of attack and retreat as they were damaging in casualties and confusion.

64

Yet doggedly the Spanish pressed on and finally came to Taos, the fortified village where Popé, leader of the 1680 rebellion, had planned and directed his successful attacks on the cities and farms. Despite heavy losses and uncompromising resistance, de Vargas and his soldiers finally broke through the defenses, captured or killed all of the inhabitants, and burned the town.

That was late in 1694.

That should have ended the matter.

But it did not.

Next year, the natives rebelled again. And again they were repulsed in a series of bloody battles.

Finally, by 1698, a full century after de Oñate's founding of the first city in the territory, Indian resistance had been reduced to sporadic attacks by small bands of bareback raiders, mostly pilfering from the horse herds and sheep flocks of the Spanish settlers, and New Mexico became a land of pastoral semi-tranquility and slow agrarian growth.

While Don Diego de Vargas Ponce de León was having his troubles resettling New Mexico, another Ponce de León —this one Alonso, a frontiersman by birth and a man already known for daring exploits fighting Indians—was successfully challenging scattered French outposts in Texas and securing that territory for Spain. And it was Alonso Ponce de León who provided the seed for the herds of wild cattle that, more than anything else during the first half of the 18th century, marked the incursion of the Spanish into Texas.

When Alonso Ponce de León led the first trek of missionaries, soldiers, and 700 mules and horses across the Rio Grande in 1689, and, bearing eastward, crossed the Nueces, Frío, San Antonio and Guadalupe Rivers, he also brought a large herd of cattle, and it is said that at every river, from the Rio Grande to the Louisiana border, he turned loose a bull and a cow, a stallion and a mare.

Whatever horse and cattle seeding Alonso Ponce de León actually did, the first missions established on the Nueces

River in 1690 had at least 200 head of cattle, which the Indians scattered before they could be successfully bred or eaten by the padres.

In three years, both the missions and the cattle were abandoned, and the escaped cows learned to follow the shrinking waters of the summer heat as the buffalo did, and then drift southward, humped up and shivering, before the whipping winter wind, finding refuge and breeding ground in the hospitable river bottoms.

When, in 1716, the Spanish established permanent missions and colonies in Texas, wild horses were running loose by the thousands in the Nueces region, with wild cattle thick in the brush of the Trinity River bottoms. Among the fat, fast, spotted bovines were black Castilian bulls, broader of chest, stronger of leg, and longer of horn than any on the ranges or in the rings of Spain.

But in the first half of the 18th century, as New Mexico and Texas were beginning to come to life as centers of Spanish influence, the bright promise of Florida had long since begun to fade, and, with the dissolution of the missions in Georgia and the Carolinas, following the revolt of 1680, prospects became increasingly dark.

Still, Florida continued to be strategically necessary to the protection of trade from Mexico and the West Indies, and it also was an important pawn in the game of international power between Spain and France and England. In fact, it was just those factors that caused the residents of Florida to forsake agriculture and industry and to depend on the *situado*, or government subsidy, buttressed by trading in slaves, in shipwrecking, and in traffic with pirates, for their livelihood.

In 1504, at the death of Governor Pedro Menéndez, the *situado* had been 33,000 pesos for 150 soldiers; by 1660, the *situado* was 65,000 pesos but the number of soldiers had also doubled; and at the opening of the 18th century, for 350 soldiers, their families, the friars, and a few royal functionaries amounting to approximately 1,600 residents, the governor received 81,000 pesos yearly.

Thus, the *situado* was never great enough to sustain the populace, and by 1750—when it had risen to 116,127 pesos —longtime residents had decided to develop what had started out as spasmodic trading with privateers and other occasional vessels into a permanent industry in the manufacture and sale of ships' stores on a large scale.

The swamps and forests of Florida had the natural resources to produce tar and pitch for shipbuilders, and the tall pines in the mountains of the interior toward Georgia could be worked into superb masts and spars, which could easily be floated to the coast on the rivers flowing into the Gulf or into the Atlantic.

The developing industry was truncated, however, by the ceding of Florida to England in 1763 and the withdrawal of almost all Spaniards to the West Indies for 20 years. On the return of Florida to Spanish rule in 1783, shipping patterns had changed, and the economy of Florida relapsed to the cultivation of small farms, shopkeeping, and labor at odd jobs—except for a developing major fishing industry on both the Gulf and Atlantic Coasts, an enterprise that had been initially undertaken and then sustained by an enclave of Majorcans who had come to the area before the English period, who had stayed despite the withdrawal of most other Spanish, and who formed the nucleus of Spanish-speaking people under the second Spanish regime.

During the years of Florida's shuttling between Spanish and English rule, in New Mexico, heart of the Spanish territory in the Southwest, generation merged into generation in a pastoral pattern of life that was a blend of the Old World and the New, of the religious and the secular, of the Spanish and the Indian, that shaped itself gently to the contours of the land, and, away from the scene of the clash of nations and off the track of major migrations, settled comfortably into the timeless terrain.

Towns were clusters of adobe huts, low silhouetted where
the curve of a stream made for the best prospect of water
the year round. Joined to each other around a central plaza
or square, the huts, from a distance, could not be distinguished from the earth out of which they had been made.
Between the hamlets and the limitless grazing ground
beyond were scattered fruit trees, a few scraggly rows of
beans and corn, ground-hugging plots of squash, and patchy
fields of wheat.

A few Spanish came with *mercedes*, or land grants, ranging in size from a few hundred acres to vast holdings of
more than a million acres. With them settled and merged
the Mexican Indian, the Pueblo, the Navajo, the *mestizo*,
and the mulatto. And the result was a blend of culture and
custom, with only the Spanish language and the Catholic religion dominant, and even those shading into new forms
adaptable to the people and the place.

In some of the pueblos under the spiritual control of the
padres, the *alcalde* or administrative officer, either Spanish,
or, in the smaller municipality, *mestizo*, was supported by
the farmers, who usually provided butter, beans, *tortillas*,
and one sheep a week. The peons and Indians also took care
of the *alcalde*'s house, cared for his farm, and wove the
cloth from the wool of his sheep.

In other communities, there was a cooperative system in
which a *mayordomo de la acequia*, or ditchboss, supervised
the irrigation, from river diversion to reservoir building, and
from canal construction to water apportionment. Each landowner worked on the ditches in proportion to the acreage
he farmed himself.

Families were interrelated, goods and services were exchanged, and trading expeditions to other communities and
even into Mexico were organized cooperatively. Often, the
field hands, herders, domestic servants, and other laborers
were close relations of the large landholder, or *patrón*.

Social life grew out of church festivals, and luxuries were
simply necessities in short supply—for the truncated grow-

ing season, the thin soil, and the limited rainfall, together
with the lack of tools and trade, made simple existence both
a struggle and a victory.

By 1744, there were 771 households, or about 10,000 persons, in the territory of New Mexico. The four principal cities, Santa Fe, Santa Cruz, Albuquerque, and El Paso,
housed two-thirds of the people, while the remainder lived
on *haciendas* and *ranchos* ranging from five to 46 families
each.

There were 25 Franciscan missions, each administering
from 30 to a hundred families. Nineteen of these missions
were in the upper district between Isleta and Taos and between Pecos and Zuni, and six strung out along the Rio
Grande below El Paso.

At El Paso, in addition to the irrigated fields of wheat and
maize, there were vineyards, which produced wine reminis-
cent of the Spanish homeland. There were annual fairs at
Taos, and the Spanish practiced trading with the Indians,
with annual expeditions south to the Jumanos in central
Texas, east to the Pawnees and Arapahoes beyond the Arkansas, and west to other Indians as distant as Lake Utah.

At Albuquerque, the Spaniards wove woolen and cotton
fabrics. Northward the farms of cotton, wheat, maize, and
truck products flourished, with cattle, goats, horses, mules,
and poultry abounding.

Farther north yet, beyond Taos and Soledad, was the
sheep country, where the owner, or *rico*, controlled vast
herds in an easygoing way, using Pueblo Indians, men of
mixed Indian and Spanish blood, and even Spanish peasants
to serve as shepherds, grazing flocks over sprawling grants
of thousands of acres of land.

Under the *rico* and his peon crew, the Churro grew har-
dier than his European ancestor. Storm, blizzard, drought,
careless tending—all were part of his way of life, and his
short legs carried him on great seasonal marches from the
high mountain valleys in the summer to the lower plains and
prairies in the winter. Although his fleece continued poor,

his meat became more succulent, and—seemingly to offset the quality of his wool—he began to propagate an abnormal number of twins, so that no matter what threatened—bears, wolves, wildcats, or panthers—his *rico* could depend on a growth in numbers each season.

After 1750, there was a brief flurry of Spanish influence in Louisiana, which had always been a French settlement, and which, even under Spanish rule, remained continuously and characteristically French. But Spanish rule did come to Louisiana on March 5, 1766, when Juan Antonio de Ulloa arrived in New Orleans as the first Spanish Governor of Louisiana. And a major infusion of Spanish-speaking people took place in 1770, when some 1,500 Canary Islanders settled in the Louisiana territory.

Back in Texas, stock ranches spread out from the Goliad mission down the San Antonio River. The mission of Espíritu Santo, alone, claimed 40,000 cattle by 1770, some branded and some unmarked, all running loose between the Guadalupe and the lower San Antonio. Although there were no bull rings, there were the "days of the bulls" with the big blacks being ridden, roped and pull-tailed as they plunged and bellowed and tugged, their coats glistening under the excited goading of their riders, captors, and tormentors. Along the Brazos River and up to the Texas Colorado, huge herds, roaming wild and free, provided sport for Spaniard and Indian alike. Rangier, swifter, and more dangerous— with their long, sweeping horns—than the buffalo, the wild cattle came to outnumber their native cousins. But it was not for their meat that the wild cattle were prized; rather for their hides and tallow. So, after a major hunt, the plain would be dotted with carcasses, and the scavengers and the earth would wax fat.

Thus it was that from Florida to Arizona—where a presidio called Tubac had been established in 1752—the second half of the 18th century saw the flag of Spain flying over relatively secure, established settlements. The days of exploration were over, and the task now was to try to make a living through farming, ranching, or commerce.

But out on the Pacific Coast, land exploration and settlement were just beginning. On April 11, 1769, Juan Pérez, a native of Majorca, dropped the anchor of his small ship, *San Antonio*, in San Diego harbor. The *San Antonio* was joined on April 29 by the *San Carlos*, and on May 14 by a detachment that had come overland from the Baja Península, or Lower California.

Commanded by Captain Fernando de Rivera y Moncada, the marching unit consisted of 25 soldiers, two muleteers, and 42 Christian Indians, who, it was believed, might prove useful both as interpreters and as assistants in converting the natives of the north, to say nothing of performing the drudgery of the expedition. De Rivera also had nearly 400 domestic animals, which he had gathered from the missions as he went along, together with farming implements and staple provisions.

Finally, on July 1, 1769, another land expedition under the Governor of the Province, Gaspar de Portolá—and including Father Junípero Serra (see Appendix for biography), president of any new missions to be founded in Alta California—arrived at San Diego.

The convergence of these four companies, two by sea and two by land, marked the first permanent physical occupation by the Spanish of what is now the State of California, and completed the string of permanent settlements that, by 1770, extended from St. Augustine on the Atlantic Coast through New Orleans, San Antonio, Santa Fe, and Tubac to San Diego on the Pacific Coast.

But de Portolá's governorship of California and his establishment of a permanent Spanish settlement in that territory came just six years too late to bring the whole southern face of what was to become the United States under Spanish rule at that time. For in 1763, Spain, yielding to the pressure of English colonists pressing south from their settlements along the Atlantic Coast, had ceded the territory of Florida to England. Florida was ceded back to Spain in 1783, so that the Spanish settlements were finally complete from coast to coast.

However, in Philadelphia in the year 1776—the year that saw the Spanish founding San Francisco, California, and Tucson, Arizona—the Declaration of Independence had been signed by representatives of the 13 small Eastern seaboard Anglo colonies. By separating themselves from England, the colonies, without knowing it, linked their future to the West. And an eventual clash was inevitable between the Anglo and Hispanic cultures, with distant Spain a diminishing influence and the United States a young, virile nation, backing up the actions of its individual citizens with political fiat and military power.

Initiative and impact were, of course, with the upstart colonies and their rugged, rough frontiersmen, whose heavy boots left Anglo imprints across the plains and mountains, whose big voices and tall tales drowned out the softer language of native and Spaniard alike, and whose voracious appetite for possession devoured land, wildlife, natural resources, and all ethnic values and pride except their own. Nonetheless, three centuries of Spanish influence and involvement had planted deep and scattered wide the crops, the herds, the genes, and the culture that derived from the Spaniards' European homeland and drew sustenance and substance from the earth and from the ethnic interchanges of the New World. The cumulative effect of these ingredients constituted an almost immovable object blocking the Anglos' irresistible force.

Indeed, the 18th century was the Hispanic century in the territory that was to become the United States. The marks that had been made on the land in that time were indelible and iridescent. And the first half of the 19th century promised to be as rewarding.

 Alta California

In Alta California, mission building was the major Spanish mark of the last years of the 18th century and the first years of the 19th. There, the missions were just getting started as they were being ended and secularized in Texas and Arizona—around 1770—and long after they had ceased to function in Georgia, the Carolinas, and Florida. Yet it was the missions of Alta California that provided the prototype Spanish missions of romantic tale and legend, whose image and influence shaped secular as well as sacred structures through the subsequent centuries.

But the first settlement at San Diego was hardly a model for what followed.

The two ships that had first dropped anchor off San Diego in April 1769, the *San Antonio* and the *San Carlos,* had missed the harbor on their first pass and had poked among the coastal bays for a considerable period of time before finally arriving at the spot they were looking for. And the two land parties that had been part of the same expedition —the party under Captain de Rivera and the other commanded by Captain de Portolá—had found the way up the

Baja Península tortuous and barren, so that, by the time de Portolá's party arrived, almost three months had elapsed since the *San Antonio* made landfall. During that time, all that Pérez and de Rivera had accomplished was the erection of a few huts and a stock corral. Their principal occupation had been to care for the sick and bury the dead, the *San Carlos* having arrived with every member of its crew ill or dying from scurvy.

With the arrival of Governor de Portolá's party, the company was complete; but of the 219 individuals who had comprised the four units, 93 had died on the journey or shortly after arrival.

Finally, however, on July 16, Father Serra, president of the yet-unfounded mission, using one of the small huts as his church, raised a cross beside the flag of Spain, and preached the first sermon to the natives, dedicating the mission-to-be to San Diego de Alcalá.

In order to attract the natives, the missionaries had brought along a supply of trinkets and pictures. In addition, whenever any Indians ventured close, the missionaries gave them bits of cloth and food. As a result, a constant procession of Indians moved in and out of the area, and there were always quite a few sitting silently, watching the activities of the missionaries and the soldiers and the sailors.

But Governor de Portolá's objective was far more ambitious than the simple founding of a mission at San Diego.

Two days before Father Serra's dedicatory ceremonies, the Governor had moved out northward, at the head of a company made up of Father Juan Crespi and other friars, followed by a pack train of one hundred loaded mules, with muleteers and a soldier guard. Under the command of Captain de Rivera, a rear party of soldiers, friendly Indians, and spare mules and horses followed at a distance calculated to provide for their safe escape in case the main body was attacked.

Prior to his departure, de Portolá had sent the *San Antonio* back to Mexico for supplies and a crew for the *San Car-*

los, which rode empty and unmanned at anchor in the San Diego harbor.

De Portolá's objective was to found a mission and build a presidio on the bay of Monterey, which had been so glowingly described by Vizcaíno a century earlier.

Along the fertile coastal plain, de Portolá and his party found good water, verdant pasture and friendly Indians. Plodding comfortably through what is now the San Bernardino Valley, they had reached the Los Angeles country when suddenly the horses and mules reared and plunged in terror and the foot soldiers fell, frightened, to the ground, which heaved and shook in the first California earthquake experienced by other than the native Indians.

The quake lasted, as Father Crespi, historian of the expedition, expressed it, "about half as long as an Ave Maria." Then the earth was still, and the muleteers were calming their pack animals and the riders were calming their horses. Within ten minutes, order was restored.

And then the earth shook again!

When finally the earth ceased its trembling, the company found that the quakes had caused no real damage, and the party moved on through an area heavily populated by the Santa Barbara Indians, beyond the later site of San Luis Obispo, to what was eventually to become the southern end of Monterey County. It was a spot marked by a hulking mountain, whose steep cliffs were undercut at the base so that they actually jutted out over the sea and effectively blocked any further advance up the coast.

Turning inland across the Nacimiento and San Antonio Rivers, de Portolá followed the Arroyo Seco and eventually reached the headwaters of the Salinas River near Soledad. The mountains were barren of vegetation and animals; deep gorges sliced across every path; and men, mules, and horses clambered one precipitous rock wall and up the other side only to find over the next ridge that the arroyo had made a sharp turn and had to be crossed and recrossed again and again.

From the crest near the San Antonio River, Father Crespi looked out in all directions and could see nothing but mountains extending to the horizon. Exhausted and discouraged, struck by debilitating scurvy, the de Portolá party followed the Salinas River for six days and came to its outlet on a disappointingly unprepossessing bay.

After a brief rest, de Portolá and his entourage continued northward up a beautiful stretch of coastline. No longer a flat, fertile plain or a seemingly impassable mountain barrier, the route ran through a forest of magnificent evergreens, whose straight, branchless trunks—larger at the base than a brace of mules and stretching high to the sky—were capped by lofty tufts of huge cones and green needles, which dropped from the trees and carpeted the ground with a deep fragrant softness. De Portolá called the trees *"palo colorado,"* or "red timber," for these were the giant redwood that still grace the Pacific slopes of northern California.

Above the present site of Santa Cruz, they came to a high point, where they could see and recognize Drake's Bay, the best-known point along the coast, since it had been visited by many navigators over the years. Knowing they had missed Monterey Bay, which lay south of Drake's Bay, they pitched camp at Point Pedro and sent hunting parties out to seek game to replenish their nearly exhausted food supply.

The hunting parties, under Captain Ortega, followed the signs of game up into the mountains and came suddenly to where the land dropped away to the shores of a huge quiet harbor dotted by a pair of islands and almost completely closed off from the ocean by two headlands, which stood like the columns of an entryway and glowed invitingly in the rays of the setting sun.

Ortega's discovery was, in a very real sense, the fulfillment of the Spanish dream, for his party had stumbled upon San Francisco Bay and the Golden Gate, destined, less than 80 years later, to be the portal to the California gold fields, and, even more importantly, to shelter through all the years that followed, a golden harvest from international commerce by sea and by land.

With the location of San Francisco harbor in their minds and on their maps, de Portolá's party, its larder restocked, headed back south, still searching for Monterey Bay. They did not find it, but they planted a cross on the shore of the bay at the mouth of the Salinas River.

De Portolá's expedition was gone for five months, and at San Diego mission, illness and death had continued, with 50 burials during the period. In addition, the Indians, who had at first been so pleased with the gifts of trinkets and cloth and so intrigued by the activities of the garrison, had begun to demand more food and cloth. When gifts were not forthcoming, they began to help themselves from the meager stocks of the settlers. In greater and greater numbers, the Indians began to overrun the camp; and, in order to keep them off, the soldiers began to fire over their heads and at their feet.

Although the noise of the gunpowder at first frightened the Indians, they soon saw that no damage resulted, and one day they mounted a sudden raid on the camp, pillaging the huts and stripping clothing from the invalids. Physical resistance by the guards was answered by a volley of arrows from the raiders, and, with three wounded and one dead, the Europeans aimed their guns directly at the Indians, killing three and wounding several others. The Indians retreated; and after that, an uneasy truce prevailed, with the Spanish treating the wounded Indians, and the other natives keeping their distance. But, though the company survived, supplies continued to dwindle, and the situation was so inauspicious that the missionaries did not gain a single convert.

De Portolá, discouraged by his failure to find Monterey Bay and appalled by the state of things at the San Diego mission, determined to abandon camp and return to Mexico. But the friars, Crespi and Serra, despite their total failure as missionaries to this point, were determined to remain as long as possible. They persuaded de Portolá to make one last try, and, in February, he dispatched Captain de Rivera with 19 men to Lower California for stock and supplies. Still, by early March 1770, long before de Rivera's expected return, conditions became so precarious that de Portolá ordered preparations to break camp permanently on March 20.

During the last ten days before that date, Serra and Crespi led the other members of the religious community in prayers and fasting, hoping for some last-minute sign that would persuade Governor de Portolá not to carry out his planned exodus. But no sign was forthcoming, and, as the sun went down on the evening of March 19, preparations for the journey were complete, and the hopes of the priests set with the sun.

Then, in the clear twilight, white sails appeared against the blue, at first just a small dot on the horizon, but growing steadily larger and bearing straight for the camp. As the stars came out overhead and the moon rose over the inland hills, the ship standing in from the sea was revealed as the *San Antonio*, which had been sent south so many months before for men and supplies to support the founding of the mission and presidio at Monterey.

Juan Pérez, commander of the *San Antonio*, had been sailing under those orders directly for Monterey, but had put into the Santa Barbara channel for water, where he had lost his anchor and had been told by the natives that the Spanish land expedition had returned south months before.

Pérez did not totally accept the Indians' information about the expedition's return, but the loss of his anchor persuaded him to put back to San Diego for another anchor before returning northward to Monterey. Had it not been for the accidental loss of the anchor, the *San Antonio* would have missed the Monterey expedition and would have returned to San Diego too late to prevent the abandonment of that enterprise, also.

As it was, the arrival of the *San Antonio* on the wings of night was taken by the faithful friars as a sign that their prayers had been answered, and the supplies and men that had been brought by the *San Antonio* were taken by Governor de Portolá as the practical necessities required to keep the colony alive.

Not only that, but both the missionaries and the secular governor agreed that they should take advantage of the fresh supplies and the personnel to try again to establish a mission and presidio at Monterey.

Analyzing all the evidence of their journey, the explorers concluded that the bay at the mouth of the Salinas River must be, despite its unprepossessing land prospect, the Monterey Bay that Vizcaíno had so over-enthusiastically described. They decided to do exactly what they had planned to do on the previous trip. The *San Antonio*, fully supplied and manned, moved out of San Diego harbor on April 16, with the commander, Pérez, and the missionary, Junípero Serra, aboard. On the following day, Governor de Portolá again set out northward by land, with Father Crespi in his entourage.

On May 24, the de Portolá party arrived at the point where they had set up the cross the previous fall and found it adorned with sticks, arrows, feathers, meat, fish, and clams. With the assistance of the natives who had made these offerings to the unknown god of the Europeans, they stacked great piles of firewood on the rocks to make a clear identification of the entrance to the harbor, and when the sails of the *San Antonio* broke the horizon a week later, they lighted the piles of wood, and the ship made an easy entrance to the bay and was soon riding comfortably at anchor.

The company made camp in a little ravine under the branches of a huge oak tree. Father Serra and Father Crespi hung some bells on the oak branches, and, by moving the branches, made the bells peal out, loud and long. The company assembled on the beach, the priests chanted the *venite creator spiritus*, planted a cross, and Father Serra said Mass; the dedication was completed, as Father Crespi reported it, "amidst the thunder of cannon and the crack of musketry, followed by a *salve* to the Image and a *te deum laudamus*." Then Governor de Portolá took formal possession of the land in the name of the Spanish king, Carlos III. He unfurled and planted the Spanish flag beside the cross, thus founding presidio and mission at the same time in the same spot.

Back from the beach, de Portolá built a few huts. Father Serra dedicated one of them as a church. Then the whole encampment was enclosed by a palisade.

Chapter *8*

High Tide

In 1770, *to control a territory that extended some 400* miles from San Diego north to Monterey, there were only 43 Spanish soldiers in Alta California. Of missionaries, there were even fewer.

Rounding out the complement of less than 200 non-natives in the territory were sailors from the supply ships, and a few stock-herders and settlers.

Except for the priests and the officers, all the non-natives were *mestizo* men. Most of them were illiterate. Many of them were ex-convicts who had chosen exploration rather than incarceration—a rugged, ragged, unruly band.

Despite the fact that not a single conversion took place during the first year of the mission at San Diego—and the initial baptism at Monterey's San Carlos Mission was not until December 26, 1770, six months after the mission's founding—Father Serra moved ahead and established two more in 1771, one at San Gabriel, the other at San Fernando. And in 1772, he founded the San Luis Obispo mission.

But after five years, at the end of 1773, the record of the

Alta California missions was very meager, particularly compared with the conversions claimed in the early centuries by the missionaries from the Atlantic Coast through the wastes of New Mexico. Only 491 California baptisms had been recorded in the five years, and those were mostly children. There had been 62 marriages in the same period, a number that probably represented the total adult converts.

The padres had followed all the traditional methods of constructing a hut and calling it a church. They had displayed banners and pictures. They had gained the natives' confidence with gifts of food, trinkets, and bits of cloth. They had talked about the Gospels, and had persuaded the Indians to help with the work around the mission buildings.

And the methods had seemed to work, since the Indians were numerous and friendly, and they had accepted the increasingly lavish gifts with every evidence of sincerity. But they still steadfastly refused to move to the next stages, which had apparently been so easy in the past in other places.

When the supply ships were late in coming—as they almost always were—the missions were in deep trouble, because their over-generous gifts to the Indians depleted their stocks to a desperate state. Since the missionaries neither knew much about farming, nor could rely on help from the Indians, the few seeds they planted usually failed to germinate; and, if they did germinate, they failed to yield crops. Yet all around was lush vegetation, visible evidence of the richness of the soil.

Not only did the missionaries of those early years fail to convert the natives and fail to grow good gardens, they also failed as stock breeders. Five hundred domestic animals had been brought from the Baja Península in the original expeditions, but Spanish deserters took with them as many head of horses and cattle as they could separate from the herds, and the natives quickly developed a taste for succulent Churro sheep. While the stock had increased spectacularly in New Mexico and Texas, a census of California's cows, sheep, goats, pigs, donkeys, mares, colts, stallions, and mules in 1773 totaled only 616 animals at the five missions—a slight increase, but nothing to get fat on.

The year 1773 was, therefore, a crucial one in the affairs of Alta California.

Fortunately, at that time there was a new Viceroy for New Spain in Mexico City, Don Antonio María Bucareli y Ursúa, a man who was determined to do everything in his power to make Alta California—and, indeed, the whole of the Pacific Coast area—a province of Spain, rather than of Russia or of England, both of which, through explorations and colonization, were moving down on the Spanish domain from the north.

To expand territorial claims and protect what territory he had, Bucareli, in 1773, ordered three expeditions crucial to the future of Alta California.

First, he appointed Captain de Rivera to be Governor of Alta California and ordered him to proceed with new settlers up the Baja Península.

He dispatched Juan Pérez on a voyage of exploration far north of any points thus far reached by Spanish ships.

And he authorized Juan Bautista de Anza (see Appendix for biography), commander of the Arizona fort of Tubac, to seek a viable land route from Arizona to California as an alternative both to the sea supply route—ineffective because of the small size and limited number of ships and the violence of storms—and the peninsula supply route—ineffective because of its lack of water, foliage, and friendly natives.

De Rivera's mission was just a holding one, to demonstrate governmental support rather than abandonment of the Alta California outpost. The other two were expeditions of discovery in the grand tradition of the past.

Pérez, on his first voyage, simply nudged northward through stormy seas to a point off the northern tip of what is now Queen Charlotte Island, almost due west of the port of Ketchikan, southernmost city in Alaska, and considerably

north of the scimitar-shaped Aleutian chain reaching out in
a series of rock steps toward the continent of Asia and the
land mass of Russia. Coasting south, Pérez found storms still
obscuring the land, and he returned to San Blas on the Baja
Península to outfit a more elaborate expedition.

Inland, Fray Francisco Tomás Hermenegildo Garcés had
been probing westward between 1768 and 1773, following
the Gila to its mouth in the Gulf of California, then going
farther west across the desert that was to become the fertile
Imperial Valley. On his journeys, Fray Garcés had discovered San Felipe Pass in the San Jacinto Mountains, and then
he had returned to Tubac.

As a result, when de Anza set out from Tubac on January
8, 1774—at the same time that Juan Pérez was making his
first voyage to the north Pacific—he enlisted Fray Garcés as
an associate to lead his company of 34 over the same route
and beyond. Anza crossed the San Jacinto Mountains and
reached the mission of San Gabriel by March 22, and then,
with six soldiers, pushed on to reach Monterey on April
18—while Pérez reached the northernmost part of his voyage by July 22, by which time de Anza was comfortably
back in Tubac.

The next year—in March 1775—a sea expedition of four
ships set out from San Blas to sail even farther north than
Pérez had sailed in 1774. The ships were to make landfalls
and take possession of the country in the name of Spain.

De Anza started on his second trip on October 23, 1775,
with 240 persons, including three missionaries—one of them
Fray Garcés—ten veteran soldiers—including one lieutenant and one sergeant—and 20 recruits to provide the first
garrison at the projected presidio of San Francisco. There
were also ten soldiers to provide protection on the return
journey, 29 wives of the garrison soldiers—only Lieutenant
Murraga being unaccompanied by his wife—136 additional
colonists of both sexes, 20 muleteers, three cattle herders,
four mission servants, and three Indian interpreters.

The settlers and soldiers were all paid in advance—not in

money, for fear they would gamble it away—but in supplies and equipment. Thus, the train was heavily loaded with clothing—from shoes and boots to petticoats and hat ribbons, arms, riding equipment, household equipment, and food.

The sea expedition under Lieutenant Bruno de Heceta, with Juan Pérez as second in command, comprised the frigate *Santiago*, the tiny (36 feet long) schooner *Sonora*, and the familiar *San Carlos* and *San Antonio*.

The *San Antonio* proceeded only as far as San Diego, with supplies for the southern missions. The *San Carlos*, under Juan Manuel de Ayala—who transferred from the *Sonora* when the original commander of the *San Carlos* became insane—had as its mission the exploration of San Francisco Bay.

De Heceta and Pérez on the *Santiago*, and the *Sonora*, now under the command of Juan Francisco de la Bodega y Cuadra, sailed on to the distant north.

During the month of July, 1775, de Heceta, Pérez, and de la Bodega made landfalls in northern Oregon and in the Grays Harbor area of southern Washington. On July 17, they viewed the mouth of the great Columbia River, 17 years before the American Captain Robert Gray made the same discoveries and recorded them in his name.

Farther south, de Ayala set sail from Monterey on July 27 and was at sea when, on July 30, a great storm parted the *Santiago*, with de Heceta and Pérez, from the *Sonora*, commanded by de la Bodega. On August 5, de Ayala, severely wounded by the accidental explosion of a loaded pistol left in his cabin by the insane former commander of the *San Carlos*, put his helm over and stood in toward shore, successfully passing through the strait and past the pillars of the Golden Gate, anchoring near the present North Beach in San Francisco Bay.

At almost the same time, de Heceta and Pérez were entering a small sound on the western shore of Vancouver Island and taking possession in the name of Spain of what was to be named Nootka Sound by the English navigator James Cook.

Nootka was the northernmost settlement actually claimed by the Spanish, although de la Bodega continued on in the tiny *Sonora* almost to the 58th parallel, well above the present southern boundary of Alaska, and landed twice on the journey to take technical possession for Spain.

De Heceta landed at Nootka, but the sickness of his crew forced him to turn back, and he arrived at Monterey on August 29, 1775.

De Ayala spent the month of August and most of September exploring and mapping San Francisco Bay, taking soundings, probing as far as the mouth of the San Joaquin River, and naming geographical points. *Nuestra Señora de los Angeles,* the name he gave to the great island just inside the strait, is still called Angel Island; and *Isla de los Alcatraces,* (Island of the Pelicans) is a name preserved until today as Alcatraz, although the Spaniards applied the name to the island now called Goat Island instead of to the small dot of land surmounted by the ex-prison that now bears the name.

De Ayala left San Francisco Bay on September 18, and the following day he anchored at Monterey, calling the Bay of San Francisco the best he had seen from Cape Horn north, and describing it as "not one port but many, with a single entrance." He praised the bay as a good port, "not only because of the fine proportions which it offers to the site, but also because there is no scarcity of good water, wood, and stone for ballast. The climate, though cold, is entirely healthful, and is free from the annoying daily fogs experienced in Monterey."

With the arrival of the *Sonora* in Monterey on October 7, the great voyages of 1775 were completed, but the high point of Spanish exploration and settlement in the territory that was to be the United States was not reached until the first month of the next year, when de Anza and his settlers arrived from Arizona.

Leaving Tubac on October 23, 1775, de Anza had de-

scended the Santa Cruz River to the Gila and then on down
that river to where it joined the Colorado. At this stage of
the journey, there was plenty of water, but forage was thin,
and members of the company, still not hardened to cross-
country travel, easily fell ill.

The special problem of this expedition was that many of
the women were pregnant, and two gave birth to children
during that first stage of the journey, delaying travel because de Anza felt that the mothers needed four or five days
rest before riding horseback again.

On November 28, de Anza had come to the Colorado at
the point where he had crossed it on the previous trip. But
now the river had deepened, and there was no way to get
across except by raft, and no rafts were available. Building
them and guiding them across without loss of personnel,
equipment, and animals would be both doubtful and time-
consuming.

Nonetheless, while searching for another way to cross,
de Anza had a cabin built for the two friars—Garcés being
one of them—who, with three interpreters and four servants, were going to stay with the Yuma Indians for further
exploration.

The hut was the original building for the settlement of
Yuma.

Upriver a short distance, de Anza located a place where
the water divided into three shallow branches, and he was
able to transport his entire company across on horseback.
Early in December, therefore, the de Anza expedition
moved out into the Colorado Desert.

On his previous journey, de Anza had become completely
lost among the terrible dunes, where the shifting sands had
virtually obliterated all trails. The pack mules had been exhausted; the horses had become ill from eating a poisonous
weed where there was no water or other pasturage. De
Anza had wandered for six days, eventually arriving back at
the point where he had entered the desert. Deciding to go
around rather than across the desert, he had taken about

half the men, the strongest horses and the ten best mules, together with provisions for a month, and, after six days of hard riding, had arrived at good springs and pasturage near the foot of the Sierra Nevada.

Now, confronted by the same desert, he divided his company into three relays, each to march on successive days, in order to give the few water holes in the desert time to refill between uses.

Leading the first detachment, de Anza struck out again into the blowing dunes. Knowing now his destination, he pushed relentlessly forward, and in three days reached the cool wells of Santa Rosa. Two days later, he was camped at San Sebastián, at the foot of the Sierra Nevada, where he waited for the other relays to catch up.

Only one had any trouble. The third unit, under Lieutenant José Joaquín Murraga, had suffered from intense cold, and Murraga had severe pains in the head and ears; he later became totally deaf.

With members of the company ill from thirst and cold, the 200 cattle dehydrated from being without water for four days, the horses and mules exhausted, de Anza found the prospect of the snow-covered mountains ahead a grim one. Yet the trek down river from Tubac had been difficult, the swollen river menacing, and the desert threatening in its barrenness and cold—and still they had survived.

Instead of complaining and foreboding, there was singing and dancing, and on December 19, de Anza's party started the ascent.

Now came rain and snow and temperatures that to the travelers from Arizona—and the almost tropical Sonora—were frigid beyond belief.

On Christmas Eve, as the company huddled deep in the canyon that de Anza knew led to the pass across the mountains, the third child to be born on the journey chose to arrive; but this time, after only one day of rest, the expedition pushed slowly on.

On December 26, just below what de Anza knew was the

summit, the earth began to tremble and shake—just as it had for de Portolá. Rocks, dislodged from the cliffs above, thundered down the slopes toward the men, women, and animals. For four minutes the chill grip of total terror held the company in its grasp. And then it was over, and they made their last assault on the mountain, coming to the saddle of the pass and over and down into a country of trees and grass and warm sunshine.

On January 4, 1776, they arrived at San Gabriel. Although 90 cattle had died from cold and exhaustion in the crawl up the mountain slope, de Anza's company now numbered 244 persons, counting the new babies and the Indians who had joined along the way, four more than the 240 they had started with—and they had left a mission detachment of nine at Yuma!

However, de Anza's troubles were not over, for the Indians of the area had attacked the mission of San Diego two months before, and, except for de Anza's arrival, might well have wiped out the garrison.

As it was, de Anza spent almost two months helping Governor de Rivera insure that the hostilities had ceased. Then he had to chase deserters from his own troop, particularly five muleteers who had run away with some of the best horses of the expedition. De Anza himself had become seriously ill, but he refused to give up, and late in February, he set out with a number of families from San Gabriel. Sloshing through driving rains, the company reached Monterey on March 10. Then, on March 23, taking only a few men with him, de Anza struck out for his final destination, San Francisco.

De Anza explored the bay shore to the junction of the Sacramento and San Joaquín Rivers and then marched back to Monterey. Having selected the site for the San Francisco settlement, he had accomplished his mission, and on April 14, 1776, he moved out toward San Gabriel, then back over the trail to Sonora.

Governor de Rivera then ordered Lieutenant Joaquín

Murraaga to take de Anza's group of soldier settlers and their families and move on to erect the fort at the San Francisco site.

The company arrived on June 27, and quietly went about the work of building huts and the palisade for the presidio. The work was well under way on July 4, 1776, when, on the opposite coast of North America, a group of Anglo pioneers were signing their Declaration of Independence. On September 17, 1776, the presidio was formally dedicated, and the consecration of the mission, San Francisco de Asís, was solemnized on October 9.

Also in July 1776, that month of decision for the mostly unexplored territory that was to become the United States, Father Francisco Silvestre Vélez Escalante, accompanied by Father Francisco Domínguez and six other men, set out from Santa Fe to explore a northern route overland to the coast. Although Vélez turned back before crossing the mountains, he did journey well out into the area of Utah, clearly demonstrating that an overland trail was feasible in that area.

With the founding of San Francisco, the major elements of Spanish settlement in the New World were complete. There were, of course, more colonies to be established, more missions to be founded, and a period of peace and growth to be enjoyed; but these were rather a filling-in than expansion.

On February 3, 1777, Felipe de Neve arrived at Monterey as the new territorial Governor. On November 29, 1777, he presided at the founding of the Pueblo of San Jose, and on September 4, 1781, he founded the Pueblo of Los Angeles. The settlers who formed the nucleus of these colonies were poor people, as had been those who comprised the earlier pioneering companies. Very few were actually Spanish, but were *mestizo* or mulatto. And, while the animal stock finally began to proliferate with the expansion of the missions so that by 1784—the date of the death of Junípero Serra—there were 5,384 cattle, 5,629 sheep, and 4,294 goats in Alta California, the non-native population multiplied very slowly. (See Appendix for additional information on this period in the biography of Doña Eulalia Fages.)

In 1790, counting *mestizos* and mulattoes, there were still only 970 Spanish-speaking people in Alta California.

Yet, in a sense, despite the small population, that year 1790 was the acme of the Spanish period, since the year before an event had occurred in the cold, foggy far north that spelled *finito* to Spanish expansion. The beginning of the end of Spanish dominance on the Pacific Coast had taken place in such a way that virtually no one knew it had happened, and no one could possibly have sensed the significance of the action.

In 1789, Captain Esteban Martínez, a Spanish navy commander, seized four British ships anchored in Nootka Sound, alleging that they were lying in the waters belonging to the Crown of Spain.

Martínez had sent the ships off to Mexico under armed escort, but the British government had immediately demanded not only the restitution of the ships but also possession of Nootka Bay. The British threatened that if such actions were not taken immediately, they would attack Spanish possessions in both North and South America.

The attacks did not come, and diplomatic exchanges piled up. But on March 28, 1795, to avoid major confrontations on several fronts, the Spanish government ordered the release of the British ships, and the flag of Spain was raised for the last time on Nootka Island.

From that time on, it was all downhill for Spain in the territory north of the Gulf of California and the Gulf of Mexico.

part 3

 *The Rancheros*

Chapter 9

Hispanic Hiatus

For three centuries, Spain had provided the primary European influence across the southern face of what was soon to become the United States of America. True, there was the French enclave in Louisiana and along the shores of the Mississippi, and for a brief period, the English had taken over Florida; but from the time Columbus made his first landfall in what he called the West Indies in the last decade of the 15th century until the irresistible Anglo thrust in the 19th century, the land was Spain's.

However, the Spanish also controlled all of Mexico, Central America, and most of South America. In comparison, the barren southwest prairies, the swamps of Florida, and even the enticing harbors of Alta California and the rest of the West coast to Nootka Sound, seemed unproductive, unpromising, and, ultimately, far removed from any effective base of military or economic operation. As a result, both the distant rulers and the adventurers—some clinging to the coasts and others clawing desperately for a livelihood from the deserts—began to lose interest in the physically and fiscally enervating prospect of struggling across the barrier hills and mountains that lined the West coast and East coast and rose high just north of the Southwestern settlements, in the vague hope that things would be better in the unknown interior beyond.

And so the 19th century, which was ushered in by the ceding of Nootka Sound to the British, saw the Spanish-speaking people seeking to exploit the natural and imported resources of the places where they were, rather than seeking to extend their thin line of settlements even more thinly across greater distances. Thus, it was not the Hispanos but the Anglos of the brash new United States, moving west across the Alleghenies from the Eastern seaboard, who occupied the rich heartland, which had lain for those three Spanish centuries just beyond the horizon of their vision and endurance.

The most notable thing about Spain's three centuries, however, was not that her rulers and her adventurers failed to totally explore and exploit the territory that was to become the United States, but rather that so puny an expeditionary force, representing such a decadent and dying sovereign state, should have been able to make such a lasting impact on so vast a land. And it was the period of the early 1800's—when the power of Spain itself faded into insignificance—that provided the generative gap necessary for the enduring qualities of the Hispanic culture to strengthen and survive side by side with the native culture. And the Hispanic culture also developed a tenacious resiliency, which permitted it to bend but not break before the alien Anglo assault that eliminated the buffalo, corralled the Indians onto barren reservations, furrowed the prairie, gouged metals from the subsurface strata, and sucked oil from the bowels of the earth.

But in the first quarter of the 19th century, no one would have mentioned a "Hispanic culture."

In the first quarter of the 19th century, there were just the Californios, the Nuevo Mejicanos, and the Tejanos.

In the first quarter of the 19th century, each was isolated

from the others, and each—except for an occasional visitation by traders of various allegiances—was separated from every other major influence.

In the first quarter of the 19th century—though Florida and Louisiana swiftly became part of the expanding United States—there was a moment of glorious Hispanic hiatus westward to the Pacific.

But far back, before all this, the process that had produced a Spanish-speaking people—who were, nonetheless, not Spanish, and whose language, though more Spanish-derived than anything else, was not Spanish, and whose culture, including religion, art, and family relationships, though seemingly more Spanish than anything else, was not Spanish—had begun with the first landfall of European ships in what they called the West Indies.

Far from home, the European men, mostly Spanish, some aristocratic, some poor and illiterate, immediately made union, formal and informal, with native women. Much of this activity derived from the exploitation of female slaves by the European masters; some derived from en route cohabitation by soldiers and settlers passing through to a real or imagined El Dorado beyond; some resulted from permanent or semipermanent liaisons, legalized by official act or passage of time. In any event, the effect was the emergence in a few generations, in that part of North America south of the present-day United States, of a cultural-racial group distinct from the native Indian and also distinct from the invading European, involving mostly persons of European male and native female parentage but also involving persons of European or native parentage only, whose heritage, nonetheless, was in the territory of their birth rather than their ancestry, so that their emergent culture was a mixture of European and Indian.

When the conquistadores turned northward, their entourage was composed of representatives of this new Mexican culture, as well as native Mexican Indians not yet assimilated into the Mexican culture, and representatives of their own group, still Spanish in orientation and in fact.

Both combat and cohabitation marked the path of the conquistadores, the padres, and the soldiers and the settlers who accompanied or followed them. The product of combat was death and destruction. The product of cohabitation was new life and growth. The common product was resentment and misunderstanding, resulting in a separation that survived even the mutually repressive force of the future Anglo invasion.

In New Mexico, for example, the number of individuals with just a Spanish ancestry declined over the years in direct relation to the increase in population in the territory. At the same time, the Pueblo Indian population remained nearly stationary. And the number of persons of mixed ancestry increased rapidly, so that by 1846, when there were probably only a thousand people of pure Spanish ancestry in the territory, there were 60,000 of mixed ancestry.

Language, religion, and other aspects of culture also became mixed. By the first quarter of the 19th century, the language of the "Spanish-speaking people" was a mixture of Castilian Spanish, Mexican-Indian, and occasional words from the various languages of the nomadic and sedentary tribes in that area of the United States. As contact with roving Anglos became more frequent, Hispanicized English words were also adopted into the language, and over the years the actual "Spanish" became a multiplicity of localized dialects, with considerable variation from Texas through New Mexico and Arizona to California. Likewise, the practice of the Catholic Church altered with the impact of the native religions and the life styles of the mixed-heritage communicants.

The key characteristic of the Spanish-speaking people and their culture as it developed during the first quarter of the 19th century and continued on into the 20th century was heterogeneity.

Yet with all the diversity that characterized the heritage and life style of the Spanish-speaking Americans, the combination culture was totally alien to that of the Anglo invaders, whose scouts were already infiltrating the territory and reporting back on the curious customs of these sons of the conquistadores.

The squeeze took place as the mid-19th century approached, with the Anglos moving out of the wooded areas of Louisiana and eastern Texas, across the Texas Colorado River, between San Antonio on the north and Matagorda Bay on the southeast, onto the open prairie where, in 1830, some hundred thousand head of cattle grazed. Those along the timbered territory had been brought in by the French of Louisiana or the Anglos from farther east, but those westward between the Nueces and the Rio Grande were of practically pure Spanish stock, so that four-fifths of the cattle in the area were Spanish.

At San Antonio, the Spanish-Mexican civilization, tired of a hundred years' exposure to attacks from the Plains Indians out of the north, crumbled before the onset of the Anglos. Only an impoverished, illiterate 2,000 or so remained by 1836—many former Mexican soldiers, and others, tattered civilians who had not the enterprise either to fight or to move back toward the Rio Grande.

Beyond the Nueces, however, the country was too rough and too far from the high plains for the Comanches, and the settlers prospered in peace. The Mexican government, once it had achieved its independence from Spain in 1810, rewarded its supporters with huge land grants, and herdsmen and *vaqueros* crossed the Rio Grande in large numbers to care for the sheep and the cattle.

The *rancheros* prospered, the *vaqueros* developed into a middle management class; together they looked to Mexico for laborers to do the menial tasks. Gradually there developed an almost feudal system in which the landowners lived in luxuriously furnished flat-roofed stone haciendas and left the operation of the *rancho* to the well-paid *vaquero* who sold high-priced goods on credit to the peons who lived in one-room, thatched-roof *jacales* and were not allowed to

garden for themselves or own anything other than a few
chickens, a pig, and a goat.

When the Texas revolution erupted in 1836, the Nueces
valley became the scene of a border war between the Texans of the Colorado and the Mexicans of the Rio Grande.
Many of the landowners abandoned their ranches and much
of their stock and escaped back across the Rio Grande. The
Texans declared all unbranded cattle to be public property,
and they redistributed the land among themselves. But in
the territory between the Nueces and the Rio Grande, many
Spanish-speaking people remained. A few Anglo cattle barons moved in and took over the role of the vanished landowners, the peons accepting them as patrons and protectors
and the Anglos accepting the peons as the labor force and
not encouraging further infiltration by other Anglos.

As the main thrust of the cattle ranch business turned
northward to the rich grazing lands of the buffalo and the
dying threat of the Comanche, the Texas border territory
quieted down to another peaceful period of almost a hundred years. Many of the Anglos married Mexican women
and adopted the cultural customs of their wives. The descendants of the earlier landowners, for the most part, had
been educated in private or parochial schools close to the
Rio Grande or in Mexico. This new breed, with its Anglo
infiltration, continued to be oriented to Mexico. If the children attended school, they were instructed in the Spanish
language; if they traveled, they went to Mexico. With only a
few rich landowners, Mexican or Anglo, in control, and
many peons to do the work, the Tejanos in the lower Rio
Grande Valley developed the first Spanish-speaking middle
class in the territory of the United States.

Here, then, in the Texas borderlands, was a Mexicanized,
Spanish-speaking enclave, the first Spanish culture group to
confront the Anglos, to absorb some of them, and to continue in the traditional ways down to the 20th century, despite the militant and uncompromising thrust of the Anglo
invasion.

* * *

In California, the first half of the 19th century was, in a very real sense, *the* Spanish period.

Almost all the romantic sterotypes that are recreated today in the fiestas and parades on holidays, and the image that the non-Hispanic North American carries in his mind—and that the tourist seeks and usually finds because it is commercially recreated for him—is of the Californio in those few, sun-drenched, halcyon years between 1800 and the discovery of gold at Sutter's Mill.

By the turn of the century, 18 missions stepstoned north along the California coast from San Diego to San Francisco, their names now the sentimental commonplaces of song and story: San Luis Rey, San Juan Capistrano, San Gabriel, San Miguel, San Juan Bautista, and the solid place names of San Fernando, Santa Barbara, San Luis Obispo, and San Jose. Only three more were to be built—Santa Inez in 1804, between Santa Barbara and San Luis Obispo, and San Rafael and San Francisco Solano in 1817 and 1823 in the territory just north of San Francisco Bay.

Except for the initial missions at San Diego, Monterey, and San Francisco Bay, the selection of sites for subsequent settlement followed only after considerable exploration, examination, and evaluation. The padres carefully sought out the most fertile valleys, the most commanding promontories, and the most useable harbors.

Since the mission property included not only the mission site itself, but also the tillable lands and great pasture fields for the mission herds, the Franciscans extended their claims so that the lands of one mission reached to the boundaries of the next; and since no civil town could legally be founded within five miles of a mission, the friars effectively prevented occupation of the rich coast lands of California except by their own neophytes and their own selected laity.

In conjunction with the missions, however, there were also the presidios, or military-political garrison towns. As the missions had at their heart the characteristic adobe church, the presidios had a barracks for the soldiers, the necessary public buildings, and a *castilla* for the cannons.

In connection with the presidio, there was also a *rancho del rey*, or king's farm, which was used to pasture the horses and other stock belonging to the fort. The commandants of the presidios were authorized to make grants of land to soldiers and other settlers, and so small villages soon formed around each presidio.

As a result of the general overlapping of the land claims made by the missions and the presidios, there was constant bickering between the Church and State. However, since the friars actually never were given title to the land but only authority for its use, and since the military commandants did not formally provide clear land grants to the soldiers and settlers who squatted around the presidios, the arguments were never resolved. In general, the priests managed to remain dominant because of their direct contact with the Indian neophytes who occupied most of their lands and tended their stock and farms, after the priests finally began to make converts.

Life on the missions at the turn of the century was highly regularized. The Angelus at sunrise was the signal for priests, overseers and neophytes to join in the church for the one-hour morning Mass. After breakfast, the overseers divided the native neophytes into work crews and dispatched them to the fields or to the workshops for seven hours of labor. Around the missions were the vegetable gardens and the orchards, watered by long irrigation ditches running from the dammed-up creek or river. Far out on the great *ranchos* roamed the cattle, sheep, and other stock of the mission. To keep the buildings in repair, neophytes quarried stones, made adobe brick and dried it in the sun, hewed timber from the far forest and transported it to the mission village, where other natives worked at the forge, tanned leather for saddles and shoes, and spun the thread from which to weave cloth for clothing and blankets.

Perhaps the most romantic of all the stereotypes to hold

over from the first quarter of the 19th century was that of the *rancho*, with the *patrón* in his *hacienda* and his vast holdings tended and occupied by his peons. Actually, there were relatively very few California *ranchos*, and even these were relatively short-lived; yet their impression is indelibly imprinted on the landscape. Some of the most famous of the *ranchos* were those of Manuel Iento, which embraced all the land between the Santa Ana and San Gabriel Rivers, and extended from the sea to the hill land on the northern frontier. Then there was the San Rafael tract, extending from the left bank of the Los Angeles River to the Arroyo Seco, this *rancho* granted to one José María Verdugo. Only five such grants were made prior to 1800. After the turn of the century, however, the grants proliferated, and it was not uncommon for a *rancho* to have 20,000 sheep, 15,000 cattle, and several thousand horses. On the great Vallejo Rancho of Sonora, there were 300 men tending the 146,000 acres of grazing land.

But though the presidio and *rancho* and mission lands were vast, there were only 1,200 non-native people in the whole of Alta California in 1800. And despite the fact that the actual number had tripled by 1820, the men in the non-native population numbered only around 500, the same number as had constituted the population 50 years before, when the non-native population had been almost entirely male. Thus, even at the height of the Spanish period in California, the actual productive and leadership force of Spanish and *mestizos* was a mere fraction of the mission, town, and *rancho* population, made up mostly of natives working under Spanish-speaking people's supervision; and control of the total population was in the hands of a few military commanders, a few priests, and a few *gente de razón*, the large landholders of direct Spanish lineage.

The breakdown of this structure started with the secularization of the missions. Despite their control and use of almost all the fertile lands along the coast, the padres had never actually been given title to even one acre of land, and in 1820, a decree that had been passed by the Spanish Cortes in 1813 finally reached California, ordering the friars to immediately cease governing and administering the property of the Indians.

The wars of liberation of the Mexican and Spanish-American colonies from the Spanish government prevented the carrying out of this order, but when the revolt from Spain was complete, the Mexican government enacted similar laws.

Between 1836 and 1842, the missions were completely carved up, with only the land on which the church stood remaining to the friars; and even then at least five of the missions were completely deserted in the process.

The Indians, who were to be the beneficiaries of the land and stock under the government decree, felt that both they and the padres were being robbed, and proceeded to decimate the livestock and destroy the property. By 1839, two thirds of the cattle, three quarters of the sheep and half of the horses had been butchered, and by 1845, the original herds in excess of 150,000 head had dwindled to 50,000. Of 15,000 Indians who had been part of the mission system, virtually all had disappeared into the mountains, onto the *ranchos,* or into the lower class of the pueblos by 1847.

While the Indians were being dispersed and the missions eliminated as an economic and political force, the *ranchos* were multiplying, with more than 800 sharing in the distribution of some 8,000,000 prime acres. Then, through sale, or seizure, or marriage, the *rancheros* began to combine, with some families getting several massive adjoining parcels, constituting *ranchos* of more than a quarter of a million acres each. By 1846, the power of California had settled on 46 individuals, self-made opportunists, who effectively ruled the territory.

It was indeed the peak of influence for the Spanish grandees, the *gente de razón;* the *ranchero's familia* extended outward from his *casa,* and included children, in-laws, other relatives, orphans, Indian servants, and the residents of the nearest village.

Despite the real estate enterprise and opportunism of a few, the essential characteristic of life in California—once the mission system had been destroyed and before the Anglo invasion, in turn, destroyed the life of the *rancho*—was that of *buena vida*.

The economy depended almost completely on the production of cattle for the hides and tallow trade, for which Anglo ships were now making the trip around the Horn from the eastern United States and back. There were also sheep whose wool was converted into clothing by the natives and the peons. And both cattle and sheep grazed and increased on their own in the fertile green valleys and provided even the herdsmen with a life of relative ease under the warm sun.

Olive groves, started by the padres, prospered. Green fields, requiring only sowing and reaping, yielded rich harvests. The finest products of the Industrial Revolution, brought in the ships for trading, provided luxuries unheard of on the frontier a few years before.

While the peons were still plowing with crudely constructed wooden plows with primitive points, attached to the horns of oxen, the *gente de razón*—señores, señoras, señoritas alike—appeared in the most extravagant costumes, the men, particularly, affecting bright jackets, silk sashes, velvet pantaloons, and embroidered shoes, with native *serapes* draped around their shoulders. Riding, gambling, dancing, and the giving and receiving of hospitality were the greatest pastimes of the *rico* class, the landowners.

Mañana was, indeed, time enough to think about the future.

But *mañana*, alas, was already here! it was in the golden motherlode over which they had been riding for their entire period of occupation, yet which they had never seen nor suspected because they were looking for evidence in the baubles of the non-gold-using coastal Indians, and because, in the golden sunshine, they had lacked the incentive that had driven de Soto and Vásquez de Coronado and the other conquistadores to follow even a golden lie to the bitter end in the clay pueblos of Cibola and the mud huts of Quivira.

Chapter 10

Gold!

Gold was discovered at Sutter's Mill by an Anglo in 1848.
By that time, the Californios—most of them individuals of
Spanish or Mexican or mixed Spanish-Mexican-Indian heritage who either had been born in California or had come
there to settle permanently and now considered themselves
natives—had increased to around 12,000. They had survived such periods of natural disaster as the time between
1826 and 1830 when there were twenty-two months—almost two of the four years—during which no rain at all fell,
wells and springs dried up, and horses and cattle and sheep
and goats either died by the thousands or were destroyed to
save what pasture there was for the remaining flocks and
herds. Again in 1840 and 1841, 14 consecutive months went
by without rainfall.

Politically, California had become a province of Mexico
rather than Spain when revolutionists had secured the Spanish New World's independence in 1821. Then, at dawn on
June 6, 1846, a group of Anglos in California launched the
Bear Flag Rebellion and declared the establishment of a
new Yankee Republic of California, independent of Mexico.

One month to the day later, Commodore John Drake Sloat arrived in Monterey Harbor, and posted a proclamation ending the Republic and making California a part of the United States, promising everyone the rights and privileges of citizenship.

A succession of commanders issued a succession of varying proclamations, prompting guerrilla action by the Californios, all of which resulted in 1847 in the Treaty of Cahuenga, again establishing equality for the Californios, most of whom returned quietly to the pleasures of *rancho* life.

Finally, in 1848, the Treaty of Guadalupe Hidalgo—the general treaty between the United States and Mexico that established from that time on all except a small stretch of the boundary between the two countries and provided for complete citizenship for all Spanish-speaking residents of the United States territory—appeared to settle permanently the equality of the Californios and the Yankees.

But 1848 was also the year that gold was discovered at Sutter's Mill.

Californios were among the first to succumb to the lure of the gold fields.

And they were also among the first to strike it rich.

Don Antonio Coronel (see Appendix for biography), leading a group from Los Angeles, picked up 45 ounces of gold in one day. A member of his party picked up one nugget that weighed 12 ounces. Still another, digging below a boulder, which had once blocked a rushing mountain stream, loaded a trowel with nuggets he found only three feet under the surface. A Californio who bought the claim extracted 52 pounds of gold in eight days and then sold the claim to another Californio who also came out of the hills bowed with the weight of the gold he had mined.

In that year of 1848, 1,300 Californios participated in the bonanza.

At last, the dreams of the conquistadores were being realized.

The prospect was indeed a golden one. The fact that by

the end of the year some 4,000 Anglos had arrived at the diggings—a few coming overland by various routes, others having come around the Horn by ship—did not seem in any way threatening, since these Yankees were not very successful at locating pockets of nuggets nor were they skilled at all in separating tiny flakes of gold from the river sand when nuggets were not to be found. The 1,300 Californios took out fully as much wealth in the year of 1848 as did the 4,000 Anglos.

California belonged to the Californios, and the Californios were full-fledged citizens of that land of freedom and equality, the United States of America.

But the 4,000 Yankees who arrived in 1848 were but a few drops presaging the deluge. In the next year—1849—alone, 80,000 more crossed the plains and mountains or sailed almost halfway around the world to join in plucking the golden nuggets from the golden soil. With them came 8,000 Mexicans—mostly from the mines and villages of Sonora, the metal-rich northern province of Mexico—and 5,000 South Americans—mostly Chileans and Peruvians, men also skilled in wresting precious metals from the earth.

By 1852, the immigrants seeking riches in California numbered more than a quarter of a million.

The sheer magnitude of this inundation has been virtually unmatched in all history, and the immediate consequence was a violent clash of cultures, which provided the prototype for the recurring racial riots and unrelenting discrimination characterizing Anglo-Hispanic relationships in California through the succeeding 120 years.

Although the Sonorans came armed with a knowledge of the basic prospecting and mining techniques of probing for nuggets, panning for flakes, and grinding heavy ore between massive flat boulders turned by a mule plodding in a circle while harnessed to a long spoke attached to the rocks—techniques the Anglos immediately picked up and perfected—their initial "luck," born of the skills they brought with them, made them objects of great Anglo jealousy and resentment. Besides, their sandals, sombreros, and puffed-out pantaloons made them visible objects of ridicule.

The Chileans' skill as miners and in such essential activities as bricklaying and baking made them valuable workers in the gold fields, but their language and their customs set them apart and they huddled in their own "Little Chile" at the foot of Telegraph Hill in San Francisco.

At first, the idea that these Spanish-speaking foreigners were grabbing the gold away from the newly arrived "true citizens" propelled companies of vigilantes into the saddle to drive the "greasers"—Anglo epithet for all Hispanos—from Sutter's Mill, from the Sacramento River area, and, indeed, from California. But caught in this massive harassment, by the color of their skin and the sound of their voices, were the original Californios, and there was no return to the gold fields for them for repeats of their 1848 successes.

Nor was there peace any more on their *ranchos*. For out of the mining country came the vigilantes to plunder the stock and harass *patrón* and peon alike. And out of the mass came squatters to settle on the land of the *ranchos* and claim it for themselves under the Homestead Act that had operated in the settling of the prairie land to the east. And out of the trauma and terror came newly formed bands of *bandidos*, swarthy Spanish-speaking plunderers who swarmed down on Anglo settlements when they were handy but also rustled the herds of the *ricos* and distributed their largess to the poor.

Fleeing from the chaos, Sonorans by the thousands trekked from the gold fields back across the wastes to the land south of the border where their color and their clothes and their language were acceptable.

Californios, in as much danger of getting shot, beaten, or lynched, as the Mexican *cholos*—literally, "scoundrels," but applied generally to all migrants—kept to their homes and their haciendas.

Then, suddenly, good Yankee common sense began to

prevail: with the Mexican buyers gone, food stocks began to gather dust on merchants' shelves, and mining equipment rusted in the yard and in the field; crowbars that had been selling for $8 could not be moved for 50¢; in just three southern counties Yankee merchants counted their losses up and found the figure was running around $10,000 a day.

More than that, an Anglo miner who would work for as little as $3 a day at the manual labor of mining was difficult to find; either he was out prospecting on his own—frequently for less daily take-home but with the chance of striking it rich—or he was drifting back toward the fertile valleys to stake out for himself a homestead on one of the pleasant *ranchos* where he felt quite sure he would be able to gain effective title when the Californios' claim to the vast lands proved to be couched in vague terms with invisible boundaries or based not on written documents at all but on some alleged verbal grant.

Not only would "greasers" work for a dollar in food, with just a few flakes of gold thrown in, but they would also spend the gold on the spot, drinking, gambling, and dancing. The Yankee worker, on the other hand—if he could be found—would hoard his meager earning and either send it back to the rocky soil of New England or carry it back himself, thus leaving another pick and shovel and crowbar to rust beside the mine shaft.

Besides, the Mexican *arrieros* were the best mule skinners in the world, proud of their tough and mangy pack animals, skilled in prodding them across the roughest terrain and through the dust and drought of the desert or the snow and wind of the mountain.

With all that economic evidence, the Anglo mine-operator or merchant began to understand the patrón-peon relationship and to practice it, with great profit and a widening gap between boss-"gringo" and worker-"greaser" the result.

Yet there was still one more step in this 1850 model of racial bigotry.

Over the years, from the time of the Manila Galleon in

the 1500's, a small community of Chinese who, for one reason or another, made the journey on their own initiative or were brought by cheap-labor seekers across the Pacific, had grown up in each of the seacoast towns. Since the gold strike, their numbers had increased in proportion to the number of all other immigrants.

Even more than the Mexicans, the Chinese were men of labor, tough and enduring, willing to work for a pittance and able to keep alive on scraps. Not as skilled at mining, they nonetheless worked longer and for less than the Spanish-speaking labor force and therefore settled at the bottom of the human order, to be despised there as coolies even by the peons with whom they rubbed shoulders.

Thus, despite his own persecution, the Spanish-speaking person, Californio and Latin American alike, could turn the bitterness of his language on the visibly ethnically outlandish Oriental and his illiterate "pidgin" English.

There was still a period of fiesta and fandango for the city *rico* and the *ranchero*, with cattle and goods selling at inflated prices to the newly arriving Anglo hordes.

But by mid-century, California was effectively lost to the Californios.

On the land of the *ranchos*, the pattern was like that of Vicente Lugo and Don Julio Verdugo: In 1850, Vicente had a 10,000-acre *rancho*, fat with cattle; drought wiped out his herd, so he leased part of his holdings to some Anglo sheep men and managed to hold on to 800 acres surrounding his family *casa;* however, in order to live, he had to sell his remaining land, and, by 1870, was reduced to 400 acres, the rest going at $8 to $10 an acre. Don Julio, as late as 1861, was operating the Rancho San Rafael—which today constitutes Glendale and a portion of Burbank—and he was surviving; but just ten years later, the 36,000-acre spread had been reduced to a mere 200, as he had been forced to parcel it out in order to pay his debts and buy his bread.

By the end of the 19th century, except in the crumbling mission walls and in the bright color and gay music of fiesta

days, the romantic Spanish period had vanished, leaving behind only the names of people and places to remind the
Mexican miner, farm hand, and laborer that their language
and their ancestors had once been the dominating force in
this land of dust and drudgery.

Chapter 11

Pastoral

I n New Mexico—at that time essentially all the territory between Texas and California—the 19th century was also a time for the final flowering of the Spanish-speaking culture before destruction by the Anglo traders and settlers.

But in New Mexico, the Anglo impact was blunted by the lack of a single, dramatic focus, such as cattle-raising in Texas and gold-seeking in California. The thin soil, the arid climate, and the vast lands—which could be reached and crossed only on foot, on plodding horseback, or on creaking wagons—provided an unpromising and uninviting prospect to the Anglo hunters for furs, gold, or mercantile wealth, and even less to the stolid Anglo farmer whose greatest desire was six feet of loam in which to plant his seeds.

And yet this unpromising, uncompromising land nurtured the largest Spanish-speaking population and sustained the most Spanish of all the Spanish-Indian cultures that developed in the original Spanish settlements from Florida to California. There were more missions in the New Mexico territory than in all the rest of the Spanish-settled areas across the United States put together.

114

By 1827, New Mexico had a population of 44,000, ten times as many as California or Texas, and the language and customs of the people remained more 16th-century Spanish in the early 19th century than had even the language and customs of Spain, itself.

Yet, of course, only a very small percentage of the New Mexico population were actually directly descended from Spanish forebears; they were much more Mexican and Pueblo Indian. Their language, too, had picked up Indian elements. But, overall, Spanish influences were dominant, and of these, the Church was not the least influential.

The New Mexico missions, however, had never achieved the influence nor the wealth that those in California had wielded, since they had not exercised control over land, agriculture, stock-raising, or the lives of neophytes. The mission church had been just a church, and the priest, in effect, a parish priest, with the Indians remaining at home in their pueblos and the settlers building their own towns and developing their own farms.

Because large-scale administration had thus never been the lot of the New Mexico padres, they had concentrated on conversions, and on the establishment and perpetuation of religious traditions and church participation. In addition, since there had not been great mission herds and vast mission lands to divide up in compliance with the secularization orders that had caused so much violence and displacement in California, the end of the mission era in New Mexico had left hardly a trace in the sands; and life in the pueblos, in the Spanish-Mexican villages, in the fields, and on the ranges proceeded as it always had, with the padre ministering to a flock that had always been people, and the flock providing for the livelihood of the priest and the continued existence of the Church through contributions of food and labor, but not through the total subjugation of lives.

The lifelines of the New Mexico settlements and farms were the faint traces of shallow streams, sandy rivers, and the laboriously constructed and tenderly tended irrigation net that dated from the days of Juan de Oñate's first settlement. Land rights, therefore, were anchored at the water's edge: individual land grants ran narrowly back from a thin slice of the riverbank, a watering spot at the edge of a stream, or a portion of the *acequia madre*, or "mother canal," serving the irrigated lands.

Uprange from the privately held, water-based strip farms were the farm plots and grazing lands held in joint tenancy by the whole community.

Individually interdependent but collectively isolated from other settlements, New Mexican townspeople and farmers survived by unremitting toil, propagated new generations by intermarriage, and passed on to their children equal shares of the strip lands running down to the water and equal rights in the grazing land stretching out over the hills.

Sunday Mass, with its processional, its ceremony, and its symbolism, was at once their theater and their salvation. The fact that the padres—with no supervision possible from either Spain or Mexico and little incentive to enterprise other than insuring continued contributions to the church— possessed themselves of wives, sired children, and grew fat and lazy on the fruits of others' labor, had no negative effect on church participation by the New Mexican *compadres*, peasant brothers on the land for whom their way of life was the only way of life.

And the lore of the fathers—passed on to the children by demonstration, command, and story—became the law—accepted and unquestioned because it provided for survival, and there was nothing else.

But in addition to the townspeople and farmers, there was another totally different culture that grew up in New Mexico in the early part of the 19th century; this was the culture whose economic lifelines were not those of the watercourses but rather of the sheep trails.

In New Mexico, sheep generated the largest land grants

and contributed to the widening gap between rich and poor, the *ricos* and the *pobres*.

In the early 1800s, people like Don Bartolomé Baca, Governor of Spanish New Mexico—who, in 1819, received a grant in the Estancia Valley between Albuquerque and the Manzano Mountains, of 1,282,000 acres, where he ran 2 million sheep requiring 2,700 herders—epitomized the *ricos*. Slightly smaller, but still immense, was the domain of the first governor under Mexican rule, "El Guero" (The Blonde) Chávez, who held title to over a million sheep. And then there was the Spanish soldier, Antonio Sandoval, who was awarded nearly a half million acres right in the middle of the old Baca grant by a subsequent Mexican governor, Manuel Armijo, himself the owner of more than 250,000 sheep.

In the sheep culture, the *rico*, holder of a large land grant, owner of thousands of sheep, was the lord of his domain, the law over all the people who tended his flocks. And, since labor was the cheapest commodity in the territory, the organization was elaborate and many hands did the work for their *patrón*.

At the top was the *mayordomo*, operating boss of the sheep empires. He hired and fired his subordinates and made the rounds of the sheep camps to check the condition of the flocks and the monthly accounts of those under him.

His chief assistant was the *caporal*, who supervised three *vaqueros*, each of whom, in turn, was in charge of three *pastores*, the latter being the actual herdsmen responsible for up to 2,000 sheep. The *caporal* ranged widely, keeping an alert eye for disease, directing the herds to new ranges, watching the level of water in the streams and at the water exacting detailed reports from his *vaqueros*.

The *vaquero*, for his part, moved constantly between the flocks of his *pastores*, each of whom never left his little band, following them on foot, keeping them together with the help of his dogs, protecting them from wild animals, and bedding down with them at night.

At the base of this pastoral pyramid was the tough and lowly Churro, his scraggly wool still the weaving staple for Spanish and Indian culture alike, his succulent meat still the choicest in that land of jack rabbit and rattlesnake.

Although the wages of the *pastor*—$5 to $8 a month—and his nomadic life were not conducive to a permanent home or planning for future security, the day-to-day prospect was not unpleasant: beans were 2¢ a pound, and native wines were cheap and plentiful; homemade deerskin moccasins protected the feet; calico and unbleached muslin provided shirting at a few cents a yard; and the fleece of sheep provided ample protection against the chill of the winter winds. No section lines nor boundary fences limited the movement of the flocks, and the *patrón* was always ready to advance a few *reales* for emergencies. Always in debt, the *pastor* and his family were seldom in despair. Indeed, the sun smiled on the sheepherder of the early 1800s.

Nor was the path from poverty to plenty totally closed for the *pobre*. There was what was called the *partido* system, by which a poor youth could contract with a rich stockman to take care of a herd of a thousand ewes and ten breeding rams, not for money but for lambs. Since the practice was to let the breeding rams run with the ewes, lambing was a year-round activity, with two or three lambs being born each day, which the shepherd could force the ewes to suckle much more easily than if a larger number of offspring arrived at approximately the same time.

The shepherd and rich *patrón* would share the lambs and the wool from the flock, keeping the original one thousand capital stock intact. Thus, over a period of time, if weather and wolves were willing, the poor young man could increase his wealth, hire others to do his work, and, perhaps, contract with other poor young men to start their flocks on the same basis, so that he, himself, would eventually be a *patrón*.

Actually, things seldom worked out so neatly. In the beginning, the poor young man, in addition to contracting for the sheep, would also take a loan of actual cash against the flock's increase, so that he could marry, perhaps build a small house, and pay for the necessary help to care for the sheep and shear them at wool time. Despite the fact that the contract would call for repayment in lambs or wool of the advanced money, such were the demands on the *pobre* for food, for church contributions, and for family that he seldom caught up with his interest payments, let alone payments to reduce the capital advance. In addition, wolves and weather usually made inroads on the flock; and, even more certain, bands of Apache raiders would cut in and out of his herds, carrying off his profits.

So, like the village *compadre,* the New Mexico sheepherder, in those first years of the 19th century, lived a life of isolation from all except those overseeing him or whom he was overseeing; and his language, his customs, and his hopes remained those of his father and his family and his neighbor.

For the *ricos,* life, though hardly a physical struggle for survival, was not the cultured security of the wealthy Tejanos of the lower Rio Grande, with their proximity to both Mexico, with its luxuries and educational institutions, and the Gulf, with its easy trading; nor was it the romantic *rancho* life of the Californios, with their silks and satins and other evidences of *buena vida,* secured from the Yankee trading ships in exchange for cowhides and tallow.

For the first half of the 19th century, the Nuevo Mejicanos had one avenue of trade: south to the mining towns of northern Mexico, and beyond to Veracruz, Guadalajara, and even to Mexico City. The *conducta,* an annual caravan participated in by virtually every *rico* family in New Mexico, formed each year in March. Two hundred thousand to a half million sheep were herded in the van, some from the *ricos'* own stock, others picked up from the less affluent *rancheros* for less than a dollar a head, to be sold in Sonora, and other centers, for $3 and more a head. Besides sheep, the traders were accompanied by burros, bearing woolen textiles, buffalo hides, furs, and vegetables. The round trip took seven months, and the traders would not return to the territory of New Mexico until sometime in September, bringing fruit, Brazil wood and other scarce items, and herding cattle to supplant the meager New Mexico stocks.

Because of the barren land and the rigors of trading, the New Mexico *patrones* lived in houses hardly more luxurious than those of their peons—although larger. Thick adobe walls enclosed corridors of barren rooms, which surrounded a cottonwood-shaded courtyard; and another passageway led to a similar enclosed square where the slaves were quartered with the carts, wagons, and other impedimenta of ranching.

Cooking was done on primitive stoves, and the *ricos*—like the Indians from whom they learned and the *pobres* whose labor sustained them—squatted on the hard-packed earth floors to eat; and they spread blankets on the ground to sleep, since even if there had been lumber, there were few tools or cabinetmakers to construct furniture and no ships or wagon caravans to bring such items from the Anglos to the east or the Mexican artisans to the south.

There were no schools in the territory, no newspapers, no books. Whatever knowledge of the past survived was passed on from generation to generation by word of mouth.

But in the great low houses and around the lonely campfires in the hills, a rich heritage of folk tales, riddles, myths, proverbs, and games was kept alive, along with folk songs and poetry, Spanish in origin but Mexican in the retelling. At the same time, intricate handicrafts, husbanding the scarce natural resources, led to the production of silver and gold filigree work, to small carvings and paintings of saints, and to ornaments fashioned from tin by the *pobres*, who were trying to emulate the silver accouterments in the homes of the *ricos*.

Most of all, weaving emerged as the finest of all the New Mexico art in the mid-century period, which followed the opening of the Santa Fe trail and the introduction of Yankee money and goods, in place of the bartering of essentials, which had constituted the Nuevo Mejicano trade up to that time.

Even the Yankee traders, however, found little in the barren land to keep them there after they had disposed of their goods; and they returned home with the money, the furs, the animals, and the buffalo rugs they had acquired. Throughout the 19th century, except for their periodic visits to such centers as Santa Fe and El Paso del Norte, the Anglos left the territory to the Indians, the *mestizos,* and the Creoles.

Among the Spanish-speaking population, only an occasional individualist utilized the essential openness of physical, social, and economic environment as the route from poverty to riches, from impotence to power. Such an individualist was Don Manuel Armijo. The exact details of his journey from obscurity to notoriety have been embellished over the years by legend and lore, much of his own devising, but there is no doubt about the trace of the journey itself.

As a young man, Manuel, a superb horseman, found employment working one of the herds of cattle which sought for a time to occupy the uplands with the Churro sheep. Conscientious and industrious, he was valued by the *ranchero* who employed him, and achieved the level of *vaquero.* But Manuel sensed that cattle would not win the grazing lands, and when he heard that a wealthy *hacendado,* or large plantation owner, named Francisco Chávez, was joining with two other *ricos* to purchase 36,000 head of sheep to send south to Durango and Zacatecas in northern Mexico, Manuel left the cattle herd in the mountains east of Albuquerque and went down to the town to apply to Chávez to be one of his shepherds.

Conscientiously and diligently, he trudged in the dust behind the sheep, south from Albuquerque to El Paso and across the Rio Grande to the edge of the Jordanda, the vast desert waste between El Paso and Laguna de los Patos. But Manuel had not walked those weary miles in silence. He

and another sheepherder had plotted to leave the encampment and, disguised as Apaches—the feared Indian raiders
who harassed *pobre* and *rico* alike—swoop down on the
flock, drive off the remaining shepherds, and, discarding the
disguise, take the sheep on to Durango to sell them as their
own.

His first venture in private enterprise was successful, and
Don Manuel decided to do further business with Francisco
Chávez, whose own practice was to add to his flocks by
buying at very low prices the sheep of his desperately poor
neighbors; as a consequence, the Chávez herds were so vast
that it was impossible for the *hacendado* or his *vaqueros* or
even his *caporales* to positively identify individual sheep as
being his or someone else's.

Gradually gathering around him an enterprising but
wine-thirsty lot of mobile *pastores,* Armijo cut into the
flocks of the elderly Chávez, driving the sheep off to his own
mountain pastures, and then herding them back at sale time
and collecting cash for the sheep that had been stolen from
Chávez' own herds.

Wealth, followers, and influence growing, Armijo entered
the political arena at the time of Mexico's wars of independence. He became Governor of New Mexico, a position he
held throughout the entire Mexican period, ruling like the
bandit king that he was, exacting duties of $100 per wagon
from the Yankee traders who survived the trek from St.
Louis to Santa Fe, executing, in public ceremonies, those
who displeased him, and levying taxes upon *pobre* and *rico,*
upon *hacendado* and poor *ranchero,* as moods of the moment impelled him.

But such was the openness of the New Mexico environment that despite its cradling and nurture of such as Armijo,
no one man or, indeed, no combination of men or governments could directly influence or dominate the day-to-day
activities or even the life cycle of the villagers, the farmers,
and the nomadic *pastores.*

So, as the old adobe brick of the missions, of the forts, of the *haciendas*, and of the small houses and barns slowly softened into dust under the hot New Mexico sun, the dry winds, and the passing of years, the Nuevo Mejicano ignored the corruptness of his governors and his priests and turned more and more to his own family as the unit of existence. He subsisted on his *atole*, his *frijol* and his *chile*, scooped up by his woman's parchment-thin *tortilla*, speaking the Spanish-Indian of his fathers, and passing the language on to his children, along with the songs, the tales and traditions of his father and his grandfather before him, unchanged through the years, as generation followed generation through the late 1800's. The peaceful round of existence was broken only by sporadic Apache attacks and the gambling and drinking and dancing and trading at the annual Taos fair and on the fiesta days around the village churches.

Thus it was that the Tejanos retreated from central Texas Texas to the lush lower Rio Grande and established a cattle *ranchero* culture, leaving, by the end of the 19th century, only peon remnants of the days of Spanish dominance in the city of San Antonio and across the vast reaches of the Anglo-dominated Texas prairies.

Thus it was that the Californios succumbed to the massive Anglo invasion in search of bonanza gold at mid-19th century, to compete with the Chinese for the bottom rung of the social and economic ladder in the cities, on the farms, and at the mines, while the *ricos* watched their vast holdings disappear under the squatter's plow and in the Anglo courts.

And thus it was that the Nuevo Mejicanos retreated into their family units, their language, and their religion. Except for occasional Yankee dollars received in the Santa Fe trade and from work in the mines—which provided a steady but unspectacular stream of silver for the artisans and the Anglo mints—they continued their life of self-sufficiency and barter, protected from the surging turbulence of Civil War and

Industrial Revolution that was sweeping the rest of the United States into the 20th century.

But before the end of the 19th century, a new wave of Spanish-speaking immigration into the territory of the United States was building up. Its first lappings on the shores of Florida began in 1868, when a Spanish cigar maker, Vicente Martínez Ybor, from Havana, Cuba, opened a branch cigar factory on Key West, Florida. The move was patriotic, coinciding with the start of a ten year Cuban war against Spain. It was also economic: the United States placed a heavy import duty on Havana cigars; by moving to Florida, Ybor evaded the import duty and was able to undersell his competitors. Naturally, other cigar owners followed his lead, and there began an exodus of cigar makers and their families from the Cuban towns of Santiago de las Vegas, San Antonio de los Baños, Bejucal, Guines, and Havana, itself. They came first to the Keys, and then surged north to Tampa, a small town four blocks long, set in the Florida wilderness, which rapidly expanded to a thriving city with the arrival of new thousands of Cuban tobacco industry people.

In the same period, Puerto Ricans were making their roundabout way to California, their first stop being the sugar cane fields of Hawaii. Basque herdsmen were emigrating from the Spanish highlands to the rugged coasts of northern California and Oregon, and inland to the lush sheep-grazing land around what is now Boise, Idaho.

While the Puerto Ricans in California and the Basques in the Pacific Northwest added new elements to the Spanish-speaking population and extended the Spanish-speaking settlements into areas previously not reached, the Cuban cigar makers' migration to Florida added even more.

For the Cubans came out of a culture where literature, history, and philosophy had thrived in a small geographical area. Cubans had maintained ties with Spain, with mainland Mexico, and with the developing Anglo nation to the north through the years from the early settlements following Columbus's first voyages, through the Empire years and the glitter of the Spanish galleons—with the excursions of Ponce de Léon and Pánfilo de Narváez and his treasurer, Núñez Cabeza de Vaca—and through the years of the African-Yankee slave trade when the New England slavers made their stopovers in the West Indies, exchanging people for rum, and developing a taste for those long, hand-rolled, slow-burning Havana cigars.

As a consequence, not even the lowest-paid Cuban factory hand was willing to accept docilely his job, his pay, and his meager living quarters as the horizon of his existence; nor did he accept the petty government officials, or their political bosses, or even the Spanish monks as divinely appointed overlords whose word was law and whose law was to be obeyed without question.

The Tampa-based transplanted Cuban cigar makers immediately formed Los Caballeros del Trabajo, a branch of the Knights of Labor, and the first trade union in southern United States. More militant was the name a new group took in 1886: La Resistencia. By 1900, the unions were strong enough and bitter enough to initiate their first major strike, one that failed but was only put down by the overwhelming bloody power of the owners, resisted militantly by the strikers.

In the same spirit of group action for individual welfare, in 1892, José Martí, later to be called the "George Washington of Cuba," selected Key West as the site for the founding of his Partido Revolucionario Cubano, an organization that provided the focus for the plotting of the Cuban revolution that broke out against Spain in 1895 and for the development of sympathy and support throughout the United States—all of which culminated in Cuba's independence, and in the annexation of Puerto Rico as a territory of the United States at the conclusion of the 1898–1899 Spanish-American War.

And so, 400 years after the first Spanish landfall in the

New World, a new century ushered in a totally new period in the history of the Spanish-speaking people in the territory of the United States.

Like the original explorations, the new period began in Florida, with bloodletting and conflict.

Elsewhere across the southern face of the United States, some Spanish-speaking people still occupied a few *haciendas* and dressed in Castilian splendor, but most toiled in dusty fields, slept in crumbling adobe shelters, watched with their dogs over highland herds of feeding sheep, or occupied shacks and shanties in the incipient *barrios* of burgeoning industrial cities.

To both *rico* and *pobre*, the strike and the Cuban revolution were distant, virtually unnoticed events of little or no significance in the affairs of family, church, and neighborhood. And yet the era of militant self-determination—which those two events at the turn of the century characterized—was to be the significant contribution to themselves of the Spanish-speaking people in the United States during the next 70 years.

Part *4*

 *The Migrants*

 Iron Horse

The horse was probably the most important Spanish import to the southwestern territory of the United States; since, for good or for ill, it provided the means for the initial dominance of the conquistadores, the transport of supplies and settlers, and the mobility of the Plains Indians.

The "iron horse" was the most important Anglo importation to the same region; for the long-range, rapid mass transport, which the railroads provided, precipitated economic and cultural changes that altered irrevocably the shape and substance of life for people not only in that territory but throughout the United States.

For the Spanish-speaking people, the "iron horse" provided, first of all, jobs. With pickaxe and shovel, the peons leveled or built up the roadbed across the prairies, made the deep cuts through the hills, and hacked rights-of-way from the brinks of precipices. With axe and saw and mule, they felled trees and dragged them and shaped them for ties and for trusses, spinning spidery trestles across small gullies and great canyons. With sweat and sledgehammer, they drove home the spikes, which held the shining rails in place for the puffing monsters and the creaking boxcars and the plush-padded passenger coaches to follow along the trails once trod by Juan de Oñate, Juan Bautista de Anza, and Fray Francisco Vélez Escalante, so many years before.

But laying the rails was not the end.

For storm and sun and heavy pounding of steel on steel eroded gravel and earth, weathered wooden ties, loosened heavy spikes and rusted shiny rails. Constant care and repair was necessary over every inch of the thousand-upon-thousand miles of track to insure the safe journey of the produce and people.

Natives of the territory were not available in sufficient numbers to perform the tasks of shepherding the rails, so straw bosses and supervisors looked south across the Rio Grande, south from New Mexico and Arizona to Sonora and Chihuahua, and there they located a vast reservoir of unskilled laborers, peons who responded to promises of one American dollar a day in cash in exchange for their vigilance, their strength, and their physical imperviousness to the heat and dust and drought, through the desert stretches of the Santa Fe and the Southern Pacific rights-of-way.

The first of the Mexican section hands responded to recruiters and crossed the border at El Paso in 1900.

The 20th century Mexican migration had begun.

Awaiting the newcomers and their families were the boxcars that were to become their homes. From El Paso they rattled and bounced in the dirty springless conveyances north and west, sprayed by smoke and cinders from the soft-coal-burning steamers that had replaced the picturesque wood-fueled puffers of the Civil War era, until their wheeled home was uncoupled and shunted off on some nameless, cheerless siding from which they would set out each morning thereafter to walk the track, test the ties, tighten the rails, and jump from the right-of-way to stand in the thunder and dust of the heavy-laden freight or speeding passenger trains that it was their job to keep moving.

At the far terminus of the transcontinental lines in California, the Southern Pacific and Santa Fe reached down along the Baja Península and beyond the mouth of the Colorado to the shores of the Gulf—where Núñez Cabeza de Vaca had consummated his eight-year trek four centuries earlier—for additional Mexican labor to man their shops and walk their rails.

By 1906, two and three carloads a week were chugging into southern California, establishing boxcar and tent *colonias,* and then reloading for transport to remote spots in Colorado, Wyoming, Utah, Montana, Idaho, Oregon, Washington, Kansas, and Nebraska.

In 1908, 16,000 Mexicans were recruited in El Paso, alone, for railroad employment. By 1910, 2,000 a month were crossing the border to set out on their boxcar journeys to a land where their language was neither understood nor spoken, to a place where the dollar a day that seemed so grand and the work that seemed so special were both disdained and despised, just as they would be despised by the Anglo inhabitants of the cities and towns and ranches, which they would live in, visit, or pass through.

In east Texas, at the turn of the century, cotton was king, as it was all across the states that had been the Confederacy over beyond the Mississippi River. When the seemingly insatiable demands of the New England cotton mills, the New York garment manufacturers, and the export markets pressed plantation owners for increased production, the cattle country beckoned and King Cotton moved westward behind plows that turned the prairie sod to farmland, where seeds transformed vast, grassy grazing lands to bushy fields whose blooms burst white under the Texas sun.

Mexican peons crossed over at points all along the Rio Grande and traversed the broad plains to meet the cotton—planting, hoeing, harvesting, and then returning home with Yankee dollars in their pockets.

Closer to the border, the Reclamation Act of 1902 and the completion, in 1904, of the St. Louis, Brownsville and Mexican Railway, spurred landowners in the Lower Rio

Grande Valley to use federal funds for the development of large-scale irrigation projects and to plant table vegetable crops, which could be whisked to metropolitan centers on the railroads' refrigerator cars. The key to success in these enterprises was the Mexican laborer, whose knowledge of irrigation techniques dated back to conquistador days, and whose experience and environment prepared him for the stoop labor, the hand planting and weeding tasks under temperatures of 100° and above that constituted truck gardening in that area.

One other legislative event near the turn of the century also contributed spectacularly to the Anglos' intense recruitment of Mexican immigrant labor in the first decade of the 20th century. In 1897, Congress placed a 75 per cent tax on the importation of foreign sugar. The result was the birth of the United States' sugar beet industry.

In California, growers immediately turned to the resident Spanish-speaking population, the Mexican immigrants in railroad labor camps, and additional peons recruited from the northern Mexican plains to perform the tedious hand labor of blocking and thinning the sugar beet fields in the spring, and harvesting the mature roots in the fall. By 1906, the sugar beet acreage in the United States had more than tripled from the 135,000 acres planted in 1900.

So aggressive had California railroad and agricultural interests been in recruiting immigrants from Mexico that the Mexican immigrant population in California quadrupled in the decade from 1900 to 1910, 8,086 being the immigrant population at the turn of the century, a number that had increased to 33,694 ten years later.

The traffic across the border into Texas, of course, had gained momentum earlier because of the railroad building and the development of the cotton fields in former cattle country, so that there were already more than 70,000 Mexican immigrants in Texas in 1900. That number, however, had increased to more than 125,000 by 1910. And from about 20,000 in Arizona and New Mexico at the turn of the century, the Mexican immigrants numbered more than 40,000 ten years later.

Thus, as the United States entered the second decade of the 20th century, the habit of looking to Mexico for cheap hand labor to perform the menial tasks necessary for new agricultural and industrial enterprise in the southwestern United States was effectively established.

And everybody was happy.

The railroads were running and carrying the produce from the Lower Rio Grande farms to the metropolitan markets, carrying the cotton from central Texas plantations to the New England textile mills, carrying the sugar beets from the California fields to the newly built refineries.

And the Mexican immigrants had railroad cars and tents and shacks in their developing *colonias* to live in, and good jobs and good pay. . . .

Only nobody was quite that happy!

The railroads were going to the expense of hiring contractors to recruit Mexican help for them, but just when the Mexicans had begun to learn their jobs, they heard of other jobs in the truck gardens and in the cotton fields and harvesting sugar beets, and so the railroads had to go back to the contractors to recruit more Mexican workers for the section gangs.

And it was the same with the truck garden owners, the cotton plantation operators, and the sugar beet growers: the crew they had for the planting might disappear to some other farm or even back across the border just when the weeds needed to be chopped, and almost never were they around for the harvest. The constant struggle and expense to keep the field hands on the line took time away from the more important task of marketing, and tied up money that should have been used for expansion.

And the Mexican immigrants?

At first they thought they were well off, but then they began to notice that no one else would do the work they were doing, and the dollar a day they got was a lot less than what others were getting for work that was not nearly as strenuous and looked to be a lot more desirable.

In 1903, more than a thousand Mexican sugar beet workers in Ventura, California, joined together to strike for better working conditions and more pay. They lost their jobs, and many of them were deported back to Mexico.

But the trouble had begun.

It was sporadic and ineffectual, and most of the Mexican immigrant workers continued to do their daily work with other Mexicans, eat their daily meals with other Mexicans, return to their boxcars and shanties with other Mexicans, and sing their Mexican songs, and talk their Mexican talk, and drink their Mexican wine, and give nobody any trouble.

Except that Mexican workers employed in the construction of the Los Angeles electric streetcar line started a strike, which was followed by others and came to a climax when the *Los Angeles Times* was dynamited in 1910.

The unsuccessful strikes—by the Cuban cigar makers in Florida and the sugar beet and electric railway workers in California—showed that not all of the new immigrants were docile, subservient, and unambitious peons, as their employers had initially believed them to be.

However, the strikes were also symptomatic of concerns much deeper than simply wages and working conditions.

By 1910, the shape of things to come for the Spanish-speaking people in the United States during the first half of the 20th century was already clear. The new immigrants were being brought in to do menial jobs that the Anglos would not touch. They were being brought in to work for wages below those that Anglos would accept. Even in situations—such as in the Nevada mines—where Anglos and Mexicans worked side by side at the same tasks—there was one scale of wage for the Anglos and a lower scale for Mexicans.

When immigrants were imported in groups by contractors, they were transported in those groups to work areas and dumped, still in groups, into shack towns on the edges of larger communities where their language, their dress, and their poverty set them apart and held them together, looking and sounding different from the rest of the community.

Along with their inability to speak English and their dark complexions, the Mexicans were generally short in stature so that their fair-skinned Anglo neighbors literally looked down upon them.

But it was not only their Anglo neighbors who avoided and despised them: the Spanish-speaking residents who had preceded them resented the new immigrants almost more than the Anglos did.

The sons and daughters of the early Californios, the Nuevo Mejicanos and the Tejanos, had been gradually making new lives for themselves in the last half of the 19th century. Then the Spanish-speaking dominance of the Southwest had been shattered by the westward Anglo migration, and they had found themselves—as had the long-time Californios in the gold fever of 1849—grouped with "foreigners." Their dark skins set them apart and barred them from Anglo restaurants, Anglo theaters, Anglo schools, and Anglo neighborhoods.

So, there were widening differences among members of the Spanish-speaking community, although they were forced together by the "they-all-look-alike" syndrome of the Anglo community.

And both the lumping together and the breaking apart were to be intensified during the next 50 years.

Another complicating factor during the first quarter of the 20th century was the revolutionary movement against the government of Cuba and against the regime of Porfirio Díaz in Mexico. Among others, Ricardo and Enrique Magón—who were exiled by Díaz for the publication of a Mexico City newspaper called *Liberación* and the organization of a revolutionary movement called the "First Liberal Congress"—agitated from St. Louis, Missouri, and Douglas, Arizona. Eventually, in Los Angeles, they organized the

Mexican Liberal Party and undertook an abortive invasion of Mexico on May 8, 1910, seizing Mexicali and Tijuana, just across the border, but retreating—when neither financial nor physical support was sufficient to hold the towns—to Los Angeles, where they were eventually convicted of breaching the neutrality laws of the United States and sentenced to two years in a federal penitentiary.

When Ricardo died in Leavenworth prison and his body was returned to Mexico for burial, he had become a national hero, but his revolutionary activity and that of others caused great tensions along the border, where the Anglo economy and dominance were threatened by the Mexican violence. Shootings of Anglos by Mexicans and of Mexicans by Anglos, for no other reason than that of mutual suspicion, became common. Cattle rustling on both sides of the border to take advantage of inflated prices brought on by the unrest both at home and in Europe boosted property losses into the hundreds of thousands of dollars. Texans suspected the Mexicans of conspiring with the Germans after 1914 to provide an entryway for the Kaiser into the rich heartland of the United States.

When Pancho Villa raided a town in New Mexico on March 9, 1916, the United States government responded by sending General Pershing into Mexico to hunt him down.

In that same year, however, Ezequiel de Baca was elected Governor of New Mexico—the first Spanish-speaking citizen ever to be *elected* to such high office in the United States.

But the two most important events during the decade 1910–1920 affecting the Spanish-speaking people in the United States took place in 1917.

Most obvious was the entry of the United States into the European war, an event that, by involving so many Anglo working men directly in the war effort, created an apparently imperative need for additional Mexican immigration to provide for the production both of foodstuffs and industrial items.

The second event was the act of Congress granting citizenship to inhabitants of the territory of Puerto Rico. With citizenship, Puerto Ricans were free to travel between their island and the United States without the delays and restrictions imposed by the Immigration Service. Coinciding with the need for workers on the mainland, this act engendered an immediate movement of several thousand Puerto Ricans to the legendary metropolis of New York, where they hoped to better their financial and social condition.

From every point of view, the Puerto Ricans should have had a better chance than had the Mexicans. Education and individual enterprise had long been values in their island homeland, whereas the Mexican immigrants—even though the majority of them came from urban rather than rural areas—were frequently illiterate, usually undernourished, and all were a product of a society and political system that sought to erase individual characteristics of economic or social initiative and enterprise.

But the Puerto Ricans, who disembarked so hopefully from the ships that had carried them up the coast of the country to which they now belonged as full-fledged citizens, found themselves still regarded as aliens, their swarthy complexions and their non-Brooklynese English setting them apart and closing apartment house doors and avenues of employment to them as effectively as if they were violating statutes by being there.

Some, less dependent on the immediate securing of work than others, took advantage of the rail net that fanned out from New York to seek employment in less hostile areas; and such was their mobility that, by 1920, there were Puerto Ricans living and working in 44 of the 48 states.

A substantial group also followed the route established earlier by the sugar cane workers, and joined other Spanish-speaking peoples in the beet fields of California; so that, next to New York, California had the largest continental Puerto Rican population for the ensuing 30 years.

In the decade 1910 to 1920, housing patterns for the

Spanish-speaking people throughout the Southwest had become fixed. Typical were the California *colonias*; and Los Angeles, the site of the greatest concentration of Spanish-speaking people, was particularly characteristic.

During most of the 19th century, Los Angeles had remained off the beaten track, a modest trading center for the southern *rancheros*, a quiet town with not much of a seaport and no close access to gold fields. As late as 1880, Los Angeles was essentially a small Mexican town, in which Spanish was the language of transaction, both for business and for casual conversation, and where, as a neighborly gesture to the Anglo minority and the Anglo wayfarer, public documents were published in English as well as Spanish.

By the turn of the century, however, the Southern Pacific and Santa Fe railroads, like great pipelines, were spewing eastern Anglos by the thousands into their western terminus city of Los Angeles, where cactus land and sand hill suddenly became valuable residential subdivisions, and the clusters of ancient adobe *casas* had to be leveled to make way for large industrial developments. The only place for the *casas'* Spanish-speaking inhabitants to move was out.

At the sites where the railroad hands had first huddled in boxcars on sidings, then moved into tents, the company had eventually built row houses, which they rented to their employees, a practice that kept the employees' pockets empty of money and returned it to the railroads' cash register to be used for future payrolls. As new hands came in, some of the old hands, feeling permanent, made deals with the railroads to buy lots around the outskirts of the campsite at a dollar down and a dollar a week—a process that, in itself, was almost as permanent as renting—and then using what was left over to build houses of their own, houses with thin wood walls, tin roofs, and one or two rooms barely large enough to shelter them and their brood.

With the turn-of-the-century land boom—spurred by railroad publicity—Anglo-built "Spanish colonial" houses began to cover vast areas, their red tile roofs surmounting white stucco walls, filling in the land westward toward the ocean, eastward toward the mountains, and north and south along the Great Valley. At one point, the middle-class development spread so rapidly that it completely surrounded a Pacific Electric labor camp, a shack court for 40 Mexican families, with outside sinks for communal washing of dishes and clothes, and four outside showers, which had hot water on Mondays, Wednesdays, and Saturdays.

For most of the displaced Angelenos and for many of the new immigrants, the privately operated house court was the best available accommodation. Built around a court and supplied by outside water faucets and outdoor toilets, the house court consisted of a series of one- and two-room connected units. With the pressure for land, these space-economical habitations multiplied rapidly. By 1916, there were more than 1,200 separate house courts in the Los Angeles area, accommodating a total of some 16,000 people, most of them Spanish-speaking. Courts in places with such soft names as Old Sonora Town, and shacks along a wooded cut called Chávez Ravine, all had dirt floors, wood-burning stoves, and meager group sanitary facilities.

Nonetheless, to the new immigrants crowded in the open doorways of the dirty boxcars in which they had traveled night and day from Mexico, these and other areas peopled by sombrero-hatted, serape-draped familiar looking figures seemed, indeed, to be wonderful cities. Belvedere, a large area on the east side, stretched before them as they rattled along the track. *"¡Qué maravilla!"* they cried when they saw it. "What a marvel!" Twenty thousand of them shared its wonders by 1920: 20,000 Spanish-speaking people in a city that was not a city, just a huddle of huts called Maravilla by those who lived there, Belvedere by those who collected the rent and governed from afar.

During the decade, the Mexican immigrant population in California had tripled, and now there were 88,881 in the state. In the same period, the Texas, Arizona, and New Mexico immigrant population had more than doubled, and now was over a quarter of a million in Texas, and more than 80,000 new Spanish-speaking inhabitants in the arid areas of the two adjoining states west.

The Puerto Ricans, however, did not have the same economic impetus to remain in inhospitable surroundings. Once World War I had ended—and the troops were returning and the jobs were being returned to the Anglos—Puerto Ricans left the fringes of Harlem and the tenements of East Side New York, so that, in 1920, there was actually a net out-migration of Puerto Ricans from the continental United States back to their island homes.

Meanwhile, King Cotton had continued his march from middle Texas into the western cattle prairies and up into Oklahoma. Landlords living in Louisiana and even north and east to Boston, as well as in the towns of Texas, gained title to millions of acres and put them to the plow. Most of the acres had been unfenced, uninhabited grazing lands, but spotted across the territory had been the homes, the churches, and the schools of the resident cattle barons and their Anglo tenants. As the migrant Mexican workers moved in behind the plow, chopping weeds and picking cotton, there was no more room for the tenants, who drifted north, east, and west, and the cattle barons retired to hotel verandas in San Antonio and Houston and fishing yachts in the Gulf.

Cotton gin plants sprouted, and Mexican migrants built their shacks around them and did not cross back over the border any more. Old towns grew, and new towns started, but the homes and the churches and the schools, once emptied of their Anglo tenants, did not fill again, because the Mexican cotton field worker came from a culture to which the school was alien and the Anglo Protestant church was strange.

By 1920, the Spanish-speaking population was no longer densest along the Rio Grande, but rather it was spread across the whole of Texas' broad lands, and the bulk of Spanish-speaking people were not the *rancheros* descended from the followers of the conquistadores, nor were they the middle-class overseers and entrepreneurs who had filled essential roles in the Rio Grande economy of the 19th century; instead, they were the poor from the urban *barrios* and the poor from the Sonoran wastelands, to whom the plantation wages and the shack-town shelters meant a step up in life.

As in most other things, Californians were not about to pass up a good thing. With irrigation, the great desert became the wantonly productive Imperial Valley.

In 1910, the first cotton had been planted in that rich soil, and, as the desperate World War I needs for cloth drove prices up, the Imperial Valley planters drove caravans of springless, hard-rubber-tired trucks to San Felipe and Guamos and other Mexican communities, where they gathered up migrant contract workers in groups as large as 1,500 and 2,000, and drove them back to the thriving cotton fields.

In New Mexico and Arizona, too, growers rushed longstaple cotton to ripening in the Salt River Valley and in the Mesilla River Valley. More than 10,000 Mexicans were recruited for the cotton picking in those areas, and others followed along on their own.

Then, when the bottom dropped out of the cotton market immediately after the war, pay went down with the prices. In 1920, 4,000 Mexican cotton pickers retaliated by going on strike in the fields, only to be arrested with their leaders and deported. Other thousands were stranded, jobless and starving, in the winter of 1921, and only through the intercession of the Mexican consul, who secured an appropriation of $17,000 for temporary relief, were they able to survive.

But the cotton panic was short-lived, and from Texas to California, King Cotton rode the big white horse, and the acres, and the production, and the workers increased. In California, the San Joaquin Valley, with its huge farm factories, became the cotton center, the 5,500 San Joaquin cotton acres of 1919 swelling to almost 175,000 acres in 1931. During the 1920s, almost 60,000 Mexicans each year rode the trucks into the San Joaquin Valley for the cotton harvest; at the peak of the season more than a hundred truckloads a day arrived in the area. At season's end, the Valley dwellers would stake the migrants to just enough tax-refund gasoline to get back to Los Angeles, where they would huddle down in the *colonia* for the winter, swelling the ranks of unemployed day laborers, and relying on welfare and charity to keep from starvation.

 *Field Hands*

As cotton was moving west across Texas, through New Mexico and Arizona, to the Coast—hand-hoed and harvested by migrant Mexican field hands—Mexicans were grubbing their way up out of the Rio Grande Valley toward the north and east, preparing the *brasada*, or brush country, for the irrigation ditches they would dig later, and for the citrus trees, and the tall palms, and the bright green papaya, and the fragrant bougainvillea vines, which they would then plant and nurture to maturity.

But first, with hand and hoe, they had to root out the thick patches of evergreen *mogote*, the sharp-thorned *coma*, the *chaparro prieto*, or black chaparral, the wild *agarita*, with its tiny black currant berries, and the rat-tailed *tasajillo* cactus.

The Anglo and his tractor and even the Anglo with his axe were helpless when confronted with the *brasada*, because to them all brush looked alike. But the Texas chaparral was a mixed grill. Each variety took its own special grubbing, and this the Mexican knew well how to do.

143

Then came the irrigation ditches and the careful nurture of the citrus to the time of ripening oranges, boughs of yellow lemons, and rich yields of green limes.

During the decade of the 1920s, thousands of acres were reclaimed from the ragweed and the cockleburs and the bitter *amargosa* and transformed to orchards that would produce cash crops long into the future.

Throughout all of this—throughout the increase in Mexican immigration, the development of new crops, the conversion of land, and the addition of the automobile and truck to the mass transportation system—there was one place—the upland sheep country of New Mexico—where life went on about as it always had for the Spanish-speaking people who inhabited the area. They tended their sheep, raised their corn and beans, went to Mass on Sunday, and spent their evenings in the *cantinas*, or canteens, operated by village *compadres*. Also in New Mexico, Octaviano Larazolo, who had been born in Mexico but had become an American citizen under the Treaty of Guadalupe Hidalgo, was elected Governor and later became the first Spanish-speaking New Mexican to be elected to the United States Senate.

Elsewhere, too, a few Spanish-speaking citizens—most of them young people who had been born in the United States—were surviving the school system. Lessons were conducted in English, a foreign language to them; history was Anglo history. The picture books had only blonde, blue-eyed children with blonde, blue-eyed parents, living in houses with white fences around their yards, and had garages with cars in them, and the children rode on bicycles and skated on roller skates and were always dressed in clean clothes and wore shiny patent leather shoes.

Among those who survived—to the sixth grade, the eighth, or even high school—some were getting service jobs in hotels and restaurants or were being hired as messengers; a boy occasionally made it as a clerk, a girl occasionally as a typist. And a few—a very few—were tenaciously struggling

on into the universities and coming out as teachers and lawyers and doctors.

But for most who wanted to do something else than walk
the rails, hoe the cotton, or harvest the sugar beets, the only
opportunity was a small *cantina* in the *colonia,* or a shop for
tourists—Anglos who more and more were coming to visit
in "Mexican town" as if it were a foreign country, where
one could get foreign food and foreign bargains and have
the thrill of hearing a foreign language spoken.

One other route out of the fields was to become part of
the transportation team and start dealing in other Mexicans,
rather than picking cotton or weeds.

In the beginning, it was the iron horse—the railroads—
that provided a place for the legal or illegal labor go-between.

As the railroads scattered Mexican section hands out
along their rights-of-way, it was inevitable that some would
end up at the eastern terminus in Chicago. From there, the
railroads that picked up the passengers and the freight to
move them on east—the Baltimore and Ohio, the Pennsylvania, the New York Central—would also pick up skilled
section hands and rail yard workers to scatter along their
rights-of-way in New Jersey and New York.

And in those industrial areas there were other enterprises
that needed cheap hand labor to do the menial and repeti-
tive tasks in the packing plants, the steel mills, and—up
around Detroit—the automobile production lines.

Then there were the northern railroads west, up through
Minneapolis to Seattle and Portland. And it turned out that
sugar beets would thrive in Michigan and Minnesota and
Idaho.

So all across the country, from the Pennsylvania steel
mills to the Detroit auto mills to the Chicago meat mills,
back to the beets and fruit and sheep of the Northwest,
there developed a burgeoning national market for mobile,
unskilled Mexican labor, preferably fresh from the *barrio* or
the *brasada.*

Although the Contract Labor Law of 1885 had set up perfectly legal steps by which foreign nationals could come into the United States to work, it transpired that throughout the first quarter of the 20th century, when the demand for Mexican labor was increasing so rapidly, it was easier for official, employer, and employee, alike, to ignore the law. Mexicans simply crossed over, officials looked the other way, and employers hired anybody available—no questions asked—rather than get involved in administrative red tape.

By the time of the 1920s, labor-smuggling had become a highly structured and lucrative business.

A border patrol was established in 1924, and an administrative order restricting wanton crossings was issued in 1929. But the "coyotes," or labor-smugglers, simply increased their vigilance against detection and increased the scope of their activities.

Entering Mexico, the "coyotes" would tour the villages and the fringes of the great cities, offering peons, for a fee of $10 to $15, not only a work contract but also safe passage across the line by guiding them to a ford of the Rio Grande at night, by concealing them in carts or automobiles or trucks, or by helping them jump the fence at La Colorada.

On the United States side, an *enganchista,* or labor contractor, would pick up the worker and either sell him directly to an employer for 50¢ to a dollar a head, or turn him over to another labor agent who would contract with employers in other areas to supply a given number of laborers at a fixed fee. These agents would then contract with the workers to transport them to their new employers, but would charge the workers for the transportation and the food involved in getting them there.

Profits in the trade were spectacular, and other, even more devious operators, began to muscle in. These "man snatchers" would raid the compounds where the labor contractors were staging their imports, and, at gunpoint, hustle the bewildered peons into trucks for transport to a barn, a warehouse, or even an open corral, where, under armed guard, they would be kept until their captors had arranged for their transport to a new employer.

And, like Manuel Armijo with Don Francisco Chávez's sheep, the "man-snatcher" was not necessarily content simply to steal from one contractor and sell to another; once he had transported his merchandise to an employer unwary enough to do business with him, he and his herders would follow up and, at night, hustle the Mexicans from their new quarters back into the trucks for resale the next day to yet another employer. By this process, the "man-snatcher" sometimes would sell the same crew to a half dozen or more employers in the course of a few days or weeks.

The long haulers, slightly more legitimate but still outside the law, would contract with beet growers in Colorado, Michigan, Minnesota, or Montana, or with industrialists in the same areas, and would pick up workers from the "coyotes" or other agents at the border, packing 50 or 60 into an open-stake truck, fitted out only with benches for sitting on and coffee cans for urinals. They would cover the entire cargo over with a heavy tarpaulin and fasten it down around the edges, so that the truck would look as if it was loaded with potatoes rather than people.

A team of drivers would head out at night, driving straight through, with stops only for fuel, staying off the main roads to avoid highway patrols, but gunning over the rough dirt and gravel country lanes to try to make the trip in 48 hours and collect their $10 a head for their human cargo and speed back to the border for another round trip. A good trucker, who did not end up in the ditch with his truck smashed and his load maimed, could average $3,000 a season, whereas the worker and his family would be lucky to come out with $300.

The Texas growers and employers, of course, fought back, guarding their crews with rifles, and sometimes discharging the weapons in the vicinity of suspicious trucks, causing frequent flat tires and occasionally retrieving a "man-snatched" crew.

But for the immigrants, the end of the line became home. Sometimes it was better than what they had left, but mostly it was the only choice they had.

Growers, seeking to keep them for the next season, would stall on the final settlement of the individual contracts, allowing the families, in the meantime, to live on in the courts or shacks they had set up for their harvest habitation.

Others, more legitimately recruited, were urged to settle permanently from the start. In 1923, the National Tube Company in Lorain, Ohio, contracted for 1,500 Mexicans; Bethlehem Steel Company in Bethlehem, Pennsylvania, imported about a thousand. Arriving by train, they were marched each morning from their boxcars to their work, with a police escort. But with regular work and regular wages, most of them gradually moved into small apartments or purchased small homes and became part of the community.

Near Chicago, the steelworkers settled down around the mills of Gary, and the stockyard workers settled on the periphery of the slaughterhouse area. At first, the packing plant workers congregated on the east side, toward the center of Chicago, but the people who were already living there made life as unpleasant as possible for them, so many moved west of the yards, only to be met with more neighborhood opposition. Landlords refused to rent to them and closed businesses and restaurants to their patronage. Eventually, the Mexicans found themselves forced south of the yards.

Despite discrimination in job choice, in housing, and in recreation, the Mexican immigrants who arrived in the farm areas and the cities of the northern tier of states, found themselves accepted as just another foreign element, disturbing to the settled customs of the community, but necessary to progress, and acceptable if they kept their place.

For their own part, the new neighbors from south of the border began to mix Mexican and Anglo patterns, buying radios and phonographs and typewriters, but demanding a

Spanish keyboard for the latter; playing tangos and Mexican marches on the phonographs; and draping the radios with colorful serapes. Their shelves would be stocked with American canned food, but *chiles* and *tamales* and *enchiladas* would always be on the table. In the kitchen, they would have gas or electric stoves, yet they would be grinding corn out back on the familiar old stone *metates*.

In New York, the 1920s saw a gradual return of Puerto Ricans, some 20,000 sifting into the garment manufacturing shops and food service industries during the ten years following the exodus after World War I. (See Appendix for biography of Pedro Canino, who came to New York in 1925.)

By 1930, the Spanish-speaking population of the United States was well over 2 million, half of them having entered the country during the last generation from Mexico, Puerto Rico, Cuba, Central and South America and other Hispanic homelands, the other half being descendants of settlers who became United States citizens as a result of the Treaty of Guadalupe Hidalgo.

But now the newcomers were creating a third force: their children, citizens by birth, no matter what the allegiance of the parents. Without the tradition of the conquistadores, and the *haciendas,* and the Spanish years, the newest generation of Spanish-speaking citizens was, nonetheless, no longer "Mexican" and, therefore, no longer willing to be called Mexican, be treated Mexican, or be Mexican.

And it was this generation that was suddenly plunged into the economic abyss of the Great Depression, and, willing or not, found themselves identified and forced to live as Mexicans.

In 1930, of the more than 2 million Spanish-speaking people in the United States, fewer than 7,000 held white-collar jobs. Of these, only 250 had gained the professional status of doctor or lawyer, just a thousand were teachers, and all the rest were clerks.

So most of the young Americans were laborers like their parents.

With their families, they lived in shacks made from odds and ends of boxes and scrap lumber, in *colonias*, on fringes of cities, where the language spoken was *pocho*, vintage North American Spanish, where the schools from which they dropped out were attended almost exclusively by other youngsters born of Mexican parents in the United States or by children of recent immigrant Mexicans, and where, despite the fact that some liked to refer to themselves as Spanish-Americans, Latin-Americans, or native Californians, all considered themselves, more than anything else, members of *La Raza*, a term expressing a cultural ethos and sense of common purpose rather than just the literal "race" or "clan."

Brothers and sisters alike, when the harvest call came, they loaded into their parents' Model T Ford or rusty old "Chevie," or they joined the herd in a labor contractor's stake truck, and headed off across the hills to follow the wheat, or the sugar beets, or the grapes or the cotton, wherever the sun had turned the crops to the color of ripening.

To the Anglos, the native-born and immigrants looked alike and sounded alike, and they were all Mexicans, or "greasers." To the immigrant, the native-born was a *pocho*, or "watered-down" Mexican. Floating between two cultures, he adopted the reachable economic values of the Anglo, while holding tight to the social values of *La Raza*.

But when the Anglo economic world collapsed in the stock market crash of 1929, the dilemma was even more complicated. The California Fruit Growers' Exchange, the Cotton Growers' Association in Arizona and Texas, and the great sugar beet companies of Colorado and the northern states found their markets drying up, as the wheat and corn farmers found the drought was shriveling their once lush fields, and the grasshoppers were stripping the stalks that were left. No longer was there the need for a constantly growing work force. There were no longer even jobs for the cheap labor that had been recruited so industriously over the years from Mexico. Now immigrant and native-born alike swelled the rapidly burgeoning relief rolls of the communities which their *colonias* ringed.

With welfare costing from $500 to $1,000 a year for each individual on relief, communities began actively to encourage the *colonia* dwellers to become *repatriados*—Mexicans who were returning to their homeland. Some *repatriados* journeyed south voluntarily in their own cars—their families and their belongings packed in as they would have been on any other journey after migrant worker jobs. Others were granted transportation expenses to the border by the welfare agency, but the money was offered only with the additional stipulation that if it were not accepted, welfare aid would be summarily cut off and there would be no transportation money to the border. In addition, there were an increasing number of Mexican nationals who were simply herded together and deported.

At the outset, the movement of the *repatriados* was slow. In the first five months of 1930, only slightly over 3,000 a month headed south. But in the summer of that year, with the prospects for harvest work fading rapidly, the number jumped to more than 5,000 a month, rising to 6,000 in September, 8,000 in October, 9,000 in November, and almost 10,000 in December. By the end of 1930, 69,570 *repatriados* had crossed the border into Mexico.

And that was only the beginning.

When the job prospects for 1931 dimmed even more, 17,000 returned to Mexico in the month of October alone, and the high tide of repatriation was reached the next month, when 21,055 individuals of Mexican descent made the journey once more to their homeland.

By spending $77,249.29 to send off one trainload of *repatriados*—starting with the loading of men, women, and children carrying bulging suitcases held together by scraps of string and rope, carrying bedding rolls, baskets of lunch, and dragging dogs, cats, and goats at the end of leather thongs or frayed leashes—the County of Los Angeles saved $347,468.41 in relief payments to the individuals crowded

onto that train who were making the return trip from Maravilla to their native towns and villages, to large cities, and to
the repatriation colonies established by the government of
Mexico.

In 1936, it was estimated that not more than ten per cent
of the seasonal labor force recruited from 1917 to 1930 still
remained available in the California fields.

By that time, however, the attitude of the remaining descendants of the conquistadores, of the native-born teen-age
sons of Mexican immigrants, and of the immigrants, themselves, had changed. From the more than 21,000 *repatriados*
in November 1931, the number had dwindled to just over
2,000 in November 1933. And the docile subservience,
which the Anglos had come to expect in their Spanish-
speaking laborers, had virtually disappeared.

At the height of the harvest in June 1933, 7,000 members
of *La Raza* got up off their knees and walked out of the celery fields, the onion patches, and the berry orchards of Los
Angeles County. It was the largest strike of agricultural
workers ever to take place in California up to that time.

When, in the fall of the same year, a series of farm strikes
was called by the Cannery and Agricultural Workers' Industrial Union, three-fourths of those who walked off the jobs in
the San Joaquin Valley were Mexicans who had joined the
union to fight against race discrimination, poor housing, and
low pay.

Although those strikes, and the third, also in 1933, in Imperial Valley, failed, and the workers went back to the
fields, their eyes still smarting from tear gas and their bodies
aching from the clubs wielded by sheriffs' deputies, there
was little doubt that the period of repatriation was over.
Now the immigrant *cholos* and the native-born *pochos* who
remained to do the stoop labor needed by the agricultural
enterprise of the Southwest—while throwing epithets at
each other—were determined to achieve an economic par-
ity for their work with other laborers, and to stand tall after

working hours because they had stood tall and demanded their rights from their boss.

In 1936, there was the spectacle of 2,000 celery workers confronting 1,500 armed police, with a pitched battle ensuing when the police attacked a barricaded barn; and arrests and injuries were too numerous to tally. And in Orange County, 200 citrus crop workers were arrested and charged with criminal acts by a judge operating in an outdoor bullpen set up as a courtroom. As the 20-million-dollar crop over-ripened on the trees, submachine guns, rifles, and shotguns struck up a barrage that made the old vigilante days pale by comparison.

Not alone in California did the Spanish-speaking field workers strike.

In 1933, 50 cars bearing members of the Asociación de Jornaleros formed a caravan that toured the entire Lower Rio Grande Valley, protesting anti-union activity. In 1934, West Texas sheepshearers picked up their clippers and walked off the job, and more than 6,000 pecan shellers stopped cracking nuts in protest against San Antonio sweatshop wages of two to three cents a pound for their work. In Idaho, Washington, Colorado, and Michigan, the sugar beet workers demanded more pay, better housing, and an elimination of discrimination.

In New Mexico, 300 coal miners—part of several thousand who were striking—built shacks on a piece of company property which they named "Chihuahuita"—since most of them had come originally from Chihuahua—and rioted when they were faced with eviction by a New Mexican politician who had bought the property from the mine company. Jesús Pallares (See Appendix for biography), one of the miners, organized 8,000 Spanish-speaking people into the Liga Obrera de Habla Española, and developed enough power to win relief for the strikers and the abandonment of proceedings against the squatters. But Jesús Pallares, himself, was arrested and deported to Mexico.

With the gradual recovery of the economy, the Spanish-speaking people in the United States, like their formerly unemployed Anglo neighbors, began to go off relief. Some moved out once again on the seasonal journeys that characterized the life of the agricultural worker. Others returned to the laborious digging, and chopping, and pounding of tie and spike to keep the shining rails solid under speeding trains. Then there were those who again undertook the probing and blasting and shoveling in the dark, deep drifts of the mines. And the rest went about all the other menial tasks that still remained the staple of employment for the *cholos,* and the *pochos,* and all of the Spanish-speaking residents of the United States.

In just one area of employment there seemed to be some hope that a change would be made through government intervention. The Sugar Act of 1937 was designed to promote the production of sugar in the United States by providing a subsidy from the federal government to growers of cane and beet sugar. However, in order to get the subsidies, the growers were required to pay all workers no less than an annual wage set by the Department of Agriculture. The idea was clearly that the benefits of the subsidy should go to the sugar beet laborers, as well as to the farmers and the processors.

In order to be sure that the Department of Agriculture's wage would be arrived at through democratic processes, there were to be open hearings at which any interested party could testify; and the wage, itself, was to be only a minimum, not a standard for the industry.

Unfortunately, things did not work out that way.

The highly organized growers and refiners packed the hearings. The laborers frequently were not represented at all, but if they were their spokesmen often proved incompetent to deal with the kinds of complex factors that the bureaucrats and the industrialists discussed: production costs, sugar content, yields, and probable prices. In addition, the wage that was established was almost universally used not as a suggestion, but as the *only* wage; and since it was government sanctioned, the workers were led by the growers to believe that it was a wage required to be paid and to be accepted, by order of the United States government.

So, as the depression decade of the 1930's drew to a close, the situation of the Spanish-speaking people of the United States was much different from what it had been in previous decades, and yet it was exactly the same.

Mexican immigration and repatriation had slowed until there was almost no movement at all.

Those who remained had become increasingly more militant, many joining unions, engaging in strikes, and pressing for legislation to improve their economic and social status.

Among themselves, the Spanish-speaking residents of the United States sought to emphasize differences rather than similarities. They called themselves Spanish, Spanish-Americans, Hispanos, Latin-Americans, Mexicans, Mejicanos, and Chicanos. There were *pochos* in California, *manitos* from New Mexico, Tejanos from Texas. And then there were the Puerto Ricans, the Cubans, the people from the countries of Central and South America, and the Españoles from Spain.

And there *were* differences.

There were those who had ceased to have any identity at all with the Mexican-Indian heritage, and had become, in fact, Anglos.

Those who were called Spanish were very close to the line: usually native-born, well-educated, and adapted to the Anglo society, speaking little or no Spanish and having very little to do with those who did speak Spanish.

The Spanish-Americans, or Hispanos, who lived in New Mexico or southern Colorado, and the Latin-Americans, who lived in Texas, spoke more Spanish than English, although their language was frequently an Americanized Spanish, which neither Anglos nor Mexicans could interpret easily. These were the people who had long lived in the territory of the United States, struggling against weather, poverty, and Anglo ostracism to establish an identity that was not Mexican nor Anglo but was uniquely their own.

The Mejicanos, product of the *colonias* and *barrios* and border towns, proudly spoke Mexican Spanish, and were a composite of native- and foreign-born, determined to make it in an Anglo society on their own terms, not on Anglo terms.

The Chicanos, stooping over in the fields and working the grape arbors and the orchards, were beginning to flex their collective bargaining muscle and to link arms in a *campesino*—man-to-man—relationship against the exploiters of their labor.

The *pochos*, the *manitos*, the Tejanos—each identified with the locale of their work and their ways and developed distinct argots that set them off verbally, as well as geographically, as very special people.

But despite the differences, the end result was the same: Anglos saw only Mexicans. Mexicans occupied a subordinate status in the Anglo socioeconomic scheme of things.

And so the work went on: the tiring, tedious tasks of stoop labor, piecework pay, and migrant living.

For the young people of the fading 1930s, however, there were two new routes to a kind of self-respect.

With men on the march again in Europe, there was the expanding United States military machine, where every private had equal pay, equal food, and equal non-status, no matter what his heritage. Enlistments were brisk at Fort Sam Houston, Fort Bliss, and the presidio at San Francisco.

In the cities, the swing era youth culture was giving way to jive, jitterbug, and bop. Matching the frenetic movements was the development of exaggerated clothing styles, young males appearing in long suit coats, with pants pegged at the cuffs, draped at the knees, and deeply pleated at the waist; heavy low-hanging watch chains matched long, well-greased duck-tail haircuts.

These "draped," or "zoot-suited," boys were accompanied by girls in tight short skirts, transparent blouses, black stockings, perilously high-heeled shoes, and elaborately high-piled hairdos.

In the tradition of their elders, the young people spent most of their free time outdoors, congregating on street corners for conversation, crowding the sidewalks as they moved from one group to another, visibly filling the warm southwestern afternoons with their stylized clothes and their self-conscious swagger. And with the new militancy of their parents and the new militancy of their country, some of the youth adopted a militancy of their own, gathering in gangs, fighting each other, fighting outsiders. The most violent, the *pachucos*—a term whose origin is vague but was probably applied to border bandits in the previous century —mixed burglary and the beating of both *barrio* residents and Anglos—apparently indiscriminately—with their gang fights.

And this was the manner and mood of the Spanish-speaking people of the Southwest when Japanese dive bombers suddenly appeared over Pearl Harbor and catapulted the United States into World War II.

Chapter 14

 *War!*

In landlocked New Mexico, the National Guard had two Coast Artillery battalions, the 200th and the 515th. As the United States tooled up for coming conflict in 1940, these two National Guard units were activated and dispatched to the Philippine Islands. Their selection was one of the more logical moves in the military, in that these New Mexico National Guard units were made up largely of Spanish-speaking personnel, both officers and enlisted men.

When the Japanese invaded and conquered the Philippines, more than a quarter of the men captured or killed in the last-ditch fighting on Bataan Peninsula were United States' soldiers whose native language was Spanish, although their native land was New Mexico.

On October 29, 1941, President Franklin Delano Roosevelt pulled a capsule containing a slip of paper with a number on it from a great bin of capsules, and initiated the United States Selective Service. In Los Angeles, Pedro Aguilar Despart looked at the number of his draft card. The number on the slip of paper President Roosevelt removed from the capsule and the number of Pedro Aguilar's card were identical: 158. Pedro Aguilar was No. 1 in the draft for what was to be World War II.

At mushrooming Army camps across the country, post commanders were faced with groups of wiry, eager young draftees who had been born on *ranchos* and raised on the move as part of migrant farm-working families. Following the furrows from planting to harvest, and never pausing in one place long enough to learn any language except that of their parents and their parents' friends, many of these draftees could speak no English and understand little. Yet, organized into special platoons led by officers who had a smattering of Spanish, they emerged from the 13-week training cycle with both a knowledge of the fundamentals of soldiering and also an operational knowledge of conversational English. Moved into predominantly Anglo units, they performed not only adequately but often brilliantly.

In addition to the expansion of the armed forces, part of the United States' tooling up for war involved the expansion of defense industries.

Trucks, tanks, clothing, construction, munitions, and the manufacture of massive quantities of the essentials for millions of men on the move, required the recruiting not only of skilled labor but also of men and women who could effectively man the proliferating production lines. There the quickly learned task of adding a single piece to gradually growing identical structures moving at a regular pace in an endless procession—self-propelled or pushed—required no knowledge of the English language, of mathematics, or of other academic skills; but rather demanded manual dexterity and a tolerance for monotony, repetition and tedium— occupational aptitudes that the residents of the *barrios,* the *colonias,* and the migrant worker camps had, out of necessity, developed to a high level of efficiency over the years.

Responding to government pressure for speed and volume production, manufacturers were able to negotiate contracts based on cost plus a fixed profit percentage, so that keeping wages down was not necessary to fiscal survival. As a result, unskilled laborers were able to move from the field to the factory and earn more in a week than they had earned previously in a month. And with production lines running around the clock—three shifts in 24 hours—the whole family was employable, individuals sometimes holding down more than one job.

Moreover, the accelerating assembly line did not discriminate among Anglo housewife, Spanish-American field hand, off-reservation Indian, northern migrating Negro, newly arrived Puerto Rican, Filipino, Chinese, or individuals with any other ethnic background. Side by side they stood, labored, and received their wages, the only distinction being the actual effectiveness with which each individual performed his or her ritual tasks.

Just one group was not there: in California, the Japanese-Americans, virtually without exception, were removed from their homes and transported to barbed-wire enclosed "relocation centers." (Other Nisei fought with great distinction in Europe.)

But the military moved not on manufactured goods alone.

In mess halls multiplying across the land, men who had never actually experienced a balanced diet in their lives responded to the regimen of physical exertion from reveille to retreat by developing increasingly insatiable appetites. As a result, food production, itself, became a major defense industry.

But many of the migrant farm and field workers who had been in such a satisfactory surplus during the 30s had now migrated to the more lucrative fields of factory and fabrication plants. Now the Fruit Growers' Exchange, the Associated Farmers, the Cotton Growers' Association and the Sugarbeet Producers again needed help—the kind of help that the great migrations north from Mexico in the first third of the 20th century had provided: hardy, hungry, herdable help.

And the government responded.

In August 1942, the United States and Mexico entered

into a formal agreement regarding the recruiting of Mexican labor for wartime employment. The Farm Security Administration (FSA) was made responsible for working out the details of insuring that Mexican laborers would not displace labor already available, and that employers would not use this new source to lower wage standards and increase profits.

The FSA responded swiftly and efficiently. In just one month, they had developed a method of entering into individual agreements with workers to provide free transportation to and from their homes, subsistence en route, and minimum guarantees on wages and working conditions. The FSA confirmed these guarantees through agreements with the various farm organizations seeking recruits for their labor force; and Mexican consuls and labor officials were authorized to make inspections and investigate complaints to make sure that all agreements were carried out.

On September 29, 1942, the first trainload of 1,500 Mexican *braceros* pulled into the station at Stockton, California, to be met by a flag-waving reception committee, a band booming out Mexican and American melodies, the speeches from national, local, and Mexican government officials, as well as farm organization and worker spokesmen. On the sides of the Pullman cars that provided the transportation were the chalked words, *"De las Democracias Será la Victoria."*

As the workers fanned out to farms where they would be employed, they were met by recreation leaders and teachers who greeted them in Spanish and outlined the opportunities for fun and knowledge that would be theirs along with the work and wages, so that when they returned to Mexico, they would be ambassadors of good will.

By the end of 1942, 4,203 *braceros* had entered the United States farm labor pool. In 1943, 52,098 additional *braceros* joined them.

But in Los Angeles, in August 1942, at exactly the same time that the United States government and the Mexican government were working out the final details of their agreement on the *bracero* program, events of a very different nature were taking place.

On August 1, 1942, Henry Levas, a young Mexican-American, member of a group known as "The Thirty-Eighth Street Gang," took his girl for a drive to a water-filled gravel pit on the east side of Los Angeles, which—since "Mexicans" were not allowed to use Los Angeles public swimming pools or parks—had been adopted by Spanish-speaking youth—non-gang members as well as gang members and *pachucos*—as their own swimming pool and parking place.

When members of a rival gang started a fight with Levas, he and his girl retreated. But later that evening, Levas went back to get even, reinforced by several carloads of his own gang.

The gravel pit was deserted, so the group decided to crash a party at a nearby house, an action that precipitated another fight. Neither the fight nor the party amounted to much, so Levas and his gang pulled out and went home.

However, early the next morning, the body of José Díaz, a member of the "Downey Boys," the gang that had attacked Levas and his girl friend, was found lying on a dirt road near the Delgadillo house, where the party had taken place. Díaz was still alive, but died at General Hospital without ever regaining consciousness.

In dressing up his story about the finding of Díaz's body, a reporter identified the old gravel pit as "the Sleepy Lagoon," and, as "the Sleepy Lagoon Case," the death of Díaz served as the spark that ignited a series of explosive events involving inhabitants of the *barrios* surrounding Los Angeles and members of Los Angeles' law enforcement agencies.

On the nights of August 10 and 11, 1942, members of the police departments of Los Angeles, Monterey, Monte Bello, and Alhambra, together with detachments from the Los Angeles sheriff's office and the California Highway Patrol, blockaded the main streets running through all of the Los Angeles *barrios*, ordering occupants of cars entering or leaving the neighborhoods to get out and submit to search of their persons while their cars were being searched by other officers.

Six hundred people were arrested "on suspicion." All but 175 were subsequently released, those remaining being charged with possession of knives, guns, chains, dirks, daggers, and such other possibly dangerous weapons as tire irons, jack handles, wrenches, and other tools normally carried in any car.

Twenty-four young men were alleged to be members of the "Thirty-Eighth Street Gang," and all were charged with the murder of José Díaz. Two of the 24 demanded separate trials, and the charges against them were later dropped. Of the rest, five were acquitted; five were found guilty of minor offenses and committed to the Los Angeles County jail; nine were found guilty of second-degree murder plus two counts of assault and were sentenced to San Quentin Prison; and three were convicted of first-degree murder. The lengthy trial filled 6,000 pages of transcript, but no evidence placed any of the defendants at the actual scene of the alleged crime, no murder weapon was produced, no one was identified as having seen the crime, and there was no proof that Díaz actually was murdered. He had been drunk, had repeatedly fallen to the ground, and his injuries were such that his death could have been caused by one of the falls or by his being struck in the darkness by a car; the two companions with whom he had left the party were never called to testify at all.

The defendants were not allowed to sit with their attorneys and were denied haircuts and clean clothes for several weeks. The verdict, finding most of them guilty, was returned on January 13, 1943.

The war in the Pacific was still going badly, and tension along the California coast was intense. Soldiers and sailors and marines were sweating out their last days before embarkation to the war zone. Civilians were pouring in from the Midwest and South, tired, confused, and hungry, looking for work in the defense industries and the shipyards—where huge batteries of lights lit the keels of Liberty ships and the skeletons of bombers, and the harsh, incessant pounding of rivet guns shattered the former quiet of night and added to the clamor of day.

In this supercharged, round-the-clock atmosphere of national shock and individual uncertainty, the defense workers' industry and the military personnel's creased uniforms, scrubbed faces, and short-cropped hair, contrasted vividly with the apparently loafing, drape-clad, greasy, ducktail hair-styled young men of the *barrios*. Moreover, these *pachuco* types, whether actually members of vandal gangs or not, seemed to be claiming the favors of the *pachucas*, the high-heeled, short-skirted sensually attractive girls of the *barrios*.

By April 1943, when a large group of sailors and marines decided to make a good weekend out of their last liberty before shipping out and went to clean up 200 "zoot suiters" in Oakland, California, the "hot summer" had started. In May, the scene was repeated in Venice, California, and in June, the riots spread across the country.

On the evening of June 3, 1943, 11 sailors ventured off the well-lighted streets of downtown Los Angeles into the center of one of the city's worst slum areas. On the same night, members of the Alpine Club, a non-gang group of *barrio* youth, met in a police substation at the invitation of the the police captain to discuss how best to cope with gang fighting in the neighborhood. At the end of the meeting, the boys were taken in squad cars to the corner nearest the slum neighborhood where they lived, and were dropped off in the darkness.

Later that evening, the sailors, one badly hurt, the others cut and bruised, limped into another substation and reported they had been attacked by a Mexican gang that outnumbered them three to one. About the same time, members of the Alpine Club were limping into the shacks where they lived, reporting that they had been attacked by hoodlums who they were certain were not of Mexican descent. At the substation where the sailors had checked out their battle scars, a detective lieutenant and 14 policemen set out to clean up the gang that had attacked the sailors, but they found no one to arrest.

The next night, June 4, 1943, some 200 sailors hired a caravan of 20 taxicabs and headed through the center of Los Angeles toward the eastside *barrios*, laughing, shouting, enjoying themselves. At one point, a police car barred the way and nine of the sailors were taken into custody—later released without charge—and the rest of the cabs proceeded. When the lead cab came abreast of a lone, drape-clad, dark-complexioned boy, the whole caravan of cabs emptied, and the sailors charged the boy, leaving him badly beaten and bleeding, lying on the pavement. Four attacks later, the cab caravan swung back to the Naval Armory; the Shore Patrol took over, arrested 17 of the sailors, and sent the rest back to their barracks; while ambulances picked up the two 17-year-old youngsters, a 19-year-old, and a 23-year-old adult who were lying where they had been left by the sailors.

But that was not all.

The next night, June 5, 1943, several hundred service men linked arms and moved through downtown Los Angeles four abreast, threatening anyone wearing "zoot suits." In a bar on the east side, a group of sailors ordered two drape-clad customers to remove their clothes. One refused, and they knocked him down, tearing his clothes off forcibly. The other did disrobe, and the sailors ripped the clothes to shreds.

On the night of June 6, more carloads of sailors toured the area, followed by police, who arrested 44 severely-beaten *barrio* residents but no sailors.

All this, however, was just preliminary.

On the evening of June 7, thousands of civilians joined with soldiers, sailors, and marines, to march through downtown Los Angeles, beating every "zoot suiter" who was unwary enough to be abroad, crashing into movie palaces, forcing the ushers to turn on the houselights, and then dragging any drape-clad patrons out into the streets. The mobs stopped streetcars, leaving "zoot suited" riders half naked, bleeding, and bruised. Police seemed helpless to stop the violence, and so the military finally decided at midnight to declare the entire downtown area of Los Angeles out of bounds. The rioting then spread to the suburbs, where it continued for two more days.

On June 9, 1943, "zoot suit" violence broke out in San Diego; on June 10, in Philadelphia, clear across the country; on June 15, in Chicago. On June 20–21, 1943, Detroit was the scene of the most disastrous riots in 25 years; and, in Harlem, damages totaling nearly a million dollars resulted from a few hours of "zoot suit" rioting in that summer of 1943.

The hysteria eventually subsided, but the festering scab of prejudice was a visible, vicious thing, and no amount of verbal salve or racial rationalization was going to heal it.

Then, on July 1, 1943, the *bracero* program—which for nine months had been gestating exactly as it had been conceived, under the prescriptive care and guidance of the Farm Security Administration—was ripped from its womb and handed over to the War Food Administration (WFA), whose role was emergency production, not long-range planning.

To accomplish its mission, the WFA turned primarily to large farm employers. By holding prices high and guaranteeing purchase of all crops, and by paying all transportation and administration expense for the *bracero* program—while fixing farm wages at a low level and immediately deporting any workers who attempted to jump from farm to industry—the WFA provided a secure subsidy, which yielded huge profits, to wartime farm-factories.

Despite its corruptive aspects, however, the *bracero* program provided better conditions for the migratory workers than any they had previously enjoyed. Liveable camps, medical care, accident insurance, and guaranteed minimum wages attracted more than 60,000 *braceros* in 1944 and twice that number in 1945. Working in 21 states, they produced crops that were worth more than a half million dollars in 1944; and, with 10 per cent of their wages being deducted and transmitted by the federal government to compulsory savings accounts in Mexico City, the *braceros* contributed huge sums to their families and to the economy of Mexico. A separate program brought 80,000 Mexicans to keep the Western railroads running during the whole period of national emergency.

Also in 1942–1943, while the *bracero* program was tooling up and the "zoot suit" fuse was sputtering to an explosion, Mexican-Americans were contributing to the war effort overseas. (So were other citizens of Spanish descent; see Appendix for biography of Puerto Rican Horacio Rivero, Jr.)

Taoseno Joe Martínez had left the warm hills of New Mexico to work in the sugar beet fields of Colorado. When the war came along, he enlisted and was shipped to Alaska, where, in the only battle of World War II in what is now part of the United States—the Battle of Attu, in the frigid, foggy Aleutians—he was killed. But in the Battle of Attu, Joe Martínez so distinguished himself that he was posthumously awarded the Congressional Medal of Honor.

Private First Class Manuel Pérez, of Oklahoma City, killed in the Battle of Luzon, was also posthumously awarded the Congressional Medal of Honor.

Sylvester Herreras, of Phoenix, Arizona, survived to accept his Medal of Honor in person, but the presentation was made to him while he was sitting in a wheelchair, for he had lost both his legs in the heroic action which led to his award.

Sergeant José Mendoza López, of Brownsville, Texas, one of five Texans of Mexican descent to be awarded the Congressional Medal of Honor, had just returned from a goodwill tour of Mexico arranged by the United States Army, when he entered a restaurant in a small town in the Lower Rio Grande Valley.

"No Mexies in here," the paunchy man behind the counter said, as he turned from the grill, wiping his greasy hands on his already dirty apron. "This joint's for white folks only. Get out."

Sergeant Mendoza left, but only because he did not want any food prepared by the "chef" in that restaurant. His protest through Army channels, however, took some of the complacency from some of the Anglos in the area.

Sergeant Macario García, another Texas Medal of Honor winner, was visiting his parents, who were working in the beet fields at a place called Sugarland in his home state. He dropped into the Oasis Cafe for a cup of coffee and was greeted by the "We don't serve no Mexies in here," so familiar to members of *La Raza* wherever they went in the United States.

"You'll serve me," Sergeant García said. "If I'm good enough to fight your war for you, I'm good enough for you to serve a cup of coffee to."

"Listen, you dirty greaser," the proprietor said, coming around the end of the counter toward García, "you disgrace that uniform just by wearing it. Now get out of here before I throw you out."

At a table by the window, two sailors were finishing their roast beef hot plates. "Hey, come on, give the sarge a cup of coffee," one sailor called.

"You keep out of this, sailor boy," the proprietor said. "This punk thinks just because he's got some stripes on his arms and ribbons on his chest he's as good as a white man."

He grabbed Sergeant García by the collar and by the seat of the pants and was trying to swing him from the counter stool and head him toward the door.

The two sailors were on their feet and coming over to try to stop the action. Three other customers were on their feet, too, coming from various directions toward the spot where the proprietor was still trying to unseat Sergeant García.

But before any of them could get there, the sergeant's combat-trained reflexes took over, and his left elbow dug into the proprietor's stomach. As García spun on the stool, the side of his right hand caught the proprietor on the point of the chin as he doubled forward from the punch to his stomach. A split second sooner, and García's hand would have smashed into the proprietor's throat, above the Adam's apple; as it was, the force of the chop sent the proprietor sprawling back into the arms of the two sailors.

By that time, the other customers had arrived where the action was, and García found himself struggling against the pinioning arms of two of them. Still another customer had grabbed the phone at the end of the counter and was busy dialing. For a brief time, the Oasis sounded more like a herd of stampeding Texas longhorns than a quiet cafe, and then the door burst open and a deputy sheriff charged in.

"Cut it out or I'll arrest the lot of you!" he shouted. And he had to shout, "Shut up, all of you!" several times before he got an idea of what had happened.

"Look at that ribbon," one of the sailors told him. "It's the Congressional Medal of Honor. That's the highest decoration a guy can get, and anybody who's wearing it ought to be able to eat anywhere."

The deputy shook his head. "I don't know nothing about that," he said, "but I do know this place is a mess. I'm closing it up for the night. All you guys go on home, and you," pointing to the proprietor, "lock this door and clean up the mess. The best thing to do is for everybody to forget the whole thing."

So the fracas seemingly ended.

But that was not the end of the incident.

Everybody involved talked about it, and diplomatic channels from Mexico City to Washington, D. C., burned hot over the issue.

Then Walter Winchell, with his "Good evening, Mr. and Mrs. America, let's go to press," told the national radio audience about the insult to hero Sergeant Marcario García in the Oasis Cafe in Sugarland, Texas. As a result, the sheriff, in order to "uphold the honor of the county," arrested Sergeant Marcario García and charged him with "aggravated assault."

In Los Angeles, a group of concerned citizens had reacted to the conviction of the "Thirty-Eighth Street Gang" members for the murder of José Díaz by forming the "Sleepy Lagoon Defense Committee." In October 1943, the Committee opened a nationwide campaign to raise $20,000 for an appeal of the conviction. Successful in their fund-raising efforts, they were also successful in their legal action; for on October 4, 1944, the District Court of Appeals reversed the verdict, castigated the trial judge for his conduct of the trial, and criticized the prosecution for the methods it had used in securing the original conviction.

On October 24, the charges were completely dismissed "for lack of evidence" and hundreds of Mexican-Americans greeted the boys as they emerged from the hall of justice— there was shouting, weeping, and celebrating.

It was the first *La Raza* court victory.

Part 5

The Militants

Chapter *15*

Courthouse

On March 2, 1945, Gonzalo Méndez filed a suit in the Federal courts against the officials of Orange County, California.

Méndez was a Mexican-American whose parents had been part of the great immigration of the 1920's. With them, he had lived in the shacks of the *colonia*, had been battered and bruised in the trucks of the labor contractors, had squatted over miles and miles of rows of furrows, planting seeds, chopping weeds, harvesting produce; and, in the night, he had walked blocks through rows of migrant tents and brush shelters to the distant latrine.

But Méndez had saved some pennies out of every Yankee dollar he had earned.

Méndez had opened a bank account and had earned Yankee interest on the Yankee pennies he had deposited.

Méndez had taken some of the money from his bank account and had made a down payment on an acre of Orange County's rich black soil.

Méndez had taken some more of his savings and had bought seeds; he had hoed his own furrows, had planted asparagus deep in that rich black soil, had brought the asparagus to harvest and to sale; and he had used the proceeds to purchase more acres of Orange County land.

Méndez no longer hoed his own furrows, planted his own seed, weeded his own acres, or cut his own asparagus.

But Méndez still sold the asparagus for Yankee dollars, put some pennies from each dollar into his bank account, and was a comfortably successful and accepted member of the grower community of Orange County.

But Gonzalo Méndez was not grateful to Orange County for his success.

Gonzalo Méndez took the stand in court to testify against that same Orange County in which he had achieved employer status.

"There are two communities in Orange County," he explained; "Westminister, where I live, and El Modeno, where many other Mexican-Americans live. There are two schools in each community. In Westminister, one school is close to the center of things, a handsome building set on green lawns, shaded by shrubs, and equipped inside with good lights, new desks and tables, a library full of new books, and a motion picture projector in each room. The other school is out on the edge of town, in the middle of a clay field, dusty in the sun, muddy in the rain; inside and outside, the paint is peeling from the walls; droplights hang from the ceilings, dim and sometimes not replaced when they go out; the desks are dirty and carved with initials; there is no library; there are no motion picture projectors. In El Modeno, there are also two schools. They are side by side. But one is well-equipped, the other ill-equipped, and the children eat lunch at different hours, so that one group will not be contaminated by the other. Which school in Westminster do the Anglo children attend? Which group in El Modeno is likely to contaminate the other group?"

"You contend that by requiring your children to go to the dilapidated, ill-equipped school at the edge of town in Westminster, just because they bear the name Méndez and their grandparents were Mexican, they are being deprived of an education equal to children whose names are Hansen, Evans, and O'Rourke?" he was asked.

Gonzalo Méndez smiled. "It is true that the children are selected for each school by name," he said. "But occasionally there is a Jesús O'Reilly who shows up at the new school because his mother married an Irishman, and then they have to look at his face to tell whether he belongs or must go to the dirt school. But I am not so worried about the education that my Sylvia, my Gonzalo, Jr., and my Gerónimo might get at the dirt school, because the teachers are good teachers and the students are good students. I am worried about the hatred which my Sylvia, my Gonzalo, Jr., and my Gerónimo will have in their hearts for the children who went to that new school, and I am worried about the hatred the children of the non-Anglo school in El Modeno will have for the children who always ate lunch before they did and could read the writing in their books without squinting, because the light was bright enough in their classroom."

"But Mexicans are a distinct and inferior race!" the school authorities asserted.

Noted anthropologists testified for Méndez and demonstrated that in any meaning of the term "race" the Mexican belonged to the same group as the Anglos. And Federal statutes were quoted to show that Mexicans of Spanish descent and of mixed Spanish-Indian descent were "white persons" under the naturalization laws.

"Mexican children are dirty! They have lice and impetigo! They don't wash their hands, faces, necks nor ears," the superintendent of schools testified.

"*My* children are dirty? *My* children have lice?" Gonzalo Méndez asked, spreading his arms expressively.

Méndez won his case and the case of some 5,000 Mexican residents of the Orange County school district.

In nearby San Bernardino, all "Latins" were barred from using the public swimming pools. In protest, three citizens —a Catholic priest, the Reverend R. Núñez; a newspaper publisher, Ignacio López; and a college graduate, Eugenio Nogueros—entered a successful suit in the Federal courts to require San Bernardino to lift the ban which, they pointed out, actually applied to citizens of Italy, Spain, Portugal, Mexico, and 21 South American nations, as well as to residents of the San Bernardino area.

The swimming pool case was not the only action initiated by Ignacio López, who had worked in the Office of War Information during World War II, organizing European minorities in the urban areas of the eastern United States into Liberty Bond Leagues to support the war effort. Now he used his organizational experience and his bilingual Pomona newspaper to form Unity Leagues in small towns south and east of Los Angeles. In the Unity Leagues, veterans furnished the element that fused the blue-collar worker and farm laborer into a politically active bloc, members going from shack to shack and from house to house in every area where Mexican-Americans might be, persuading them to register and then to vote for other Mexican-Americans who were willing to put their names up for Board of Education offices and City Council seats.

In Chino, California, the Unity Leagues finally elected a City Councilman; and in Ontario, and Pomona, itself, their active political participation captured the attention of the American Council on Race Relations, which sent a field organizer to advise them in expanding their organization. Soon Unity Leagues were staging voter registration drives south from Azusa and Cucamonga to San Diego.

In 1947, a committee was formed in Los Angeles to elect Edward Roybal (see Appendix for biography) to the City Council. Although the campaign failed, members of the committee determined to start a permanent political action group, which they called the Community Service Organization (CSO). Like the Unity Leagues, the CSO was determined to prod Mexican-Americans into full citizenship by getting them registered and getting them out to vote, whether or not they were promoting the candidacy of a single individual or a slate of potential office holders.

By 1949, the Community Service Organization had been so successful in its activities that it succeeded in electing Edward Roybal to the Los Angeles City Council.

But it did not stop there.

To increase the effectiveness of members of *La Raza*, the CSO instituted citizenship classes and courses in English, and later it opened offices to give Spanish-speaking people needed advice on such things as filling out income tax forms, applying for Social Security, or deciphering the instructions on some "put-together-yourself" purchase from the English-speaking world in which they had to live.

In 1948, in Texas, members of the long existent League of United Latin American Citizens (LULAC, formed in 1928) and the newly organized American GI Forum hired Gos García and other lawyers to file suit against the officials of the school district of Bastrop County, a mid-Texas community, on behalf of Minerva Delgado, a native-born schoolgirl whose grandparents—with whom she lived—had come to the United States as immigrants. Mexican-American scholar George Sánchez (see Appendix for biography) prepared the factoral brief which won an out-of-court agreed judgment requiring the district to cease segregating pupils of Latin American descent either in separate schools or in separate classes. An exception was made of the first grade, where students who had been in school for less than one year and who could not understand enough English to perform first grade work in a nonsegrated classroom would be permitted to have their own Spanish-speaking teacher for that year only.

During World War II, as during World War I, industrial and farm recruiters painted glowing pictures of opportunity to lure many Puerto Ricans to migrate from their island to the mainland United States to fill the vast manpower needs of the war effort.

In 1945, at the very peak of the manpower shortage,

40,000 Puerto Ricans made the trip, most of them settling in New York City, a large number congregating in Spanish Harlem, many more on the Lower East Side; but because of crowded conditions everywhere, they spread thinly through the boroughs. As a result, while most Puerto Ricans thought of Spanish Harlem as "El Barrio"—and, if they did not live there, nonetheless visited as often as they could, making it a center of informal social life—no major organized Puerto Rican community actually developed in New York. In other parts of the country, Spanish-speaking citizens joined labor unions, formed political action groups, and brought suit to better their education and living conditions, but the New York Puerto Ricans—although members of labor unions, Catholic and Protestant churches, and especially of "hometown" clubs representing virtually all island *municipios*— still tended to cling to family and friends in small, tight clusters, and did not move as a group toward united action on economic, social, or educational matters. Then, at the end of the war, migration slowed sharply, with many Puerto Ricans returning again to the islands.

Immigration from Mexico, however, did not slow.

While the *bracero* program had been an emergency measure, the legislation that authorized it did not cancel out at the end of hostilities. And to the Mexicans south of the border—scratching out a bare subsistence from the almost nonexistent topsoil, parched some years by the hot sun, washed away other years by torrential rains—the opportunity to augment their income (equivalent to about $250 per year) with the fabulous farm wages in the United States, ranging upward from 50¢ an hour to almost a dollar, was one to fight for, pray for, and pay bribes for.

To the truck, sugar beet and fruit growers of the United States, the seemingly limitless supply of laborers willing to work for such meager pay, willing to accept regimentation and primitive living conditions, willing to come at the last minute and leave as soon as the need was ended—with the Federal government paying for recruiting and transportation—was an operating bonanza worth all the economic and political pressure they could muster.

Highly structured, the *bracero* selection started with drawings in *rancho* hamlets across Mexico, an official placing a marble in a shoe box for each of the men of the *rancho,* white marbles in the exact number to fill the *bracero* quota for that *rancho,* colored marbles meaning no trip north that year.

Individuals reaching into the box and drawing a white marble could either take advantage of their good fortune—if they had the bus fare to take them to the immigration stations—or they could try to sell their authorization to some eager *compadre,* frequently realizing up to a thousand pesos—or about $75 U.S.—for their lucky draw. Since the purchaser of the authorization might return from four or five months in the United States with twice as much as he would make all year if he stayed at home, this traffic in authorizations was a profitable one for all.

Crowded into the lumbering buses that plied the rutted paths serving as roads in rural Mexico, the *braceros* would spend two or three days bruising their buttocks on the hard, straight-backed steel seats, with time off to sit in the shade of the bus in the daytime or to lie under the stars at night when the vehicle broke down, and the two drivers would pull out their tool kit, their welding torch, and their versatile Spanish vocabulary to get the bus patched up and moving again.

At the workers' immigration station, there would be another wait of four or five days, until their names were among the 200 to a thousand announced over the station's loudspeaker each day. During this time, food was meager and quarters were frequently the underside of porches or the warmth of doorways.

But at last there would be a place for them on the wood-slatted benches of the railroad coach, which would take them north. Through the grimy windows they could see little of the country they were passing through. There was no food to be bought on the train, and even the water spigots had stopped working.

At the border, papers were checked, baggage inspected and sprayed with DDT, and then they would push themselves into the waiting buses, in which—at last in the United States—they would travel to the processing camp where a hot meal would be available in the mess hall; doctors would thump their chests, take X-rays, check them from head to toe; and then others would take their fingerprints and their pictures. If they were not rejected for physical reasons, they would at last be taken to a large hall where the various contracts available would be read to them in Spanish and all of their questions—if they asked any—would be answered.

The last lap of their long trip would be on another bus, to the huge farm where they had contracted to work. If it was a good operation, they would have bunks to sleep on and they would follow a regime much like that of the military: up at 6:00 in the morning; line up to go to the toilet; line up to wash; line up for breakfast of scrambled eggs, sausages, and Mexican sour beans; line up to get into the field bus; line up to start down the rows of sugar beets, or lettuce, or fruit trees; line up for lunch; line up to go back to work; line up to get back on the bus after 12 hours of hot, sweaty work; line up to wash again; and line up for supper. In the evening, there was always a bunkhouse card game, and, for those not too exhausted, a scrub baseball game outside.

Payday was a time for sending money orders home, buying new boots and new decks of cards, and, that evening, a bunkhouse party lasting until exhaustion.

At the end of the season, the *bracero* would return home, anticipating the marble drawing for the next year, when, if he were extremely lucky, he might again draw a white bead; but more than likely he would not be so lucky and would either have to wait another year or two or more, or would need to bribe a *compadre* for his authorization if he wanted to return legally to the fields of the United States.

But waiting to pick a white marble, or buying an authori-

zation from a *compadre,* or even—a third way—going to the
central *bracero* camp at Monterey, Mexico, where, if he had
done military service, the Mexican was eligible to enlist as a
bracero—was too chancy, or costly, or time-consuming for
many who were eager to get across the border to the land of
economic opportunity.

So, instead, they simply swam across the Rio Grande
River, or climbed over a barbed wire fence that stretched
along the boundary between Mexico and the United States
from the Rio Grande to the Pacific Ocean. Men crossing the
river with families could use an illegal ferry—a flatboat, a
raft, or a "duck," a craft constructed of dried willow
branches held together with rope and sometimes lined with
canvas.

For the "wetback," swimming the river in the night,
pushing a log with his clothing strapped to it above the
water, or for the "aerialist," climbing the barbed wire fence
and scurrying across the open, treeless fields beyond, or for
the 20 or more men, women, and children huddled on the
makeshift raft or "duck," or overloaded boat, there was the
direct danger of drowning or being shot by the border patrol, whose rangers were constantly in motion along the
lengths of both river and fence.

Once safely across, the Mexican knew that the border patrol was still a constant menace, and added to that was the
possibility that everyone he contacted in his search for employment or in his actual work on the job might be an in-
former or a member of the Immigration Service who would
arrange his arrest and deportation.

Yet, despite all this, and the additional danger that at
every stage he might be cheated, robbed, or beaten by fer-
rymen, labor contractors, or untrustworthy *compadres,*
"wetbacks" by the thousands continued to make the jump
each month.

And, for the most part, they were more welcomed by
Mexican-Americans already in the United States, and by
employers, than were the legally entering *braceros.* For the

bracero was, in every respect, a foreigner, competing with citizens for work, taking American money back to Mexico rather than spending it in American shops for American goods, and yet protected in wage and working conditions by the law. The "wetbacks," on the other hand, usually wanted to stay in the United States—particularly those who arrived with wife and children.

For them, the crossing was just a beginning. Disembarking from raft or "duck," they would scramble in the dark as far as possible from the border and crawl into the scrub brush just before dawn to sleep from exhaustion, but wakening many times in terror at the sound of a prairie dog's bark or at the shuffling hooves and gentle lowing of grazing cattle. Toward evening, they would eat the last scraps of food they had brought with them in the blanket roll or rope-tied suitcase that contained all of their personal belongings. And then, with the sharp knives they carried at their belts, they would chop poles from the brush, forcing them into the soil in a kind of palisade, held together with vines and other poles at the top, and spread over first with brush and then with mud—the low silhouette and the materials themselves making the hut, or *jacal*, blend into the terrain as if it were just another mesquite clump.

His family sheltered and protected from discovery by the border patrol, the male "wetback" would set out the next morning to seek assistance from citizen Mexican-Americans, whose names and addresses he had been given by family and friends back in Mexico. If not caught or turned over to the authorities before making contact, the "wetback" would usually be welcomed and guided to employment by those from whom he sought help.

With food for his family and money for clothing necessities, the "wetback" tried to make himself so useful to his employer that he would be given a document stating that his services were needed "due to the shortage of skilled agricultural labor," and then he would be able to get residence papers and move his family from the *jacal* to a scrap lumber hut in a *colonia*.

Seldom, however, did the saga of a "wetback" constitute just a single foray across the border. Jobs were usually only temporary, and citizen friends did not have endless contacts: they were desperately seeking a livelihood themselves. Authorities unceasingly patrolled the area frequented by Spanish-speaking people, demanding papers and following up leads of Mexican-Americans who had taken offense at a "wetback" and reported him.

However, deportation became merely a small episode to the "wetback," who immediately plunged into the river again, climbed the fence again, or, if possessed of pesos or dollars, joined a group on a raft or "duck" and returned to the United States in style.

During the immediate postwar years, when demand was still high for seasonal labor to harvest crops for lucrative and growing markets, neither the border patrol vigilance nor local government pressure was applied too seriously in seeking out illegal immigrants.

In 1945, just 16,311 "wetbacks" were deported. As the decade of the 40s drew to a close, however, and production of food and cloth began to exceed demand, unemployment began to mount. Citizen Mexican-Americans, as well as "wetbacks" and their families, were stranded in labor camps, and relief officials found their welfare rolls doubling and tripling each month. Enforcement of immigration laws became more intense, with 224,588 illegal entrants being deported in 1949. In 1950, the number was more than half a million. (Of course, these figures are misleading, because the same individual might be deported five or ten times in the same year.)

In the East, the unrestricted postwar air transportation provided a direct bridge from Puerto Rico to Manhattan Island. In 1946, alone, 40,000 Spanish-speaking individuals made the trip from the Caribbean Sea to the Hudson River.

The industrial tempo slowed and many returned to their home island in the labor-surplus years that followed. But by the end of 1950, the United States was again plunged into a foreign war—this time in Korea—and conditions were dramatically reversed. Limitations on cotton acreage in the Southern states, from the Atlantic to the Pacific, were removed, the New England factories began to speed up their clothmaking machinery, and the New York garment manufacturers started turning out work in the form of Army uniforms at a record rate.

From a labor surplus in the first part of 1950, there was, before the end of the year, a manpower shortage. In 1951 alone, 63,000 Puerto Ricans flew into New York. By 1953, every tenth Manhattan Island resident was a Puerto Rican. From Spanish Harlem to the Bronx, tenement landlords, still strait-jacketed by rental ceilings on existing facilities, quickly remodeled four-bedroom unfurnished apartments, which rented for $38 a month, into four separate furnished rooms, with a single bath and a kitchen serving all four and each room now renting for $60 a month—more than a 500 per cent markup resulting from the addition of just a few $10 sheets of plasterboard.

Coming from a land of perpetual summer, many Puerto Ricans arrived in New York in midwinter without coats to cut the icy wind, without overshoes to wade the snowy drifts. They crowded into any accommodations they could find, and it was not unusual for a family of seven or eight to live in a single room. Double-deck beds, cots, and just mattresses placed on the floor at night but rolled up and stored on one of the beds in the daytime constituted the furnishings. Fifteen to 20 people would frequently have to line up to use the single toilet available on a floor. The few vacant lots, narrow alley ways, and the streets, themselves, would be littered with refuse, broken bottles, rusting cans, and dirty shreds of paper swirled by the gusting winds.

Despite these conditions, more than a thousand islanders a week continued to fly in, most considering themselves es-

sentially commuters, realistically expecting to get work at
$40 to $75 a week in the garment industry, radio assembly
plants, pharmaceutical laboratories, or in the food and hotel
service industries as busboys, dishwashers, maids, and bellhops; and then, as soon as their stake had grown to an amount that would make it possible for them to live better in
the islands than before, they expected to return to the Caribbean.

To this end, most were industrious workers, and many
sought to improve their saleable qualities; 11,000 Puerto Ricans attending courses in settlement house classrooms and
public night schools in the year 1951, alone. Others, giving
up the idea of getting rich quick, saw opportunity in moving
out from the New York slums to other areas. By 1953, there
were 15,000 Puerto Ricans in Chicago; 4,000 in Bridgeport,
Connecticut; 3,000 in Lorain, Ohio—a community that had
long been home to Mexican Americans—2,500 in Philadelphia; and 76 pioneering Puerto Rican families had settled in
Bingham Canyon, Utah, where, in six years, some had managed to work up from being day laborers in the copper
mines to manning the machinery at salaries of $6,000 a year
and more—as much as cabinet ministers in the Puerto Rican
government were earning at the time the migrants had left
their homeland.

By the end of the 1940s, therefore, a vast number of
changes had taken place in the lives of Spanish-speaking
people in the United States.

The decade had started with most families still trying to
get stabilized from the depression years.

Then came the war and opportunities in defense industries and on the battlefields, offset by race riots in many of
the country's large cities.

Successful court actions, economic recovery, and a new
political awareness were matched by *bracero* and "wetback" competition with Spanish-speaking citizens and long-
time residents, and acts of discrimination by some Anglos
against all "Spics."

In this setting of growing unity and economic and political effectiveness, juxtaposed with disunity among different segments of the Spanish-speaking people and continued poverty and lack of alternative vocational choices, a new group of leaders and an increasing socioeconomic stratification began to develop during the next decade.

Chapter 16

Peon, Pugilist, and Preacher

In 1950, *a young man,* 22 *years old, brought his wife and* small children to San Jose, California. After trying to raise their family by working together in fields up and down the state, the Mexican-American couple had decided to stop their wanderings and concentrate on making their living in the cotton and prune orchards around San Jose.

Ten years earlier, the young man—one of five children in the family of an Arizona farmer who toiled and barely existed on his small acreage near the Colorado River outside of Yuma—had lived briefly in San Jose. His father, finally unable to sustain his family any longer as an independent farmer, had come there at the end of a long trek following the crops from Arizona to California, living in ramshackle huts, sleeping in a broken-down old Studebaker, or huddled in a tent when nothing else was available.

Hungry but trusting, the new migrant family had found themselves almost worse off on the road than they had been on their farm near Yuma.

One labor contractor secured work for them, picking wine grapes on a field near Fresno. For seven weeks the family toiled in the vineyard, with just a $20 cash advance, because the labor contractor assured them that when he was paid for the grapes by the winery, he would pay them. But when, after picking the field clean, they went to the contractor's house to receive their big check, they found the house empty.

Destitute and desperate, the family could only turn to another labor contractor, who sent them to the cotton fields near Mendoza. It was November, cold and rainy, and there was no work at all. The labor camp was deserted, the electricity was shut off, but there was nowhere else to go. While the parents tried to find any kind of task to earn a few cents, the children, without shoes, attended school in the Mexican American annex, to keep warm, and after school, fished in the canal and cut wild mustard greens for food for the family. Finally they struggled to Los Angeles, where the mother sold crocheting on the streets.

The following winter, near Oxnard, the boy and his brother walked the margins of the highway, looking for empty cigarette packages, while the parents worked in the pea fields from 5:30 in the morning till dark. The boys eventually retrieved enough tinfoil from the empty cigarette packages they had picked up to make a huge ball that weighed 18 pounds, which they sold to a Mexican junk dealer for enough money to buy them each a pair of tennis shoes and two sweat shirts.

When, at last, the family came to San Jose in 1939, the CIO began organizing workers in the dried fruit industry, and the boy's father and uncle joined. Union members met at the boy's house and planned a strike. It failed and the union was dispersed. But the boy's father had tasted the sweet, strong stimulant of self-respect, and after that was first in line to join every new agricultural union that came along. And later, the young man, following the crops on his own, participated in his first unsuccessful collective bargaining effort at the age of 19, as a member of the National Agricultural Workers' Union.

Then, one evening in 1950, opportunity knocked on the door of the young man's shack in the crowded, impoverished farm workers' neighborhood of San Jose. Opportunity was Father Donald McDonnell, pastor of the nearby mission church, who was simply making a routine visit to the poor people in the parish.

"How is it possible for me to embrace the teaching of the Church," the young man asked, "when I am forced to live in these surroundings, to sit in the poorest seats in a movie theater, to go to a dirty 'annex' school, just because my skin is brown, my father was Mexican, and I speak Spanish as well as English?"

"Now you're talking about social justice," Father McDonnell smiled at him, "and social justice is my language. We can talk about it in English or Spanish, or, if you can keep up with me, in Chinese, Japanese, German, or Portugese."

Father McDonnell leaned back against the wall and stretched out his legs in front of the low cot on which he was sitting.

"Take Pope Leo XIII," he said. "He wrote a whole series of encyclicals, putting the Church solidly behind labor unions."

It was after midnight before Father McDonnell left, and the young man followed him to the mission church Sunday, to *bracero* camps where he helped with the Mass, to the city jail where he joined in conversations with the prisoners, to the homes of other farm workers, always pressing for more knowledge of labor history and the farm labor movement.

And two years later, the Anglo priest, Father Donald McDonnell, introduced the young man to another individual with a distinctly Anglo name, who started the young man on the road that was to lead him to change the course of history for the agricultural farm workers in California.

"This is Fred Ross, who's on the staff of the Community Service Organization," Father McDonnell said. "Fred, I'd like you to meet César Estrada Chávez."

Fred Ross hired César Chávez at $35 a week to help organize CSO chapters throughout the state. Chávez not only did that, but also spread the organization into Arizona, and in a half a dozen years had worked up from local organizer to general director of the entire organization.

While the Community Service Organization had been growing from the Los Angeles committee formed to elect Edward Roybal mayor, to a political education group, and later an economic action front under César Chávez, other Mexican-American organizations were forming, thriving, or fading.

The longest lived of all was the Alianza Hispano Americana, first organized in 1894. It was essentially a mutual benefit insurance association, with fraternal organization rituals, and some minor social service type projects, such as scholarships, and legal action against discrimination.

A middle-class civic service organization, the League of United Latin American Citizens, (LULAC), was formed in 1928 in Harlingen, Texas, combining several smaller Alianza-type mutual benefit lodges. LULAC chapters emphasized the Americanization of Mexican-Americans and generally supported conservative local government. In 1956, LULAC established a Texas preschool English program, called "The Little School of the Four Hundred," aimed at teaching 400 basic words of oral English and succeeding in preparing 95 per cent of its graduates with an English vocabulary sufficient for the students to start even with the Anglo children in the primary classes, rather than being held back because they could speak only Spanish. (See Appendix for biography of Félix Tijerina, key figure in founding "The Little School.)

Another Texas organization, formed in Corpus Christi in 1948 by a group of Mexican-Americans, was called the "American GI Forum of the United States." Rebuffed for membership in existing veterans' organizations, Texan Mexican-Americans were aroused to action when the family of a

Mexican-American war hero was refused a plot for his body in a local cemetery, with the brusque statement that the cemetery was for white people only. Under the leadership of Dr. Héctor García, they appealed to President Truman, and the Texas hero was buried in Arlington National Cemetery in Washington, D. C., with full honors and major fanfare.

Once organized, the American GI Forum spread rapidly. In less than a year, Dr. García, chairman of the board of the Forum, was instrumental in organizing more than one hundred chapters in Texas alone. Forums then sprang up in New Mexico, and soon chapters appeared in virtually every state of the Union. Many forums were just social clubs, but others became politically active, and the Forum soon employed a full-time lobbyist in Washington, D.C.

To match the social and social action groups, the educationally oriented Council of Mexican-American Affairs (CMAA) was organized in Los Angeles in 1954. Made up largely of Mexican-American veterans using the GI Bill to achieve a college education, the CMAA held conferences, discussions, and seminars to examine issues affecting the Mexican-American community, and to seek new opportunities for college-trained Mexican-American citizens.

While the organizational activity among Spanish-speaking people in the United States following World War II clearly indicated a growing unity and willingness to sacrifice individual security to achieve desirable group goals, it also illustrated a growing diversity even among those who wished to emphasize their Mexican-American identity and heritage.

Notable among those who joined none of the action organizations were the descendants of the early Spanish and Mexican-Indian settlers of New Mexico and the Lower Rio Grande Valley in Texas. In New Mexico, the Taosinos and other semi-isolated Spanish-speaking farmers, sheepherders, and village tradesmen continued the general tenor of life that had been theirs for several generations, their votes

electing occasional Spanish-surnamed public officials, their
continuing poverty demonstrating the economic irrelevance
of such superficial symbolism.

In the Rio Grande territory, descendants of the original
landholding families fared variously economically but occupied very different social positions from the Nuevo Mexicano. "Real Texans," rich or poor, held themselves to be the
elite. Graduates of Mexican or eastern United States universities, most were thoroughly bilingual. Conversing easily
with upper-class Anglos, they, nonetheless, regarded the
Anglos as beneath them in manners, morals, and mentality.
They also considered Mexican-Americans lower class, even
though they may have made it through college and into the
professions or successful business enterprise.

The grandees' children, however—despite Ivy League
degrees or sojourns at universities in France—began in the
50's to move away from their Spanish identification and to
associate more and more with wealthy Anglos and with others whose backgrounds were similar to theirs but who no
longer were acknowledging their Spanish or Mexican-Indian
background. Doctors, lawyers, business men, and academ-
ics, the college-educated, economically independent, post-
World War I-born, depression-reared, World War II-ma-
tured, Spanish-surnamed Texas aristocrats' sons tended to
blend into their Anglo surroundings. Their fathers and their
fathers' friends were the last of their lines; the mid-20th
century decade of the 50's was bringing to an end the romantic tradition of the New World Spanish grandee.

Also still strongly identified with their Spanish-Catholic
background, Spanish-speaking owners of small businesses
and medium sized farms and ranches watched with similar
dismay their sons' rejection of the old ways.

Caught between two worlds, the Mexican-American en-
trepreneur of the 1950's avoided discrimination by staying
close within his *colonia,* and by practicing the most visible
ritualistic elements of *compadrazgo,* in which the most im-

portant of his *compadres* would be the baptismal godparents of his children, and the next closest would be the children's confirmation godparents. Then, of course, the best man would be the groom's *compadre* and the maid of honor would be the bride's *compadre*. If the *compadres* were, in addition, blood relatives, such as aunts and uncles, the extended family would be a close one indeed—one unlikely to be separated by members' moving to another area or succumbing to Anglicization.

But the children, frequently college-bound, were not satisfied to come home again to run the restaurant, or tend the store, or keep track of the field hands and market produce; and the daughters of neighboring families or *compadres*—girls who had been protected and trained in the arts of cooking and housekeeping by their mothers—were not as interesting as the girls at school who knew their way around.

To the Mexican-American parent, who had struggled up from the fields to a measure of economic success and who expected respectful acquiescence when he said, *"En mi casa, yo mando"* (In my house, I command), the attitude of the son and daughter in their teens or approaching maturity in the decade of the 50's was bewildering and deeply disturbing.

Yet to the young man and woman, the mobility of the automobile their father had given them, and the communicability of the English language they had learned in school, had opened the gates of the *barrio* to a world whose horizons were wider than any their parents had imagined. There were still the rebuffs because of their color or their stature, and even among Anglo friends there was the feeling of condescension, the echo of words that might have been said behind their backs, but there were office jobs with good pay, sales jobs with large commissions, and houses with lawns and a garage, in neighborhoods where Spanish was never spoken except in jest.

For parents who had not made it quite so far—for skilled mechanics, foremen, clerks, and family farmers—the generation gap in the 50's was not so great.

Teen-age daughters willingly stayed home to help mothers with housework after school and on weekends. They increasingly took care of the younger children in order to prepare themselves for their future roles as mothers, and whenever their own mothers were indisposed, they would take charge of all the household tasks.

The teen-age boys would gather with their friends in the informal *palomilla* relationship—*palomilla* literally meaning "moths" and figuratively referring to a gathering (like moths) around the bright lights in the early evening—playing baseball, drinking beer, and talking. Most of them accepted the goal of *machismo,* or manliness, and tried to excel at athletics and at talk about sex, looking forward to a job that would give them each time and money for a *casa chica*—a mistress in a second house—to go along with a wife and family and conversation in the *cantina* with their *compadres.*

Parents and children alike in this group wore working clothes only on the job—white shirts, tie, and suit being the badge of acceptance; and aspiration beyond the *colonia* and outside the traditions of *La Raza* being cause for acid comment or even ostracism.

In the families who had taken to the road in the 20s—when cotton and sugar beets and truck gardening and fruit raising provided steady employment for workers who moved with the seasons—who had managed to survive the drought and the grasshoppers and the economic depression of the 30s, who had taken advantage of the good crops and the swing toward mechanization in the 40s and developed an understanding of the mechanics of irrigation or the operation of farm machinery, many were able to settle in a single locality in the 50s. They watched their sons and daughters grow into semiskilled jobs in factories or canneries or also succeed in the agriculture business by driving trucks or running harvesters, or even helping with the supervision of the still-necessary hand labor at the peak of the season.

They were careful not to buy anything that would seem too pretentious to their *compadres;* but they were making payments on a small frame house; they did have a second-hand refrigerator, a secondhand stove, and a used washing machine; and they drove a secondhand car. They went to church regularly, kept a family altar in the living room, and tried to be good examples to their sons, so that someday their sons might own their own businesses or have their own little acreage, and not have to depend on anyone.

Some of the children were getting through high school, but many of them had dropped out along the line, in order to help with payments on the house, or the car, or to take advantage of the opportunity to go north with an uncle or a cousin to extend their earning season. But everywhere they went—father and son and mother and daughter—the language they spoke was Spanish, the heritage they boasted of was Mexican-American, and the traditions they lived by were those of *La Raza.*

And the same was true of those who were still among the migrants, or who still, though settled in a single place, did the stoop labor in the fields and the manual tasks in the factory. Tending the fields, digging the ditches, harvesting the crops, loading the trucks, packing the fruits and vegetables, pushing the crates in the cannery, and sweeping the floors in the offices, they distrusted their Spanish-speaking foreman and called him "the wolf," or "the fox," or "the eagle." They distrusted doctors and employers, and walked off the job or just did not come back the next day, when they felt cheated or insulted.

Wherever they went, the family stayed together, and the children went to school only when they could not find work to earn money to provide for the necessities. For money was the goal of all activities, Spanish was the language for all transactions, and *La Raza* was the way of life for all *compadres.*

Their greatest concern was competition from new migrants, a very real concern when more than a million "wetbacks" came into the country to compete with the domestics in 1954, and the *bracero* invasion reached a peak of almost half a million in 1956.

With all the stratification of value and attitude, with the increasing rejection of the Spanish-Mexican-Indian heritage on the one hand and the increasing emphasis of it on the other, the essential socioeconomic fact of the three decades from 1930 to 1960 for the Spanish-speaking people of the southwestern United States was the movement from unskilled labor to operative, craft, clerical, managerial, and professional work.

In 1930, almost 65 per cent of the Spanish-speaking men in the southwest states had been employed in unskilled jobs. By 1960, only 32 per cent were still in the unskilled category, while the operative and craft percentage had moved from 16 per cent in 1930 to 41 per cent in 1960.

At the same time, the nonmanual percentage—professional, managerial, sales, and clerical—had more than doubled in the 30 years.

The change from farm labor to operative employment, however, was due to a great extent to the mechanization of the agricultural enterprise, itself. And by the end of the decade of the 50s, the actual relative concentration of Spanish-speaking people in the farm labor force had increased, when compared with other groups, rather than decreased. Spanish was still the language of the field.

While the descendants of the conquistadores and the more recent migrants from Mexico were finding various ways of adjusting to change in the Southwest, Puerto Ricans continued their two-way trek between the Caribbean island and the mainland during the 1950s. The greatest influx was almost 70,000 in 1953, dropping to around 20,000 during the slight recession the next year.

Of the 892,513 Puerto Ricans living in the 50 states in

1960, more than one-fourth had been born on the mainland. Of those who had come from the island, 85 per cent had quit their jobs in Puerto Rico, hoping to get better jobs on the mainland.

Although many who migrated in the 50s came from low-income and laboring groups on the island, only five per cent actually worked in unskilled jobs in New York: 41 per cent of the Puerto Ricans moved into semiskilled operative occupations, as in the needle trades, and about 20 per cent went into service in hotels and restaurants.

While only five per cent of those born in Puerto Rico managed to find their way to professional, technical, or managerial jobs, more than 12 per cent of those born on the mainland had reached that occupational level by 1960. Eighteen per cent of the mainland-born were in clerical and sales jobs in 1960, but less than ten per cent of the Puerto Rican born had found such jobs.

And while only ten per cent of the Puerto Rican-born New Yorkers were foremen or skilled craftsmen, 16 per cent of those born on the mainland had achieved that status.

Puerto Ricans joined unions, too. In 1959, 65 per cent of New York Spanish-language households contained one or more union members.

In 1937 a Puerto Rican was elected to the New York State Assembly. The next was not elected until 1953, but he was re-elected in 1954, 1956, and 1958. Appointed as a New York City Court Judge in 1959 he had been joined in the Assembly in 1958 by another Puerto Rican who, in turn, was joined by still others in 1960.

The Council of Puerto Rican and Spanish-American Organizations of Greater New York was founded in 1952, to "get out the vote." Before long, it began to work with parent associations, community centers, and other groups, to improve living conditions and opportunities for Spanish-speaking people in the area. (See Appendix for biography of Father Walter Janer who worked to improve conditions.)

One summer, a school playground in East Harlem, where

the school had a Puerto Rican concentration of 92 per cent, was closed because there were no funds to pay supervisors. That summer the children played in the streets and threw rocks at the school windows, breaking 238 panes. A delegation of parents sought out the school authorities to determine how much it would cost to keep the playground open, and during the winter conducted a number of drives and raised the money. Next summer, the playground was kept open, and only 23 windows were broken in the school, a 90 per cent reduction!

Such a heavy concentration of Puerto Ricans in a school was extremely unusual, however. Actually, 80 per cent of the public schools in New York City had some Puerto Rican enrollment, a situation providing both school personnel and Puerto Rican pupils with great difficulties, since very few schools had teachers who spoke Spanish, and very few of the Puerto Ricans spoke or read English.

The situation was intensified outside of New York during the decade of the 50s, when Puerto Ricans in increasing numbers moved out from the city that was the terminus for most of their flights from the island. Eighty-three per cent of the Puerto Rican population on the mainland was still concentrated in New York City in 1950, but that level had dropped to 69 per cent in 1960, and Puerto Rican persons were living in a hundred of the 101 United States metropolitan areas of over a quarter of a million population.

For the Puerto Ricans, then, like the Mexican-Americans of the Southwest, the decade of the 50s was a decade of gradual mobility. The second generation, despite crowded living conditions, low income, and inadequate schooling, was succeeding to more desirable, better paying jobs than their parents had.

But for all Spanish-speaking people, color, language, and traditional association with manual, menial tasks continued to contribute to social, educational, and economic discrimination that became more and more intolerable as individual and group expectations became similar to those of the Anglos in the communities, in the occupations, and in the schools which they shared.

As a consequence, in California, César Chávez, general director of the Community Service Organization (CSO), decided to precipitate a head-on confrontation with the power structure of the agricultural employers and the State Farm Placement Service.

Every day for several months he led a group of farm workers to the office of the local Growers' Association, where each worker filed a complaint with the California Farm Placement Service when he was not hired for a job that was being filled by a *bracero*.

Eleven hundred separate complaints were filed in this manner before an inspector from the Department of Labor directed the growers to hire local workers instead of the Mexican nationals.

The growers complied as long as the inspector was in the area, but after he left, they fired the local and hired the *bracero*.

"It's no use," CSO associates told Chávez. "The growers have all the money, all the power."

"All the money, maybe," Chávez agreed, "but not all the power. Let's plug into the power of the press."

It was not easy to persuade the newspapers and television that something newsworthy was going to happen, but Chávez and members of the CSO finally succeeded. With reporters and cameramen observing and recording every step and every action, Chávez organized a huge marching group of unemployed local farm workers to visit the fields and demonstrate visibly that the growers were using *braceros*—Mexican nationals—while local American citizens, eager to work, could not find jobs.

The power of the press proved potent, indeed. In the investigation that followed, an assistant chief of the Farm Placement Service was fired when it was proved he had taken bribes from growers, and the Farm Placement chief and two other key officials resigned under the pressure generated by the publicized documentation of the farm workers' march.

César Chávez had won his first skirmish with the growers.

In the decade of the 50s, other men and other movements were seeking focus and identities in geographical and economic situations at once totally dissimilar from each other and from those of César Chávez, and yet identical, because they were all unique, indigenous expressions of *La Causa* and *La Raza*—a goal and a group. *La Causa*, the goal, was operationally undefined, but it clearly embraced the components of self-determination and self-respect; *La Raza*, the group, was also still unformed, but it was certainly comprised of an identifiable cultural core, a language link, and a broad socioeconomic spectrum.

One man fought to find his way in the harsh white lights of a boxing ring. Cheers and boos from the darkness beyond the ropes beat on his ears as the thudding blows of his opponent beat blood from the scarcely healed scar tissue above his eyes, flattened his nose, and cauliflowered the same ears that heard the hungry howl of the human pack screaming for a kill.

Another sought to find his destiny on street corners, in *barrio* homes, in revival tents and meeting houses across the broad stretches of the southwestern United States, wherever a hand-clapping, Amen-ing group could be gathered in city, village or rural hall.

The first was Rodolfo "Corky" Gonzales, National Boxing Association's third-ranking featherweight fighter, winner of 65 out of 75 professional bouts, after picking up both a national and an international amateur championship.

The second was the Reverend Reies López Tijerina, glory-shouting Assembly of God evangelist. Illiterate at the age of 12, self-taught after that from a Spanish Bible, fired up by a church school, he set out as a circuit preacher in his early 20s to bring the Word of God to the land that Francis-

can friars had traversed with a similar mission 400 years before.

But "Corky" Gonzales and Reies Tijerina were not
finding themselves or their mission in the boxing ring or the
pulpit.

Tijerina, born in a Texas migrant farm worker camp, and
Gonzales, child of the metropolitan Denver *barrio*, shared a
heritage of poverty and of work, from the day they were old
enough to earn a few pennies to add to the meager amount
of their families' finance. Both worked at times in the Colorado sugar beet fields, but Tijerina traveled far with his migrant family, while Gonzales merely made the short trek
from the Denver *barrio* to the Colorado beet fields, with
some time in the mines and some time in the slaughterhouse, before his ring career took him to New York and
back.

When he returned, Gonzales first took the route of business and politics. A folk hero who had battled his way from
the *barrio* to the big time, "Corky" Gonzales was a success
as a service club speaker and insurance salesman, and he
rose dramatically in the Denver Democratic Party to be a
district captain, friend of the mayor, and the bestower of
party patronage before he was 30 years old. As the decade
of the 50s came to a close, Corky Gonzales owned his own
automobile insurance agency, and was proprietor of a surety
bond business. He was the epitome of the second-genera-
tion, high-school-educated Mexican-American who was succeeding, and who had a commitment to community as well
as commercial affairs.

Reies Tijerina was succeeding, too, in a very different
way.

At 18, Tijerina enrolled in the Assembly of God Bible Institute at Ysleta, Texas. Although he did not graduate, he
began a long preaching pilgrimage, during which he walked
with his wife—a former Institute student—and son from
coast to coast, sleeping under bridges, meeting in dingy
evangelist halls, giving away his clothes and possessions, and

eventually losing his wife and his ministerial credentials.

But Tijerina called himself a nondenominational minister, and kept on.

In the 50s, he joined with 17 Spanish-speaking migrant families to buy—at $9 an acre—160 arid but irrigable acres that were part of the original Peralta land grant, lying in Arizona desert between the Tortilla Mountains and the Maricopa Indian reservation.

Calling the settlement Valle de Paz—Valley of Peace—the group built a church, a cooperative store, a school, and dugout houses. But there was no peace. A housing project called Arizona City started nearby. Land values soared to $1,500 an acre. Area teachers objected to the community school, outside the established system. Tijerina was charged with grand theft for an incident allegedly involving six feed-trailer wheels. The charges were dropped. One by one the village buildings caught fire and burned to the ground. Tijerina was charged again with grand theft, this time for some stolen hardware found in the community well. His brother, Margarito, a young man who had been in trouble in the Midwest, was picked up in Valle de Paz for an Indiana parole violation. In the Pima County jail, Margarito was involved in a jailbreak, and Reies Tijerina was charged with complicity in the break. Taking advantage of a recess in the hearing on the jailbreak charge, Tijerina simply walked away and never came back.

Standing in the desert under the stars, the Reverend Tijerina prayed to his God for guidance, and, he said later, he had a vision of four frozen horses coming to life and three angels of law asking for Tijerina's help.

When the sun woke him in the morning, he was covered all over with white, fresh dew, and he felt reborn and rebaptized. He decided to search back through history to find the source of the frozen horses, to learn the law of the land, so that he could help his *campesinos*. In Mexico, he prowled the archives and found records of land grants made by the Spanish and Mexican government to the original settlers of the Southwest. Tracing the boundaries of the grants on the actual sites of farms and villages of northern New Mexico, he found there were still descendants of those settlers who knew of the grants and even had copies of the originals in their possession.

As the decade of the 1950s moved to a close, Reies Tijerina decided he had come to a beginning.

And on an island in the Caribbean, a beginning of a very different sort initiated still a new phase in the Spanish-speaking people's migration to the territory of the United States.

In 1959, Fidel Castro transformed Cuba into the first Communist satellite in the Western Hemisphere.

Almost immediately, a steady stream of refugees began to pour into Florida on regularly scheduled air flights and on boats—small boats and large boats and almost anything that would float long enough to make the run across the open stretch of water—as frantic Cubans sought desperately to get permanently away from the new regime, or fled temporarily, hoping to find a way to get back by plotting the eventual overthrow of the Castro government.

But from the start, the Cuban immigrants were very different from any other Spanish-speaking group that had preceded them. English was already a fluent second language for most of them. More than one third were at least high school graduates, and almost one sixth were college graduates. Among the refugees were doctors, lawyers, engineers, teachers, and successful businessmen, most of whom were, if not wealthy, at least among the more affluent of salaried Cubans or independent professional people. They had every reason to believe that they would be able to resume their comfortable ways once they reached the golden sands of Miami's beaches.

But there they found life not so golden, after all. For Cuban doctors could not practice in the United States without further training, and lawyers and teachers and engineers were informed that their professional credentials were also unacceptable in the United States, land of freedom and opportunity. Despite advantages of education and solvency, Cuban refugees found themselves—as had other immigrants with a Spanish language heritage—set apart as less than equal. Doctors became dishwashers, engineers became janitors, lawyers took jobs as bellhops, teachers waited on tables, and business men clerked in dime stores.

The 1950s—a decade of progress and prosperity for the United States as a whole—had been a decade of upward socioeconomic mobility for many individuals of Spanish, Mexican, or Puerto Rican ancestry. In addition, the 1950's had been a decade of growing generational differences among members of Spanish-speaking families, of resistance to racial restraints, of testing tradition and seeking new solutions to old problems.

Even with the Cuban revolution, the decade of the 50s had been essentially a quiet decade. The decade of the 60s, on the other hand, was to be a time of tension and turmoil.

Chapter *17*

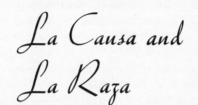

La Causa and La Raza

"*I was lost. I was in a huge room with high ceilings and* bright lights and tall windows along one wall. All around me were strangers, and up in front was a woman so tall I could hardly see her all at once. Her face was pale, but she didn't look sick, and her hair was a faded kind of almost no color at all. Her eyes were like the sky on a hot summer day, and her lips were moving and she was making sounds—so she must have been talking—but I couldn't understand what she was saying. And I cried."

The words are those of an adult recreating the first day of a Spanish-speaking child in an English language first grade classroom.

"It is especially hard on us in grade school. For example, we get in front of a classroom to read, or give a report; then we make a mistake in our English and all the boys and girls laugh. Later on, as we continue school, we hate to speak in a classroom where everyone seems to know good English. We are very self-conscious."

That was the comment of a high-school senior who knew no English before entering school.

"I remember that before I had taken Spanish lessons in high school, I spoke a kind of Spanish that now I am ashamed to hear. I used to mix my words, saying half of a word in Spanish and the other half in English. Now that I have taken two years of Spanish and I am in my third year, I recognize the terrible mistakes I used to make."

Another high-school student, crying out in anguish over her own Anglicized image of the language of her family and friends.

"The parents of Spanish-speaking students are the people that could help the most. It should be explained to these parents what their children go through. The parents should be told to speak more English."

The judgment of a son visited upon his father.

By 1960, 85 per cent of the Spanish-speaking people in the United States had been born in this country. Native Americans, they were strangers in their own land. And the only route to achievement seemed to be to reject their parents' language and even to reject their own friends.

"When I went to junior high, I started to stick around with English-speaking boys and girls, and the Spanish people would call me a 'paddy lover.' I didn't care, because I knew they were the foolish ones by not mixing."

But not all young people from Spanish-speaking families went that route.

David Sánchez, 16 years old, raised in a neat, well-furnished lower-middle-class home, in East Los Angeles—complete with a color television set and gaudy silk souvenir banner sent home from Vietnam by David's older brother—was selected as the outstanding Los Angeles high-school student in 1966 and was appointed chairman of Mayor Samuel Yorty's Advisory Youth Council. By 1969, as Prime Minister of the Brown Berets, he was demanding bilingual education, the teaching of Chicano history, the giving of voting literacy tests in Spanish, and the requirement that all police officers in the Chicano community live in the community and speak the Spanish language.

In the decade of the 1960s, the Spanish-speaking people in the United States began to flex their muscles and seek alternative ways to achieve individual and group fiscal and psychological success.

César Chávez was one of the first.

One day, in 1961, he walked into the national office of the Community Service Organization (CSO) and said to the woman behind the desk, "You probably read my letter of resignation. I am leaving. Here are the keys." He turned and walked out.

The CSO was a strong, successful organization. Its convention, which Chávez had just left, was being held in a luxurious motel. Attending, in addition to the organization officers and community supporters, were a number of local, state, and national politicians. Prior to the meeting, Chávez had argued for meeting in a cheap hall near the *colonia,* so that even the unemployed farm workers could afford to attend.

"Unheard of," he was told. "We have to build prestige. We've got community leaders and national politicians attending this meeting. We can't take them to a dump."

So Chávez walked out. There were no more farm workers in the CSO; Chávez, himself, was no longer a farm worker.

But Chávez went back to the farm. He turned down a $21,000-a-year job as director of the Peace Corps for four Latin American countries. He went back to his wife's home town of Delano and got a job pruning grapevines at $1.25 an hour.

In 1961, the Reverend Reies Tijerina was preaching the gospel of land in the adobe shacks of northern New Mexico. To Tijerina, the message of the Treaty of Guadalupe Hidalgo, ratified by the President and Senate of the United States and by the President and Congress of Mexico in February 1848, was very clear. It said that in the territory ceded to the United States, which included most of Texas, New Mexico, Arizona, and California, "Mexicans . . . shall be free to continue where they now reside or to remove at any

time to the Mexican Republic, retaining the property which
they possess in the said territories, or disposing thereof, and
removing the proceeds whenever they please." It also said
that "In the said territories, property of every kind . . .
shall be inviolably respected. The present owners, the heirs
of these, and all . . . who may hereafter acquire said property by contract, shall enjoy, with respect to it, guarantees."

The next year, Tijerina set up headquarters in an old
print shop, and on February 2, 1962, founded the Alianza
Federal de Mercedes (Federal Alliance of Land Grants),
saying to the 15 or so villagers who attended the first meeting that they were heirs to millions of acres once granted
the Southwest colonizers by local representatives of the
Spanish crown and Mexican government. He told them the
United States Forest Service had illegally occupied their
land. He told them that 19th century land barons and territorial governors had, by legal trickery, stolen their birthright
before they were born.

"It was," he said, "like talking to a block of ice. They sat
there like a block of ice. My words chipping away on that
block of ice."

But chip away he did—for three years.

As Tijerina was starting his chipping away process, in
1962, in Florida—where the first terrified flurry of refugee
Batista supporters had scurried when Fidel Castro took over
the government of the island nation of Cuba—the nature of
the refugee stream had changed. Now, with air travel read-
ily available, more than 1,800 small merchants, office employees, and skilled and semiskilled workers were arriving in
Miami each week. Since 1960, the Cuban government had
been confiscating all real and personal property belonging
to the refugees, so that, except for what they could carry
with them, the Cubans coming to the United States arrived
destitute.

Then, in October 1962, United States Intelligence discovered missile sites being built in Cuba and Russian ships
carrying missiles heading toward Cuban shores across the

Atlantic Ocean. President Kennedy placed a quarantine on the island, and for the next three years, except for government exchanges of prisoners, no direct commercial air transportation existed between the two countries, so refugees again took to large boats and small boats and anything that could float.

In the same year, 1962, César Chávez was spending all his spare time going from town to town in the San Joaquin Valley, talking to farm workers—*campesinos*—about organizing a new association, one designed to help the member with all his needs: insurance, a credit union, translation of business and tax documents from Spanish to English, guidance in getting welfare and other government benefits, assistance in solving medical problems.

Dues were to be $3.50 a month, and, after a year of organizing, Chávez was able to boast ten full-fledged members.

César Chávez's wife, Helen, worked in the cotton fields, mothered eight children, and mimeographed 80,000 cards that asked, simply: "How much do you think you ought to be paid?"

From door to door, in more than 80 small towns and labor camps, César and Helen Chávez handed out the cards. Suspicious, many *campesinos* listened, accepted the card, and closed the door. But some listened and said, "Come in."

Hungry, Chávez sometimes asked for food. "It turned out to be about the best thing I could have done," he said, "although at first it's hard on your pride. If people give you their food, they'll give you their hearts."

Finally, Chávez thought there might be enough joiners for an effective organizational meeting. Held in Fresno, on September 2, 1962, the meeting attracted 250 *campesinos* who had signed cards and who voted to establish the National Farm Workers' Association (NFWA). Chávez' cousin, Manuel, had drawn a black, vaguely birdlike object with squared wings to use as the symbol on the organization's flag.

"What is it?" NFWA charter members asked.

"It's an eagle," Manuel said. "An Aztec eagle! And when that damned eagle flies, that's when the farm workers' problems are going to be solved."

And the year 1965 was when the eagle first flew.

The year 1965 was also the year when many new movements tested their wings.

In 1965, Rodolfo "Corky" Gonzales, general agent for the Summit Fidelity and Surety Company of Colorado, district captain of the Denver Democratic Party, former Colorado Coordinator of the "Viva Kennedy" campaign, member of the steering committee for the Anti-Poverty Program for the Southwest, member of the national board of Jobs for Progress, member of the board of the Denver Job Opportunity Center, president of the National Citizens' Committee for Community Relations, and chairman of the board of Denver's War on Poverty, found himself held guilty by association with some corrupt politicians. Called "almost a thief" by a Denver newspaper, he was suddenly alone. His city hall "friends" were afraid to stand by him; his business associates were suspicious and willing to believe the accusations.

He resigned from the boards and councils and committees.

And he resigned from the Democratic Party, writing, "The individual who makes his way through the political muck of today's world, and more so the minority representatives, suffers from such an immense loss of soul and dignity that the end results are as rewarding as a heart attack, castration, or cancer!"

Then, in an old red brick building in the downtown Denver *barrio* from which he had fought his way to amateur championships, to top professional rankings, and to economic and political success, "Corky" Gonzales—once more an unemployed Chicano—founded La Cruzada Para La Justicia (The Crusade for Justice).

In 1965, Fidel Castro and President Lyndon Johnson

worked out a new agreement for Cubans to come to the United States by air. Immediately, some 200 refugees a day began arriving, most of them related to refugees who had arrived earlier. In the years between, many of their predecessors had moved out from Miami to fill jobs—in the professions for which they had been trained—in small communities all over the United States, which were experiencing shortages of doctors, lawyers, teachers, librarians, engineers. By the end of 1965, there were Cubans living in every state, including 26 in Hawaii and one in Alaska.

In New York, Puerto Rican Herman Badillo (see Appendix for biography) was elected President of the Borough of the Bronx in 1965. Also, in 1965, there were a Puerto Rican councilman, a justice of the civil court, a State Senator, and three State Assemblymen.

But on the streets of Chicago, 16-year-old José "Cha Cha" Jiménez, member of a street gang called the "Young Lords," was serving 30 days in the city jail on a disorderly conduct charge growing out of a gang rumble. Other gang members had been picked up at the same time and were serving with him. "Cha Cha" looked around; he saw that the "Young Lords"—and members of other gangs—were not the only Puerto Ricans in jail. Also locked in cells were old people and middle-aged people, people he knew were workers not criminals, and welfare mothers, whose only concern was their children, some of whom had been herded into juvenile detention centers, others parceled out to foster homes, and still others left to fend for themselves, huddled in their hot apartments, alone, hungry, and frightened.

"Cha Cha" Jiménez, who, up to that point, had turned his frustration and hatred to other gangs—the Latin Kings, the Paragons, the Black Eagles—began to think seriously of other enemies and bigger problems.

And on May 3, 1965, in a field of roses near the town of McFarland, California, Epifiano Camacho, a man who had spent his life crawling from rosebush to rosebush in the great gardens of Mount Arbor Nurseries, the largest grower of roses in California, stood up, his fingers dripping blood from the hundreds of tiny cuts inflicted by the thorns of the rose bushes he had been grafting, and shouted, *"¡Huelga!"*

At the signal, 80 other men rose from their knees.

It was the beginning of the "Strike of the Roses," first militant, nonviolent action of César Chávez's militant, nonviolent National Farm Workers' Association.

The unfurling of the NFWA Aztec eagle flag—red with the eagle black in a white circle—symbolized the beginning of a new era initiated by a new breed; but it also symbolized a tie with the ancient past, when the Aztecs, in times of peace, staged "Wars of Flowers," with marches, and orations, and flag waving—and red roses and red poppies symbolizing life and death.

The first strike was a small strike. But just four months later, on Mexican Independence Day, September 16, 1965, a meeting was held in a Catholic church hall in Delano, and more than a thousand *campesinos* pushed and shoved their way inside to vote on whether or not to strike against the Delano grape growers at the height of the harvest season.

The big strike had started with a local action by a small group of grape pickers in the Coachella Valley on the edge of the Mojave Desert. Their demand was, simply, that they be paid at the same rate as *braceros*—Mexican nationals—for the same work: $1.40 an hour, rather than $1.10.

Under the blazing desert sun, the first ripening grapes swelled to their moment of ultimate richness, hung ready to drop into the gentle hand of the experienced picker, and then, the moment past, burst, their juices falling to the thirsty ground, their bodies shriveling to raisins.

The growers capitulated.

All grape pickers in the Coachella Valley were paid $1.40 an hour.

But when the season moved north to Delano, wages for locals were posted at $1.10.

An AFL-CIO affiliated union, Agriculture Workers Organizing Committee, made up mostly of Filipino grape pickers, decided the time had come to strike. Eight hundred Filipino farm workers stood up straight and walked out of the fields on September 8, 1965.

With young Filipinos manning the picket lines, older Filipino grape pickers also stayed out of the fields.

The labor contractors turned to Mexican workers.

With the Filipinos of the Agriculture Workers Organizing Committee shouting, "Scab!" the Mexican workers, many of them members of the National Farm Workers Association started the grape harvest.

Tension grew.

And then César Chávez called a meeting of the NFWA on September 16, Mexican Independence Day.

The vote, "*¡Huelga!*"—Strike!—was unanimous.

Epifiano Camacho, fired from the rose fields for starting the "Strike of the Roses," drove his battered old car up and down the dirt lanes between the vast acres of grapes, slogans in Spanish on its sides, proclaiming, "I, too, was a virgin once!" And, in the rhetorical style of Old Mexico, he shouted at the nonunion pickers, "Are you Mexicans or what are you? Don't be slaves! Come out, you pigeon-brained sons of Satan! Join us and fight for your rights!"

A joint strike committee was set up by the Agricultural Workers' Organizing Committee and the National Farm Workers' Association; and by September 20th, more than 1,200 *campesinos* had joined the Filipinos, and the strike had become a truly big one.

But the vineyard owners, representing a business grossing more than $4 billion annually, said, "There is no strike. The *huelga* is pure myth, manufactured out of nothing by outside agitators."

At NFWA headquarters, César Chávez, the "outside agitator," representing a treasury of $85, said, "I have been a farm worker all my life."

Still, the harvest was made.

And workers, recruited widely by the grape growers' labor contractors, continued after the harvest with the tasks of making ready for a new year. They pruned the vines, they thinned them, tied them into clumps and de-leafed them. The sun moved south, the rains came, and wet wind beat at huddled pickets.

In December, Walter Reuther, president of the AFL-CIO, arrived in Delano to lead a march down the main street, culminating in the announcement that the Industrial Union Department of the AFL-CIO would provide $5,000 a month for the *huelguistas*, the strikers, so that all involved could be guaranteed $5 a week strike pay. The announcement was followed by the distribution of two trailer-truckloads of Christmas toys and turkeys. Nationally, a grape boycott was announced, and picket lines formed wherever Delano grapes were being sold or shipped.

Somehow, the winter passed, and on March 17, 1966, César Chávez began a 300-mile pilgrimage to Sacramento, leading one hundred NFWA members from town to town, hosted along the way by other farm workers. Joined by students and other volunteer supporters, the march grew, with more than 500 people walking the last miles on Saturday, April 9. Fifteen hundred attended a rally that night, and the next morning, Easter Sunday, April 10, 1966, 4,000 marchers were in the group that came to the State Capitol, where another six to eight thousand joined them.

Between Christmas and Easter, a great resurrection of hope had taken place, for on April 6, the marching strikers had received word that attorneys for Schenley Products, one of the major producers in the Delano area, had agreed to negotiate with the NFWA.

In Chicago, on a hot, sunny Saturday afternoon in mid-June 1966, the police band joined in a parade down Division Street, main stem of the northwest side *barrio* where most of Chicago's Puerto Rican population lived. The parade was the final event in "Puerto Rican Week," with singing and dancing in the streets, carnival booths along the sidewalk, and speeches by politicians and *barrio* residents.

The next day the humidity rose with the temperature, and thundershowers kept people indoors, looking disconsolately from tenement windows or crowded into doorways, waiting for a break in the weather.

An argument started on Damen Avenue, just off Division Street, and a patrolman, investigating the disturbance, thought he saw someone pulling a revolver. The police officer drew fast and shot from the hip. The sound of the shot, a break in the showers, and already hot tempers drew a crowd. The patrolman called for help, and the arrival of more officers drew out more *barrio* residents. The street was soon a mass of shouting, pushing Puerto Ricans and policemen.

The sound of sirens converged from all directions, and suddenly into the melee plunged new carloads of policemen, accompanied by snarling, vicious police dogs. A situation that was already out of control exploded into a full-scale riot. Two police cars were set afire. Bullets, rocks, and bottles turned the street into a battleground. A blue-helmeted police riot squad arrived, and was met with a barrage of Molotov cocktails thrown from roofs and windows.

Puerto Rican community leaders pleaded with the city government to get the police out and keep them out until things calmed down, and City Hall agreed. But when a burglar alarm went off, a squad car snarled into the area in automatic response, and bullets and bottles started flying again.

By midweek, massive action by major increments of armed officers had broken the large groups into small groups and had carted many Puerto Ricans off to jail. Almost miraculously, only one person had been seriously injured. But Division Street, which had always been a peaceful place, was no longer peaceful.

On the Fourth of July weekend, 1966, Reies Tijerina made the first move in bringing his Alianza Federal de Mercedes (Federal Alliance of Land Grants) to national attention. From Albuquerque, the Alianza's headquarters, Tijerina made a 62-mile protest march in two blistering hot, grueling days to Santa Fe, the state capital. Although the Governor of California had refused to meet with César Chávez's marchers, the Governor of New Mexico, Jack Campbell, did meet with Tijerina and agreed to forward the Alianza's argument to the President of the United States.

In Rio Grande City, Texas, in that same summer of 1966, the United Farm Workers' Organizing Committee had set up headquarters in the Old Mexico Theater, an abandoned movie house, and had organized a strike of melon pickers against La Casita Farms, one of the country's largest growers of cantaloupes.

Late one evening, four carloads of Texas Rangers skidded to a halt in front of the theater, smashed open the door, and, shotguns at combat ready, corralled the small group of union workers.

"Where's that son of a bitch, Dimas?" one of the Rangers rasped.

Magdaleno Dimas had been charged by a deputy sheriff —who also was manager of La Casita Farms—with disturbing the peace. His crime was shouting, *"¡Viva la huelga!"* The shout, in fact, was a crime, because the Farms had succeeded in getting a court injunction forbidding the use of the term, *"¡Huelga!"*

Dimas was not at strike headquarters. The Rangers, however, located him, visiting at the house of a fellow striker. They surrounded the house, smashed down the front door, and again charged, shotguns held waist high. By the time the arrest was made, Magdaleno Dimas had to be taken to the hospital in an ambulance, suffering from a concussion, a broken rib, and a blood clot near his spine.

In Delano, California, the year 1966 ended with the first taste of victory for the National Farm Workers' Association, when the Schenley Corporation agreed to sign a union contract and was followed by Christian Brothers, Gallo, Almaden, and Paul Masson. But the victory, though sweet, was not sweeping. The wine grape growers sold out their table grape holdings, and the table grape growers refused to negotiate. Only a few thousand of the more than a million and a half California farm workers had achieved union contracts.

So the strike went on.

And Reies Tijerina, hearing nothing from the White House as a result of his Fourth of July march to Santa Fe, made his next move in October 1966. With 350 of its estimated 5,000 to 50,000 members, the Alianza moved out from Highway 54 in Rio Arriba County, and set up tents in a mammoth natural hollow in the pastel sandstone cliffs of New Mexico, designated as a national campground and known as Echo Amphitheater. On this site, the Alianza proclaimed the re-institution of a 19th century land-grant community, San Joaquín del Río de Chama. Electing a mayor and appointing marshals with badges and loaded rifles, the Alianza proposed to repossess the 1,400-acre San Joaquín grant, awarded in 1806 by an acting governor of Mexico to a group of settlers led by Francisco Salazar.

In a gunpoint-to-gunpoint confrontation with police, the Alianzans took the nonviolent route and abandoned their campground for the time being.

Nonviolence was also at the heart of an organization founded early in 1967 in Los Angeles by David Sánchez, then 17 years old, the "exemplary young man" who was chairman of the Mayor's Advisory Youth Council. Joining with Sánchez in founding what they called "Young Citizens for Community Action," were Carlos Móntez, also 17, and Ralph Ramírez, 15.

As they discussed ways for involving more Spanish-speaking young people in their new group, Sánchez and his associates decided to change the name to Young Chicano Youth for Community Action, and they opened a coffee house, La Piranya, supported by an interfaith church group.

The idea of the organization was to discuss community issues and do something positive like taking boys and girls camping or raising money for food for the striking farm workers in Delano. The idea of the coffee house was to give teen-agers a place to do something rather than just walking the streets, lounging on street corners, smoking pot, or tanking up on wine, an activity they called the "grapes of wrath."

One of the things the group did, however, was to picket the sheriff's office to protest a case of alleged police brutality. The sheriff decided the coffee house needed looking into, so patrols went there every night, shining their lights through the window, picking up participants for selling coffee without a license, giving tickets to members of the volunteer band for entertaining without a license, and shoving out anyone under 18 for simply being there.

At one point, David Sánchez was picked up and booked, and he, along with others in the Young Chicano Youth for Community Action, decided that doing good was not enough. Sánchez, Móntez, and Ramírez changed the name of the organization to the Brown Berets, Sánchez becoming Prime Minister, Móntez Minister of Information, and Ramírez Minister of Discipline.

"We tried to bring about changes to help our people by working through conventional channels, including War on Poverty programs," Sánchez said. "But we soon found out about the insensitivity and corruption of establishment bureaucracy and left in disgust."

The Delano strike continued, bitter week after bitter week merging into months, and, by 1967, into its second and third year. But national notice involved César Chávez and his associates in more than the local action. To one of his longtime associates, Gilbert Padilla, Chávez said, "There's some problem in Texas. Go and see what's wrong."

And so, in January 1967, Padilla came to Rio Grande City, in the "Magic Valley," near the "Fun Coast" of Texas.

In that place, 18th century *haciendas* had provided the climate for the development of a "Spanish" culture that had thrived in the 19th century and had lasted into the 20th, until the Eastern and Continentally educated sons and daughters of the last aristocrats had faded into Anglo society. However, the successors to the *pobres* who had herded the cattle and tilled the soil were still there, in *colonias* of straw and mud huts, buttressed by old boards and road signs. In that land—which had been transformed by the vanguard of the great wave of immigrants from Mexico in the first half of the 20th century from cattle land to palm-lined citrus groves and rich vegetable gardens, through the grubbing out by Mexicanos of the tough Texas *brasada*, and their painstaking building of vast irrigation systems—half of the houses of the farm workers lacked any kind of water and one third of the families subsisted on welfare and surplus food.

As one of his first acts, Gilbert Padilla persuaded the United Farm Workers Organizing Committee to take legal action against the Texas Rangers. Charging 23 counts of harassment of its members, the Committee asked the United States District Court for Southern Texas to restrain the Rangers from selectively arresting and prosecuting the striking melon pickers.

Meeting with a new Governor of New Mexico, after an Alianza automobile caravan journeyed from Albuquerque to Santa Fe in April 1967, Reies Tijerina was again promised a hearing in Washington, but that was all. As a result, Tijerina announced that the Alianza would henceforth be named the Confederation of Free City States, and would hold a national conference on June 3, 1967, in the tiny community of Coyote in southern Arriba County.

At that point, District Attorney Alfonso Sánchez interrupted radio programs in northern New Mexico to announce that he considered the Coyote meeting to be illegal and that criminal charges of unlawful assembly would be filed against all persons who attended. Then, on Friday evening, June 2, 1967, the sheriff's office started rounding up Alianzans. Eighteen men were jailed; one—José María Mar-

tínez—was the great grandson of the original recipient—
José Manuel Martínez—of the 1832 Tierra Amarilla grant,
594,500 acres "for cultivation and pasturage"; another was
Cristóbal Tijerina, Reies' brother; and a third was Lloyd
Félix Martínez, a key lieutenant to Tijerina. Martínez was
alleged to have guns and ammunition in the trunk of his car,
and Cristóbal was alleged to be carrying organization charts
for Tijerina's army, along with prime objectives and lists of
members and donors to the organization.

Early the next morning, state police wearing riot helmets
and carrying shotguns, set up roadblocks outside the village
of Coyote. Through the morning, however, Alianza members filtered into the small town. Two other Tijerina brothers were picked up and jailed, but most of the time the Alianzans just stood around quietly talking as rain began to fall
from a gray sky. By midmorning, a radio announcement had
confirmed that the Governor, who initially had planned to
be at the site, was not coming. Alianza members began to
drift away.

But not all of them went home.

Word had been quietly passed that there would be a bar-
becue and swim on Monday, June 5, for anyone who ad-
journed to a *ranchito* in the nearby town of Canjilon. It was
from Canjilon on the afternoon of June 5, 1967, that Reies
Tijerina and the Alianza mounted an armed raid on the
courthouse in Tierra Amarilla, where the arraignment of the
Alianzans who had been picked up in the Friday night police action was scheduled. Object of the Alianza raid was to
make a citizens' arrest of District Attorney Alfonso Sánchez.
A warrant for Sánchez's arrest under Title 18 of the United
States Code, Section 241, which provides penalties for anyone conspiring against a citizen's rights under the Constitu-
tion, had been prepared by an Alianza lawyer.

However, Sánchez had not gone to Tierra Amarilla, but
had sent his deputy, Norman Neal. In addition, when the
raid took place, all the prisoners had been either released on
bail or returned to jail. In the confusion, a jailer, Eulogio Sa-

lazar, was shot twice but not killed. State policeman Nick Saiz was also felled by a bullet, and a reporter was abducted. In addition, there was extensive damage to police cars and the courthouse.

For a week, New Mexico was the site of an intensive manhunt, which ended with Tijerina's arrest a few minutes after midnight on Saturday morning, June 9.

And as Reies Tijerina was being led off to jail in New Mexico, "Cha Cha" Jiménez, out of jail for a brief period in Chicago, was starting to seek ways to make his gang, the Young Lords, into something more than a gang.

Organized with ministerial divisions, as other militant groups were organizing, the Young Lords made "Cha Cha" Chairman and head of the gang. He started negotiations with the Latin Kings, a 3,000-member rival gang, and persuaded them to start becoming political, also.

Looking for a permanent headquarters, they settled on the Armitage Street Methodist Church in West Lincoln Park, Chicago. When negotiations with the congregation failed to bring the kind of results they wanted, the Young Lords moved in, and, when they moved in, a solid group of the congregation moved out. By November 1968, the Young Lords had thoroughly established themselves, changed the name of the church to the People's Church, and were operating a day care program, as well as planning action to try to change other West Lincoln Park established institutions.

Also trying to change established institutions from the inside, an Independent Party in the "Magic Valley," Starr County, Texas, entered a slate in the county elections in 1968.

The farm workers' union was one of the prime backers of the new party, and the objective was to defeat Randall Nye, the county attorney who had called in the Rangers when the melon strike had begun.

To everyone's surprise, the Independent Party won the election, not only defeating the county attorney, but also winning the position of county chairman, the *jefe*—boss politician—job in the area. César Chávez's lieutenant, Gilbert Padilla, began to think there was a chance for a new life for the farm workers in "Magic Valley."

But César Chávez did not find his own cause prospering in Delano. So during the Lenten season, the fiesta of sacrifice, he began a Lenten fast for peace and nonviolence.

Back at the beginning, just before Christmas, 1966, the union had bought 40 acres of land near the city dump. The idea was to create a living monument to all who had participated in the Delano grape strike by building a clinic, a cooperative gas station, a union theater, and a union office.

By 1968, there was just the cooperative gas station and a well.

Inside the garage of the gas station, the *campesinos* built an altar for the fast. Chávez sat in the unheated garage, in the chill, damp spring of 1968, and prayed and shook from the cold.

Mass was said every day at the altar.

Hundreds of men and women came from the migrant camps, the *barrios*, and the distant hills to pray with Chávez.

On the fourth day of the fast of Chávez, Reies Tijerina, out on bail, was one of those who came to pray. The *campesinos* gathered up a collection of $500 for Tijerina's defense fund, and Chávez gave the New Mexico leader a large *huelga* flag, its black eagle spreading its wings as Tijerina draped it over his shoulders like a prayer shawl.

On the 25th day, César Chávez ended his fast by breaking bread with Senator Robert Kennedy, who stood before the wooden cross that had led the union's pilgrimage to Sacramento, and—the *huelga* flags on each side flapping in the breeze—said, "By his sacrifice, César Chávez has told the world that violence is no answer."

Violence was no answer to "Corky" Gonzales, either.

"Riots lead to the self-destruction of men," Gonzales said. "I don't think it is in the Mexican temperament to riot. We don't like to be conspicuous, or seem ridiculous. That is *ma-*

chismo. That is a man's sense of self-respect. We are men of silent violence. That, too, is *machismo.*"

But Gonzales did march. He and Reies Tijerina led the Chicanos of the Southwest in the 1968 Poor People's March, in Washington, D.C. He presented the demands of the Chicanos in a plan for the future, the "Plan of the Barrio." He demanded resources to plan family living accommodations, with parks and plenty of space for the children. He demanded schools that would be warm and inviting facilities and not jails. He demanded that Spanish be the first language, and English the second, and that textbooks emphasize the heritage and contributions of the Mexican-American and Indo-Hispano. He demanded seed money to start indigenous businesses, land reform, and a share in the wealth of the nation for all citizens.

In Denver, itself, the Crusade for Justice had bought an old church in downtown Denver, which they operated as a nursery, gymnasium, a community dining room and community center, a library, a Mayan ballroom, a kitchen, and a "revolutionary theater." In addition, in the Center—an impressive old building, with a colonnaded facade, which might have housed a branch mint or a state supreme court —the Crusade operated a legal aid service, a bail bond service, and a *barrio* newspaper named *El Gallo.* The whole thing was run without any government subsidies or rich angels. "El Centro Para La Justicia is living proof of self-determination," "Corky" Gonzales asserted. "It was built and is operated by an awakening people, a new breed. The *barrios* are coming to life."

But not all Spanish-speaking citizens were supporters of the new breed or the new ways.

Although the three United States Congressmen with Spanish-speaking backgrounds and constituencies—Congressman Henry Barbosa González of Texas (see Appendix for biography), Edward Roybal of California, and Joseph N. Montoya of New Mexico—initially endorsed the activities of the militants in their home territory, their endorsement was, at its strongest, cautious. And by the time Tijerina had become a national figure, the New Mexico Congressman, Joseph Montoya, was denouncing him as an "enemy of the United States."

In Delano, the local Community Service Organization chapter had disbanded, rather than support the farm workers. Prior to that time, the CSO had joined with the Latin American Citizens Associations, the Sociedad Progresista Mejicana, and a number of local ministers in opposition to the strike and the National Farm Workers' Association. Local women had formed a "Mothers Against Chávez" club, and visited California's governor, demanding that "tranquility be restored to Main Street." Another organization, "Men Against Chávez," denounced him as a Communist. Labor contractors and small businessmen in Delano formed the Kern-Tulare County Independent Farm Workers, and Senator Everett Dirksen awarded José Mendoza, secretary of the Agricultural Workers Freedom to Work Association, formed in February 1969, a plaque for his devotion to "freedom to work," when he completed a speaking tour for the National Right to Work Committee.

Before that, however, 15,000 Chicano students had shut down classes throughout their East Los Angeles *barrio,* in what they called "a blowout." The school strike occurred just three days after the Brown Berets' coffee house, La Piranya, closed on March 3, 1968, because of "insufficient funds and police harassment."

Police charged that the Brown Berets were "outside agitators" who caused the student disturbances.

Certainly they were there.

David Sánchez said that when the law officers "started hitting with sticks, we went in, did our business, and got out."

The Brown Berets were getting out into other areas, also. Chapters were forming in Fresno, San Francisco, Sacramento, Berkeley, Oxnard, Denver, Albuquerque, and San

Antonio. And in northern New Mexico, Brown Berets, supporting Tijerina, assisted in the organization of a new youth group, with headquarters in Tierra Amarilla, calling themselves Los Comancheros.

Then, on Friday, December 13, 1968, the jury in the five-week trial of Reies Tijerina for kidnapping Undersheriff Dan Rivera, falsely imprisoning him, and making an assault on the jail—the maximum penalty being death in the gas chamber—returned a verdict of "Not guilty!"

The next night, at Tijerina's victory celebration at the Alianza headquarters, Brown Berets stood guard.

But not all victories were lasting ones. In the "Magic Valley" of Texas, where the Independent Party had won a victory in 1968, it lost the next year, and the case against the Texas Rangers never came to trial. Gilbert Padilla went back to California, sick with frustration.

The National Farm Workers' Association had succeeded finally in gaining contracts with all of the major wine producers, but by 1969 they were in the fifth year of their strike against the table grape producers and still had no contract.

And in Denver, where "Corky" Gonzales had been so sure that there would be no riots in the *barrios*, some students walked out of the West Side High School in March, to protest what they considered were the insults of a teacher against Mexicans.

At a rally in the park, the students decided to demand that the principal have the teacher transferred. In the meantime, the principal had called for police protection, and 250 officers barred the teen-agers' path back to school. At El Centro Para La Justicia, "Corky" Gonzales heard of the trouble and rushed to the school. He found himself in the middle of a small-scale riot. Snatching a bullhorn from one of the policemen, he shouted to the students, "Go home! Go home! They'll just beat you if you stay here!"

He heard his daughter, Nita Jo, scream as she struggled to get away from a six-foot-tall policeman.

By the time the fracas was ended, 36 Chicanos had been arrested.

Next day, more than 2,000 parents, teen-agers, and teachers marched to the school to protest both the teacher's insults and the police violence.

After the quiet demonstration, most of the people left. At that point, the police, who had been standing on the periphery, moved in to disperse the rest, and suddenly there was a battle, with dozens of additional police cars called out, a riot squad equipped with mace, and a police helicopter dropping tear gas, all involved. In what the Chief of Police called the worst street fighting in the modern history of Denver, 17 police officers were hospitalized and 25 squad cars were damaged.

The trouble erupted just a week before a National Chicano Youth Liberation Conference, called by Gonzales, was to open on Palm Sunday, 1969.

It went on as scheduled!

Fifteen hundred young *campesino* activists, *barrio* gang members, *vados locos* ("crazy mixed-up kids"), university graduate school Chicanos, and even some wealthy children descended from Spanish dons, came to El Centro Para La Justicia for five days and nights of *actos, abrazos, gritos,* poetry readings, music, and the Chicano cheer *"¡Raza, Raza, Raza, Raza!"* Emotions ranged from joyous laughter to angry shouts and sentimental tears during the five days that Gonzales called "celebrating what sings in the blood of a people, who, taught to believe they are ugly, discover the true beauty in their souls during years of occupation and intimidation."

At the end of the National Chicano Youth Liberation Conference, the young Chicanos voted, almost unanimously, to accept the "Spiritual Plan of Aztlan," the name of the most ancient of the Aztec civilizations.

To close the assembly, "Corky" Gonzales read the ringing poetic conclusion to the "Plan of Aztlan":

"We are a bronze people with a bronze culture.
"Before the world, before all of North America, before
all our brothers on the bronze continent, we
are a nation.
"We are a nation of free pueblos.
"We are Aztlan!"

Chapter 18

El Coda

In May 1970, two growers, Bianco Fruit Corporation of Fresno, and Dispoto Fruit Company of Tulare, owned by Bruno Dispoto, signed agreements with Chávez's union covering about 3,000 workers and 3,000 acres in the San Joaquin and Coachella Valleys in California and at Centennial Farms near Phoenix, Arizona.

On July 28, 1970, twenty-six growers in the Delano-Arvin area signed contracts with the AFL-CIO United Farm Workers' Organizing Committee, covering 50 per cent of the table grape crop of the area.

César Chávez, his health and stamina damaged by his long fast and his long, arduous poverty, turned to the task of securing similar contracts from the lettuce growers.

Of the National Farm Workers' Association, he said, "Our goals have to be broader than the traditional goals of unions. We are a poverty union, a union made up of poor people. So we have organized a movement, a movement of the poor, where the silent hopes of many people can begin to become a real part of life."

In New York, the Puerto Rican Young Lords marched in

228

the Puerto Rican Day parade on June 7, 1970. As they passed by in their purple berets, many people lining the streets greeted them with cheers and the clenched fist salute. In both New York and Chicago, the Young Lords started free health clinics.

In Los Angeles, a group of active members of the Brown Berets removed the defiant caps with the insignia of the Holy Cross and two crossed rifles. "It is not enough to rebel," explained one. "We are searching for something more lasting, something new. Things are changing. Very fast. So whether it's violent or nonviolent, there is going to be something new to replace the old."

On August 29, 1970, 15,000 Los Angeles Chicanos joined in a parade to protest the war in Vietnam. Along the line of march, police stood by, not to clear the route but to provide "armed containment" for what was viewed as an incipient rebellion that might have to be put down by force.

Suddenly, a dispute started between a few of the marchers and a storekeeper over whether he had offered them free soft drinks or not.

Police converged on the spot, and someone said that a man with a gun had gone into a cafe. Deputies changed course toward the open door of the cafe, and one of them fired some high-velocity tear gas projectiles through the open door. Designed to pierce walls, the projectiles were accurate up to a hundred yards and could penetrate a one-inch board at that distance. One of the missiles struck and killed Reuben Salazar, a popular television commentator and columnist, who was standing ten feet inside the door. In the melee that followed, two more Mexican Americans were killed, 60 or more were injured, and 185 were arrested. At Salazar's funeral, Robert Finch delivered a personal letter from President Nixon to the commentator's widow, and Otis Chandler, publisher of the Los Angeles *Times*, spoke at the services.

Across the country, Reies Tijerina was back in prison. He had attempted to place Chief Justice Warren Burger, New

Mexico Governor David Cargo, and the head of the Los Alamos Scientific Laboratories, under citizen's arrest. He was not allowed bail because he was considered "a threat to society."

Yet underlying these sensational, explosive events, there was another kind of movement, another kind of march.

In New York, more than 10,000 businesses—from grocery stores to banks—were owned by Spanish-Americans by 1970.

In 1970, more than 60,000 young people from Spanish-speaking backgrounds were enrolled in colleges and universities in California alone.

In Miami, 6,000 Cuban businesses and more than half a million Cuban people were contributing more than $450 million a year to Miami stores, and 30 regional Latin-American offices had been attracted to the city to serve international corporations.

In East Los Angeles, 500 individuals joined together to secure a Small Business Administration loan, and built a new $1.5 million market, called El Mercado, with shops and restaurants to serve the *colonia* people. The East Los Angeles Community Union, backed by the Ford Foundation and the Federal Housing Administration, involved 40 young architects, lawyers, and business consultants in trying to create better living conditions for all people in the area.

Colleges and universities along the West Coast, across the Southwestern states, and among the large Spanish-speaking populations of the Northeast and Southeast, were establishing Hispanic, Mexican American, Latin-American, and Chicano studies programs. Conferences of educators in all sections of the country were focusing on new approaches to the education of children of migrant workers, children from the *barrios,* and children from the *colonias.*

In the United Consolidated Independent School District north of Laredo, Texas, a totally new approach was instituted: half of the teaching was done in English, half in Spanish—Anglo children and Mexican American children in the same classroom—both languages were used in arithmetic, social studies, and all other activities of the school.

"A lot of people," the superintendent said, "believed that when an Anglo child was placed in the classroom with a majority of Mexican Americans, the class level went down. But achievement tests show that the Anglo children performed better than before we started the program. The bilingual movement is catching on."

And examples were to be found in Dade County, Florida —where the Cuban majority forced such action—in California, and in New York.

But elsewhere progress was slow.

And out in the fields, in the summer of 1971, Spanish-speaking workers were still following the crops from hot, dusty sunrise to hot, dusty sunset, for wages that totaled out far below the national norm, while enduring living conditions that could only breed disease, illiteracy, and continued poverty.

Some of the leaders were fading—Reies Tijerina had been found guilty in his second major trial and faced several years in prison, while one of his brothers took over the Alianza— but new leaders were rising in new areas.

In the Yakima Valley of Washington, the summer of 1971 started hot. And Robert Trevino and Lupe Gamboa, organizers for the United Farm Workers' Organizing Committee, expected it to get hotter as they planned their campaign of "contract or strike" in the vast, $17 million hop fields of the Valley. Their next target was to be the asparagus growers.

And in the land of Quivira, central Kansas, where Vásquez de Coronado had come to the crushing frustration of the end of his quest, a new conquistador, Manuel Fierro, director of the Kansas Human Needs Corporation, was taking on no less than Senator Robert Dole, National Chairman of the Republican Party, as Fierro sought to stir the Kansas Congressional delegation into trying to solve Mexican American problems in western Kansas.

Fierro went to Kansas' Democratic governor and to the

state's Republican senators, and when he got no action from any direction, he called a press conference.

Wearing the *mestizo* insignia of Spanish-Indian ancestry around his neck, and backed by the slogans on the wall of his Garden City, Kansas, home—*Tierra o Muerte, Viva la Raza, Viva la Causa, La Raza Unida,* which were demands for land, race, cause, and unity—he got headlines.

He was very certain that his way to achieve social change was to be an antagonist—to hurl issues with force into the public's face and mind, and then to try to weave out of the center of action, so that his non-negotiable positions could be negotiated by other, more approachable groups.

As with statements made in California about César Chávez's National Farm Workers' Association, some southwest Kansas county commissioners, businessmen, and other establishment Anglos protested that, "Probably 80 per cent of the Spanish-speaking people don't like Fierro's tactics."

Farm corporation officials said, with all good candor, "The migrants, themselves, have never complained to us."

And a land manager, while admitting that the houses he had available for migrant workers were built "way back there," still held to the line that, "After all, the migrants don't have to live in them." As a clincher, he added, "I can't see we're involved at all."

In the face of gradual change—indicated by the significantly more skilled and better-paying jobs held by second- and third-generation Spanish-speaking people—and violent change—such as the high school "blowouts," the occupation of buildings by force, and bloody melees along the lines of marching men—there had been some emerging Anglo support, epitomized by Robert Kennedy's kneeling with César Chávez at the breaking of Chávez's Lenten fast, coupled with Anglo resistance and indifference, characterized by the comments of establishment officials: "They don't have to live there," and "I can't see we're involved at all."

Yet the essential situation of the Spanish-speaking people

in the United States was still that of immigrant alien almost
450 years after the first Spanish feet—those of Núñez Cabeza de Vaca—became the first immigrant feet ever to walk
the weary miles from Atlantic to Pacific and set the pattern
for the Spanish feet that would follow—the feet of soldier
and settler; migrant and missionary; *rico* and *pobre;* Spaniard, Mexican, *mestizo,* Puerto Rican, Cuban; conquistador
to Chicano.

In those four and a half centuries, other feet of other immigrants would also follow, and most would find a common
ground, a home, a new identity—American—in an assimila-
tive process once called "the melting pot."

But the new Americans would, in fact—though denying
that they did so—exclude from their common identity those
who had been Americans before them—the Indian, the Hispano, the *mestizo*—and would not welcome later newcomers from south of the border and from the Caribbean
islands, first landfall of the discoverers of the New World.
(For they would be different—in language, in looks, and in
life style!)

And the melting pot Americans were shocked when some
of those first Americans—Hispanos, Chicanos—and some of
those newcomers—Latinos, Mexicanos—turned out to be
unwilling to give up their own identity for a mythical new
one. And yet they still demanded a right to life in their own
life style! They demanded liberty to learn in their own language, to earn what others earned for the same work! And
they demanded access to the pursuit of happiness in the
same public places, and with the same respect for personal
dignity and privacy, as all other men who were created
equal!

The furious rejection by the first Americans and those
newcomers of an assimilation that had never actually been
available to them became the most bewildering anomaly of
the whole half millenium to the Anglos who had withheld
what the Puerto Ricans and the Cubans and the Hispanos
and the Chicanos were not reaching for.

What had happened to the melting pot?

The answer was clear.

And the person who said it best was Dr. Ernesto Galarza (see Appendix for biography), a man who spent his life as a farm worker, as an old-time union organizer, and as a keenly observant *La Raza* scholar—writing definitive studies of Mexican migrants.

Dr. Galarza, called "Dean of Mexican American leadership," and recognized by many young activists as "grandfather of the Chicano movement," said:

"What I see all over is something quite different from the *melting* pot.

"What I see all over is a *boiling* pot!"

*Biographies of Some of
the Outstanding Spanish-
Speaking People in
the United States*

Introduction

Here are personal vignettes of 60 individuals representing the various Spanish-speaking cultural groups in the United States, from the first Spanish explorations to the present. Hundreds of other Spanish-speaking individuals have had similar personal histories of struggle and success, and the short biographical sketches presented here simply illustrate the range of involvement in the founding and growth of the United States that has characterized the lives of Spanish-speaking people. Without attempting to be either specifically selective or all-inclusive, the author has attempted to show by dramatic example that, despite great difficulty, many people with an Hispanic heritage have managed to build careers while maintaining their own cultural integrity.

ROBERT J. ACOSTA

Teacher

Born blind, on April 24, 1939, Robert Acosta nonetheless managed to graduate from John Marshal High School in Los Angeles at the age of 18 and then go on to secure two B.A. degrees from California State College at Los Angeles, one in social studies in 1961 and one in English in 1967, to teach successfully in California public high schools, and to become a leader in student and teacher organizations. In 1968, he was named one of America's Ten Outstanding Young Men by the United States Jaycees.

Rancheros during the California period of the late 18th and early 19th centuries, the Acosta family had once held title to huge tracts in what is now known as the Pomona Valley. No longer large landholders, the Acostas still led active outdoor lives, and Robert was expected to participate with other members of the family. He learned to ride and care for horses, to join aggressively in contact sports, and to hold his own each summer away from his family at a youth camp.

In these traditions of activism and leadership, Robert Acosta founded two organizations for blind students, The Blind College Students of Southern California and the Northern California Blind Student Organization. He also initiated a professional association, The Blind Teachers of California. Then, reaching out to all young people interested in an education career, he founded the Future Teachers of America.

Still in his early thirties, Robert J. Acosta demonstrates that an individual can achieve seemingly unattainable objectives through will and effort.

MIGUEL ALVARADO
School Administrator

At the age of 25, Miguel Alvarado was a school administrator in Anaheim, California. But only 15 years earlier he had been in a class for the mentally retarded and was close to being sent to jail for stealing and for almost killing a schoolmate in a knifing incident.

Miguel Alvarado was born in Mexico. When he was nine, his parents crossed the border to El Paso, Texas. Before his first day in school, Miguel's mother told him, "Learn English. But do not forget your Spanish. Spanish is a beautiful language." On his first day in school, his teacher told him, "You will not speak Spanish. Not in class, not on the playground. Not even when you go home." And she whacked him over the head with a ruler. After his first day in school, Miguel told his mother, "You did not tell me the truth. Spanish is not a beautiful language." Miguel's mother gave him a hard slap across the face for calling her a liar.

Trapped, as he said, between two cultures, assigned to a class for the mentally retarded because he could not read or write English effectively, Miguel turned tough, picking fights in the schoolroom, in the corridor, on the playground, and in the streets. In one fight he knifed a companion so severely the boy almost died, and when Miguel's uncle came for him, Miguel knifed his uncle. A teacher sensed potential in Miguel and stayed after school to help him with his English, but Miguel stole money from her desk and then dropped out of school completely, joining the Marines and taking his frustrations and belligerence to Vietnam.

Finding violence no solution, either in personal or in international affairs, Miguel Alvarado returned to the United States, convinced that the only way to survive was through education. He graduated from high school and college, and then, as a teacher, turned to trying to find workable solutions for others. He helped transform an abandoned church building into a community center where children three and four years old could be brought by volunteer mothers each morning to start learning English. He organized service clubs for underachievers in the Anaheim schools and led them in cleaning up the *barrios* by painting the houses of the elderly, transforming garbage-strewn vacant lots into mini-parks, and holding fund-raising dances to buy clothing for threadbare children.

Miguel Alvarado learned his mother did not lie: Spanish is beautiful. But beauty is a fragile thing that needs careful nurture in a congenial culture, and he tried in a small way in Anaheim to create just such a congenial Chicano culture.

JUAN BAUTISTA DE ANZA
Explorer

Discoverer of the first overland route from Arizona to California in 1774—an event that took place two years before the United States was born, yet contributed significantly to the eventual tie between California and the United States—Juan Bautista de Anza was a member of the presidial aristocracy of the frontier provinces of New Spain.

Born in 1735 at Fronteras in Mexico to a one-time acting Governor of Sonora whose own father had been for 30 years a lieutenant and captain at Janos, de Anza entered the military service at the age of 18 and became known as a great

Indian fighter, being almost continuously involved in campaigns against the Apaches, Seris, Pimas, and Sibubapas for the next 30 years. But fighting was not his total concern. As early as 1756, when he was just 21, de Anza and another young officer sought permission to make an expedition to Colorado to determine if there were not some way of reaching California by other than the sea. Turned down on that request, and told to keep on fighting Indians, de Anza renewed and expanded the proposal 13 years later when he offered, at his own expense, to seek a link-up with Gaspar de Portolá, who had just been dispatched to try to reach Alta California by land up the tortuous Baja Península. Again directed to stick to Indian fighting, de Anza gave up on the proposal but not on the idea.

By this time de Anza had been serving as captain of the presidio at Tubac, Arizona, for some nine years, but his captaincy had never been officially confirmed. In 1770 he made a strong plea for official recognition, but did not receive it. Accustomed by this time to official rebuffs and delays, de Anza simply tried the California expedition idea again in 1772 and got tentative approval in late 1773 from the Governor of Mexico that—if the King agreed—de Anza could take 20 volunteers and, at his own expense, go directly from Tubac to Monterey and back—if there were, indeed, a route across desert and mountains—but not to try to make any settlements along the way.

De Anza did not wait for the King to say no. As a matter of fact, the King officially approved the expedition on March 9, 1774, by which time de Anza was well on his way, having left Tubac on January 8, 1774.

The journey was difficult all the way, but the worst was the "great waste of sand dunes called the Colorado desert." Of this stretch of purgatory, historian Herbert Bolton has written, "On the fifteenth of February de Anza reached the terrible dunes, where the shifting sands had completely obliterated the trails. Before night the pack mules were so used up that de Anza decided that their burdens must be lightened. Encountering now a great mountain of sand which the tired mules could not even attempt, de Anza turned south. Now completely lost in the sea of sand dunes, the animals were played out . . . there was no near prospect for either water or pasturage; in short, there was nothing for de Anza to do but to retreat to Santa Olaya."

Changing his plans, de Anza determined to try to go around the dunes, and, with just a few men, ten mules, and provisions for a month, he headed southwest and eventually made it to good springs and pasturage near the foot of the Sierra Nevada. Then he journeyed north and northwest through a pass they called San Carlos to where the streams from the snow-capped mountains ran westward. In rain and snow they surprised the garrison at the Mission San Gabriel at dusk on March 22, 1774, and by May 26 they were back in Tubac, having discovered and demonstrated the feasibility of an overland passage from Sonora to the sea.

PETER N. AQUILERA

Pharmacist

It took almost a quarter of a century, but the Aquilera brothers, of Pueblo, Colorado, parlayed an investment of $600 in 1934 to a business worth more than a quarter of a million dollars in 1957.

Prior to 1934, Peter Aquilera and his brother worked at any kind of odd job they could get just to stay alive, to stay in school, and to try to build a stake to start a business of their own. Then in 1934, in the midst of the great depression, they decided to pool virtually all of their capital— accumulated from sweeping floors, hauling ashes, and disposing of trash—to buy The Alamo, a Pueblo drugstore that had just closed its doors for lack of business. For $600 they obtained the key to the doors, the stock on the shelves, and the right to sweep their own floors, haul their own ashes, and dispose of their own trash. After becoming registered pharmacists—Peter graduated from the Capital College of

Pharmacy in 1938—they could also fill prescriptions on their own. But there were not many prescriptions to fill, and if the brothers could have sold out for ten cents on the dollar they probably would have.

Then World War II came along, and Peter practiced his pharmacy in the Pacific Theatre as a technical sergeant, while others kept the drugstore open back home. And in the business boom following the war, Peter Aquilera and his brother profited from the experience, hard work, and good will of the depression years to increase their sales and participate actively in community affairs. They opened a second store in 1957, with the total business valued at more than $250,000. After that, Peter became a director of the Mount Carmel Credit Union, a member of the Lay Advisory Board of Pueblo's Corwin Hospital, and a director of the Executive Committee of the Pueblo County Democratic Party.

ALONSO C. ATENCIO

Biochemist

When Dr. Alonso Atencio was negotiating with the University of New Mexico School of Medicine in 1969 about joining the faculty as Assistant Professor of Biochemistry, he asked to be relieved of usual faculty committee work so that he could spend time talking to Spanish-American students and prospective students about the opportunities and needs for their involvement in the health professions. The school responded by making him Assistant Dean for Student Affairs and making his talks to Spanish-American students part of his job rather than something he would have to do on his own time.

Dr. Atencio was born on June 24, 1929, in Ortiz, Colorado, just across the New Mexico line, an area very much part of the history and culture of the Rio Arriba lands. He worked with his father, tending cattle, until he completed high school at 18; then he enlisted in the United States Navy

and was assigned as a medical corpsman with the first Marine Division in Korea, an experience related to his later career, but only indirectly since, after receiving his favorable
discharge, he found himself too poor to go on to school and
without any marketable skills except those connected with
cattle ranching. For two years he earned his living—and put
what he could aside for the future—by breaking and training quarter horses.

Then, with his small stake, he enrolled at the University
of Colorado, majoring in chemistry "because I saw people in
that department that I greatly admired." He utilized his
chemistry in the laboratories of the University of Colorado
Medical School after receiving his B.S. degree, and later he
was able to combine research work in biochemistry with
work toward an M.S. in 1964 and a Ph.D. in medicine in
1967. Along the way, his studies in connection with metabolism earned him an invitation to present a paper at an International Symposium held in Gleneagles, Scotland, in 1963.
He also received a postdoctoral fellowship in biochemistry
at Northwestern University, Evanston, Illinois, before joining the Medical School faculty in New Mexico.

Dr. Atencio's major activity—beyond his direct contact
with students and his continued research in metabolism and
the relations of humans to protein synthesis—has been to assist Spanish-American students in advanced degree programs. To this end he established and became president of
the Foundation for Promotion of Advanced Studies.

"I know too many bright kids who don't get the breaks,"
he said, "and, because of the expense of postgraduate training, even those who go to college get little chance or en-
couragement to go on. 'Get your degree and find a good
job,' is the general philosophy," he said.

In addition to helping individuals achieve their highest
potential, Dr. Atencio is concerned about the lack of health
care in predominately Spanish-American areas. In Rio Arriba County, New Mexico, in 1971 there were only seven
doctors for 25,000 people. But with Federal funds new op-

portunities developed for Spanish-American students to get their medical degrees and return to their homes to practice. "People in Penasco," Dr. Atencio said, "are waiting for a girl now in her first year of medical school to finish her training and come back to be their doctor. Knowing the people, the place, and the language, she'll make a real contribution."

HERMAN BADILLO
United States Representative

Orphaned at the age of five, and passed from one relation to another from that time on until he was able to support himself as a bowling alley pinboy and lunch counter dishwasher, Puerto Rican-born Herman Badillo called no place home but lived in Caguas, Puerto Rico; Chicago; California; and finally went to New York City where he finished high school in East Harlem, went on to graduate *magna cum laude* from City College, and study nights at Brooklyn Law School, securing his LL.B. as top student in his class.

When Badillo failed to win the post of Democratic Party leader of the 16th Assembly District (East Harlem) in his first try for political office in 1961, he moved to the Bronx where the growing Puerto Rican community elected him Bronx Borough President in 1965, despite the fact that as Commissioner of Relocation—highest appointive office ever held by a Puerto Rican in New York City—he supported the West Side urban renewal project and was called by other Puerto Rican leaders, "the man in charge of minority removal."

As Borough President, Badillo refused to appear at ceremonial functions, but, instead, instituted a series of meetings in the 14 neighborhoods of the Bronx and got requests for everything from "a library in the Italian section of Throgs Neck to emergency boiler repairs in the Puerto Rican South Bronx." In his three years as Borough President, Badillo sought and got more than a billion dollars of improvements and new construction in the Bronx.

Badillo, actively anti-Vietnam War, supported Robert Kennedy and Eugene McCarthy as Democratic Presidential candidates in 1968, and, from the Democratic National Convention platform in 1968, urged the seating of the insurgent Georgia delegation led by articulate young black Julian Bond.

After losing a primary battle in the New York mayoralty campaign in 1970 and then supporting the successful Liberal-Independent candidate, John Lindsay, Herman Badillo entered the crowded Democratic primary for the newly created Triborough Congressional seat, with a constituency roughly 30 per cent Puerto Rican, 30 per cent black, 30 per cent Irish and Italian, and 10 per cent Jewish. He won by only a narrow margin, and the legality of the victory was challenged by the runner-up, but Badillo's candidacy was certified, and he overwhelmed his Conservative opponent in the election to become, in 1971, the first Puerto Rican ever to hold a voting membership in the United States House of Representatives.

PEDRO CANINO

Postal Worker

Pedro Canino became a United States citizen in 1917, when the Jones Act passed by Congress gave citizenship to all Puerto Ricans; but at that time Pedro was still a schoolboy, and his principal association with the mainland was his learning of English as a second language. It wasn't until 1925—after he had, himself, been a schoolteacher for several years—that he decided to take advantage of the "special" boat fares and the "open door" to seek more pay and greater opportunity in New York, on the island guarded by the Statue of Liberty, a landmark he first viewed dimly from the crowded deck of a ship moving slowly through the gray sleet of a bitter winter afternoon.

Following along with others from the boat who had been met by relatives and friends, Pedro eventually found himself huddled in a room in a cold-water tenement building in the area of 101st to 105th Streets off Third Avenue, where most of the 11,000 Puerto Ricans who arrived in New York in 1925 congregated, some moving into cubicles vacated by the 8,000 who sailed back to the Caribbean island in the same year and others edging the Spanish-speaking *barrio* north and west toward Central Park.

Hustled to an employment agency, Pedro was able to get semi-skilled work in the construction industry as a steamfitter. The wages—when he was working—were almost three times as much as he had been earning as a teacher in Puerto Rico, but the lifting, tugging, and straining with the heavy boilers and pipes and other equipment sapped his strength. On a winter job repairing a furnace in a flooded apartment basement in Queens, he slipped several times and fell in the icy water; knotted with cramps, he had to give up and go home to his own unheated room where he determined to find work that utilized some of his academic skills before he killed himself as a laborer.

In the Post Office Department he got lower pay but he also got security, and, because of his bilingual ability, he got jobs translating and interpreting, jobs that made him feel he was contributing something important to his fellow Puerto Ricans rather than just eking out an existence in an alien environment.

And it was his concern for fellow Puerto Ricans that, over the years, constituted the main drive which kept Pedro Canino going, because opportunities for advancement in the post office never opened up, and his top job, in the late fifties, was that of timekeeper.

But in "el barrio"—Spanish Harlem—Pedro Canino was a leading citizen. In his third floor walk-up apartment at 20 East 109th, he lived relatively comfortably with his wife and two children, his daughter eventually graduating from Hunter College and, after studying further in Puerto Rico, returning to teach in PS 108 near the Canino apartment; his son—much younger—graduating from PS 108 and going on a scholarship to the City and Country School on West 12th Street.

Whenever Pedro Canino left his apartment—to go to the store or just for a stroll—he would be greeted warmly by friends and sought out urgently by casual acquaintances and even strangers. For Pedro Canino was the driving force behind Civic Orientation Center, Inc., a place known as the "rent clinic" because it was set up to try to do something to eliminate the housing abuses that made the sheer process of living a desperate struggle for survival for most Puerto Ricans in New York.

"Forty-five wretched pigeonholes," Canino would storm, "out of five apartments! Forty-five pigeonholes renting for sixteen, eighteen, twenty-three dollars! Nine hundred dollars a week that landlord is making! More than that! And he has put in nothing! Nothing!"

Correspondence with the Department of Buildings, the Mayor, and Congressmen—ceaseless bombardment with letters, phone calls, and personal visits—were the weapons of the war Pedro Canino waged from a basement room in a building a few blocks from his apartment, where—equipped with just two old desks, a few straight chairs, and one cast-off filing cabinet, but with the volunteer help of countless other concerned citizens—he relentlessly attacked landlords who violated building codes, business ethics, and basic moral values in milking dollars from the suffering of the slum dwellers who were their tenants, until his voice and the voices of others were heard in City Hall and in Congress, and such requirements as central heating for all multiple dwellings and the outlawing of many of the most vicious profiteering practices were put into effect.

Pedro Canino, postal worker, helped many families to better lives through his selfless dedication to the welfare of his community. His Civic Orientation, Inc., was one of a continually growing cluster of organizations seeking to weld the weakness of individuals into the power of a group and thereby contribute to constructive change in society.

RAYMOND CARRASCO
Community Worker

From his role as Chief of Relocation and Community Services for the Sacramento Redevelopment Agency—in which he had to persuade people to tear up their roots in home, neighborhood, or business and move to new, strange, and unpromising surroundings—to his 1971 role as Deputy Director, Inter-Agency Committee on Mexican-American Affairs, Washington, D.C.—in which he had to persuade intrenched bureaucrats and ambitious do-gooders to surrender real or imagined power and prestige programs to the nebulous concept of effective administration—was like moving from a hornets' nest into a den of vipers, but Raymond Carrasco willingly made the move after handling the first task capably for several years.

Born in El Paso, Texas, on January 19, 1935, Carrasco graduated from Ysleta High School, Ysleta, Texas. In his first job, as a hospital orderly, Carrasco found himself caught between doctors' orders, patients' demands, and his own knowledge inadequacies. For three years, as he learned to use tact, diplomacy, reason, and skill to keep doctors assured, patients reassured, and still get the job done, Carrasco attended the University of Texas at El Paso, seeking training in psychiatric technology. A tour of duty with the United States Army Medical Corps followed; in the Army, his assignment as a psychiatric social worker tested his newly acquired knowledge and honed his mediation skills.

Impressed by apparent opportunities in California during his military service, Carrasco settled in Sacramento, started a small business of his own, and enrolled at Sacramento State College, where he received a Bachelor of Science degree in business administration in 1965. Then 30 years old and just barely out of college, Carrasco plunged himself into

Mexican-American activities, joining with others to form a council of local Spanish-speaking organizations, Sacramento Concilio, Inc. He also served as chairman of a steering committee to plan the use of one redevelopment area as a Mexican-oriented commercial and cultural center to be known as "Plaza de las Flores," a project involving some $2.5 million.

If training, experience, and demonstrated competence are any indication, Raymond Carrasco would seem to be capable of coping with hornets' nests, vipers' dens, and, perhaps, even more challenging tasks.

MANUEL A. CARRILLO

Educator

Director of the Office for Spanish-surnamed Americans, Department of Health, Education, and Welfare, in Washington, D.C., Manuel Carrillo, was born and raised in Austin, Texas, but moved to Colorado, where he received his Bachelor of Arts degree from the University of Denver and spent 17 years in public education before moving to HEW in 1970.

Fresh out of college, Carrillo lived and worked with young people for whom the traditional educational process had failed. As a Cottage Counselor at the Colorado School for Boys, he experienced both the rewarding challenge and the discouraging difficulty of trying to cope with the needs and desires of those who were determined to make it in the system and trying to make the system responsive to those needs and desires.

Continuing his own education, Carrillo received his Master of Arts degree from the University of Colorado and did additional graduate work toward an educational specialist degree. Seeking broader involvement in educational policy making, he accepted a position as co-director of Intercultural Community Relations for the Colorado State Department of Education and then as Director of Youth-Community Relations. During the 1969–1970 academic year he was

Director of Mexican-American Affairs at the University of Colorado, Boulder, Colorado.

Responsible in his job in Washington, D.C., for the coordination of all programs in HEW that relate specifically to Spanish-surnamed people across the entire United States, Carrillo brings an awareness of both hope and frustration gained from his years on the firing line in the correctional institution, the traditional classroom, and in positions of community and state-wide administrative concern.

RAUL H. CASTRO

Lawyer-Ambassador

Born in Mexico, Raúl Castro crossed the border with his parents when they immigrated to the United States, which they saw as the land of opportunity. At first the only opportunity seemed to be long hours at low pay in the fields and factories of Arizona. Castro sweated in the sun on farms and ranches and in the heat of blazing furnaces in the Arizona mine smelters while he sweated mentally over English exercise books in elementary and secondary school and over social science and law books at Northern Arizona University and the University of Arizona. While at Northern Arizona University, he sweated also under the bright lights of the boxing ring, winning the Border Middleweight Boxing Championship, and he turned professional for a short time to increase his income so he could continue his law studies.

Then the gates of opportunity swung wide for Raúl Castro. He served as Pima County Attorney, Juvenile Court Judge, and Judge in the Superior Court. He was elected president of the Pima County Legal Aid Society and was appointed chairman of the International Law Section of the Pima Bar Association. At the national level, he was designated United States Ambassador to El Salvador and then Ambassador to Bolivia.

Returning home to Tucson, Arizona, Raúl Castro combined his distinguished practice of international law with the operation of Hackney Pony Farm and continuing participation in community affairs. He headed the major gifts division of a campaign to build a new Tucson Art Center and Museum, chaired the Tucson United Community Fund Campaign, and served on the board of directors of the Boy Scouts, the Legal Aid Society, the Tucson Community Council, the National United Way and the National Humane Society.

Northern Arizona University, where Castro started his boxing career, awarded him an honorary Doctor of Laws Degree, the University of Arizona gave him its Distinguished Citizen Award, he received the Daughters of the American Revolution's Americanism Medal, and he was chosen the Outstanding Naturalized Citizen by the Pima Bar Association.

JOSE A. CHACON
Engineer

Atomic energy has been the concern of José Chacón through most of his adult life, and he was appointed to the Office of the General Manager, United States Atomic Energy Commission in October 1970. But military assignments, Peace Corps projects, Mexican-American affairs, and consumer education have also been full-time professional concerns, punctuating his engineering career; and public welfare and vocational rehabilitation have been the focus of his volunteer community service. His 1971 position, as Equal Employment Opportunities Programs Advisor for the Atomic Energy Commission combines virtually all of his activities in a single assignment.

Plunged into World War II as an aerial gunner in the U.S. Navy, Chacón received an appointment to West Point in 1947 and achieved a B.S. degree just in time to put his newly awarded commission in the United States Air Force to the test in the Korean conflict. Flying a total of 117 combat missions in World War II and in Korea, Chacón was awarded the Distinguished Flying Cross and 11 other decorations before leaving the service in 1954.

Joining the Sandia Corporation, a major contractor for the Atomic Energy Commission in Albuquerque, New Mexico, as an engineer in 1954, Chacón continued his academic work and received his M.A. degree from the University of New Mexico in 1959. At the same time he was appointed to the New Mexico Public Welfare Board—becoming Chairman before his four-year term was completed—to the Policy Board on Vocational Rehabilitation, the Governor's Institutional Council, the American Public Welfare Association, and the Cuban Refugee Committee.

In 1964, Chacón took a leave of absence from the Sandia Corportion to become director of a cooperative Peace Corps project in Perú, and in 1968 he left Sandia permanently to become involved in government administration, first on the President's Committee on Mexican-American Affairs, to which he was assigned as Executive Director in 1969, and then as Technical Assistance Officer with the Equal Employment Opportunity Commission. For the Commission he served on the staff of the White House Conference on Food, Nutrition and Health, and as Associate Director, Office of Consumer Education, President's Commission on Consumer Interests.

A native New Mexican, Chacón has varied interests that have led him to Europe, South America, and the Far East. And in the United States, wherever he has settled, he has continued his education: 20 years after receiving his Bachelor of Science degree in New York, and 12 years after achieving a Master of Arts degree in New Mexico, he became a candidate for a Doctor of Business Administration degree from George Washington University, in Washington, D.C.

J. FRANCISCO CHAVES
Political Leader

"The heretics," Francisco Chaves's father told him, "are going to overrun the country. Go and learn their language and come back prepared to defend your people."

At the time—the mid-1850's—"the Santa Fe Ring," an alliance between Anglo-American money men, lawyers, politicians, and Mexican-American *ricos* of the Rio Abajo and Rio Arriba country, controlled New Mexico. Chaves' father, a dissident *rico,* sent his son to school in St. Louis and New York. Chaves graduated from the College of Physicians and Surgeons. During the Civil War, he joined with a group of other native-born New Mexicans to fight in the Union Army.

Fully prepared with his knowledge of the Anglos' language and tactics, and with his battle experience from the Civil War, Colonel Chaves returned to New Mexico to defend his people by taking the political offensive. Running for the post of Territorial Delegate to Congress in 1867 against an Anglo-American, he found himself in a bitter struggle for ballots that was settled only in Congress where he was finally seated, despite a contested election and recriminatory accusations. In 1869, he ran again and won by a clear margin in the same kind of angry, brawling campaign. But two years later the alliance of Anglos and *ricos* was determined not to let Colonel Chaves and his Spanish-speaking lower-class constituency prevail, and violence—climaxed by the "Mesilla Riots," in which most of the nine dead and 50 wounded were followers of Chaves—punctuated the election. Chaves lost.

While he was unable to win in the territory-wide Congressional campaigns, Chaves still had his loyal local supporters and he was reelected consistently to the Territorial Senate for 12 years, leading the fight against Anglo-American bossism and seeking to destroy the "Santa Fe Ring."

He also sought and achieved the post of first Superintendent of Public Instruction for the Territory of New Mexico, and from the start set out to secure Federal funds to distribute throughout the Territory to insure equal financing for all the schools.

In 1914, Colonel Chaves was murdered. But his defense of the Spanish-speaking *pobres* against the Anglo-*rico* alliance was carried on by others, and the "Santa Fe Ring" was ultimately defeated.

DENNIS CHAVEZ
U.S. Senator from New Mexico

An eighth grade dropout, in 1901, Dionisio Chávez, one of eight children in an impoverished Spanish household, got a job driving a grocery wagon. Exposed for the first time to people from many cultural backgrounds, he came to prefer the Anglo to the Spanish way of life, changed his first name to Dennis, and joined the Democratic Party because his hero was the party's founder, Thomas Jefferson, about whom he read at every opportunity during long evenings in the public library after his day's work was done.

New Mexico was finally admitted to the Union in 1912, and Dennis was chosen by the State's Senator, A. A. Jones, to serve as his Spanish interpreter—the language of half of Jones' constituents—in his successful 1916 campaign. As a reward, Jones was able to get Dennis appointed to a clerkship in the United States Senate. In 1936, Dennis was, himself, elected to the United States Senate, culminating a career that started with the appointment as clerk, an event that spurred him to study for and pass a special examination that secured entrance for him into the Georgetown University Law School, despite the fact that he had never attended high school.

Dennis Chávez was awarded an LL.B. degree in 1920, at the age of 32. He returned to New Mexico, set up a law practice, entered politics, served in the New Mexico Legislature and, in 1930, was elected to the United States House of Representatives.

Chávez's appointment to the Senate in 1935 to complete the term of Bronson F. Cutting, whose election Chávez was contesting, caused a walkout by five leading liberal senators, but the New Mexico electorate made it official in 1938, and from that time on Dennis Chávez was New Mexico's Senator. He seldom spoke on the Senate floor and tried to avoid debate of any kind, but his tenure was filled with controversy.

For example, in 1938 Chávez sponsored a bill to set up a United States government radio station to compete with Fascist-Nazi broadcasts to Latin America; yet the next year he urged that the United States recognize Franco's Spain. In 1938, many of Chávez's relatives, friends, and political proteges were among 73 persons indicted in a WPA scandal (all but five were exonerated), and in 1944 Chávez voted to require labor unions, farm cooperatives, and other nonprofit, tax-exempt organizations to file financial reports with the government. In 1942, he urged that English rather than Spanish be the basic language of Puerto Rico, and the next year he urged that the Puerto Rican governor be native-born. In 1942, he voted against cloture to end the filibuster against the anti-poll tax bill, yet in 1944 he led the fight for cloture to end the filibuster against his own Fair Employment Practices bill.

Dennis Chávez, one of whose ancestors served as the first *jefe político* of Mexican New Mexico when Mexico won independence from Spain in 1821, was, like his ancestor, a transitional political figure; the only individual of Spanish descent in the Senate, he kept the road open for others of his heritage—although he could not see clearly, himself, where that road should lead.

ROBERTO WALKER CLEMENTE

Baseball Player

The "complete" ballplayer—at bat, in the field, on bases—super-star Roberto Clemente wound up his seventeenth year in the major leagues—all as a Pittsburgh Pirate—by being named the most valuable player in the 1971 World Series.

Born in Carolina, Puerto Rico, on August 18, 1934, Clemente spent only one year in the minors—1954 with Montreal in far-away Canada—and then was drafted by Pittsburgh. When he won the National League batting championship in 1961, he became the first Latin-American ever to hold such an honor. Ten years later he was still at the top, his lifetime batting average of .314 being the highest among active major league players.

Even before winning the League batting championship, Clemente was making records. In 1960 he hit safely in every game of his first World Series. His biggest year ever was 1967 when, at the age of thirty-three—a time when most ballplayers are looking for other jobs—he led the League in hits—209—and won the League batting championship with an average of .357.

In addition, he holds the Major League record by leading his League for five years in outfield assists. Twice he hit three home runs in a single game. He was selected to play in the All-Star Game ten times. His manager called him "the best player I have ever seen," and pitcher Sandy Koufax summed up his batting skills by saying, "Roberto can hit any pitch, anywhere, at any time . . . with both feet off the ground!"

In the winter of 1970–71, Roberto Clemente, the "complete" ballplayer, prepared for his eventful 1971 season by passing on his knowledge and developing new skills as manager of the San Juan club in the Puerto Rican League.

ANTONIO CORONEL

Teacher-Politician

Antonio Coronel did not start out to be a politician. Instead, he was a studious boy who left his home in Mexico in the 1830's to become a schoolteacher in the small Spanish-speaking village of Los Angeles in the sparsely settled far-northern territory called California. There was little money and even less interest in education in the sleepy settlement in those days, but young Coronel did manage to keep food in his larder and clothes on his back and to develop a reputation among the friendly Angelenos as a man of principle who would rather try to reason things out than to shoot first and regret afterward as was the growing custom.

In 1848, as news of the discovery of gold spread among the Californios, a group of some 30 Angelenos, Sonorans, and Indian servants persuaded Antonio Coronel to be the leader—a kind of informal patron—of an expedition to the gold fields to see if, indeed, there were wealth to be had. And, indeed, there was! First they traded baubles to some mountain Indians for gold nuggets, and then they persuaded the Indians to help them uncover more. Antonio came up with three pounds of gold nuggets in a single day, and by the end of the year was a wealthy man.

Heading back for another try at digging in 1849, Don Antonio first found himself using his good reputation to persuade a group of Yankees to restrain another Yankee from finishing the beating he had given a Coronel *compadre* in a barroom brawl, and then trying unsuccessfully to intercede when two Mexicans, a Frenchman, and a Chilean were flogged for an alleged but not proved five-pound gold swindle. After the flogging, the last two were stood, tied together, in a cart with a rope around their necks, and the horse was goaded into pulling out the cart to provide California's first lynching and to give the place the name of "Hangtown."

Don Antonio led his group to a remote northern gold field, but a hundred gringos told them the riverbed belonged to "Americans," not "foreigners," and the Californios, some of whom had been born in the territory while the Yankees had just arrived by boat, were persuaded by Coronel to give up gold mining rather than give up their lives trying to fight the "gringo" horde.

By 1852, Don Antonio, now a wealthy landowner and

community leader, returned to his first love, teaching. At the same time, he entered on his second career, politics, and, in the first Los Angeles municipal elections, he was chosen the city's initial Superintendent of Schools. The very next year, 1853, he was elected Mayor of Los Angeles and Chairman of the Democratic County Committee. In 1855, he succeeded his father as County Assessor.

But those were very troubled times, and Don Antonio, as Mayor, found himself accepting the help of Texas volunteers to protect the town from popular *bandido* chieftain Joaquín and later pleading for a closing of the breach between Californios and Americanos when the last of the *bandidos*, Juan Flores and Pancho Daniel, were being hunted down by Don Tomás Sánchez and General Andrés Pico in cooperation with the gringo government.

Don Antonio Coronel was a Los Angeles councilman during most of the 1860s, and he continued to be influential into the last decade of the 19th century, one of the few Spanish-Americans to adapt to the new gringo environment and still hold to his Mexican heritage. His real estate investments and the success of his new venture into grape-growing provided money that he donated willingly to political and social causes. His last and highest public office was that of State Treasurer in 1867. In 1873, he bought into the weekly *La Crónica*. In 1875, he served as director of the Spanish-American Mutual Benefit Society. He was the featured speaker at the September Sixteenth celebration of the Juárez Society in 1880. In 1881, he was advisor to the Los Angeles Centennial Committee; and one of his last public appearances was at the California Admission Day festivities in 1890.

JUAN NEPOMUCENCO CORTINA
Outlaw

Member of a prominent and well-to-do family, Juan Cortina was born near Brownsville, Texas, and grew up to help manage his family's extensive estates in the turbulent decade just before the Civil War. On July 13, 1859, a deputy sheriff arrested a servant of the Cortina family, and Cortina, asserting that the arrest was unjust and the result of "gringo arrogance," shot the deputy and released the prisoner, by that act becoming himself the target of Anglo law enforcers and anti-Mexican avengers.

The episode, however, stirred up the Mexican populace and Cortina found himself surrounded by volunteers eager to unleash their own vengeance. On the morning of September 28, Cortina's force was large enough and strong enough to raid Brownsville, release Mexican prisoners from the jail, plunder stores and shops, kill five Americans, and escape back into the countryside.

A spectacular horseman, Cortina, red-bearded and powerfully-built, crystalized the bitterness of the Mexican against the gringo. Bandit and cattle thief though he was, he waged his guerrilla war against the Anglo-Americans, posting manifestos and gaining recruits with speeches charging that the Anglos constantly sought to "blacken, deprecate, and load with insults" the Texans of Mexican descent. Called "the red robber of the Rio Grande," Cortina became a folk hero who for 15 years charged back and forth across the border, his followers shouting, *"¡Viva Cortina! ¡Viva Mexico! ¡Maten a los gringos!"* He raised the Mexican flag in Texas and the United States flag in Mexico. He asserted that "a multitude of lawyers" in Texas were robbing the Mexicans of their land. Cortina determined that they would not "possess our lands until they have fattened it with their gore."

Of him, one American said, "He had defeated the gringo and his position was impregnable. He had the Mexican flag flying in his camp and numbers were flocking to his standard. He was the champion of his race—the man who would right the wrongs of the Mexicans and drive the hated Americans to the Nueces."

But when, in 1873, the American government appealed to

Porfirio Díaz, President of Mexico, Díaz seized Cortina and made him a Mexican prisoner. Cortina's war was over, but the racial bitterness that had caused it and kept it alive lived on, intensified, after Cortina's death.

XAVIER CUGAT
Dance Band Leader

Son of the 20th century, Xavier Cugat was born on January 1, 1900, in Barcelona, Spain. When he was three years old, his family moved to Havana, Cuba, and there young Cugat studied classical music and art. A promising concert violinist, Cugat toured as supporting artist with the fabulous Enrico Caruso, but the combination of his sense of humor and his art training led him to desert the concert stage in favor of a drawing board at the Los Angeles *Times*, where he worked as a staff cartoonist. He gave up that job in 1928 because, as he said, "When someone tells you to be funny at 10:30 tomorrow morning—I can't do it, so I quit cartooning and start this little band of six men."

"This little band" played the music of Cuba and the Caribbean and was instrumental in popularizing "south-of-the-border" rhythms in the United States. As one writer put it, "In prewar days, under the influence of tropical decor and a couple of daiquiris, people developed a taste for Latin-American music." The band grew and so did "Cugie's" reputation until he was generally conceded to be America's "Rhumba King." His band played on radio, was featured in movies, and had its home stand at the Waldorf in New York City. Along with his music, Cugat continued his cartooning, drawing caricatures of co-celebrities to decorate the walls of nightclubs where he played, and illustrating several books.

In 1958, Xavier Cugat started his own club to feature his own orchestra, and called it, in his Spanish-pop tradition, "Casa Cugat."

JUSTINO DIAZ

Opera Singer

In 1963 a handsome young baritone born in Puerto Rico came to the mainland to study at the New England Conservatory of Music in Boston, and won the regional auditions sponsored by the Metropolitan Opera. In October of that year he made his Metropolitan debut as Monterone in *Rigoletto.*

For Justino Díaz, the young Puerto Rican baritone, the jump from island to the Metropolitan stage was not all that simple. It was a steady grind of study and performance, with summers at Tanglewood, testing himself against other talented young people, singing with the New England Opera Theater, with the Boston Symphony, and the Central City Opera Festival. Then more study at the highly selective Metropolitan Opera Studio.

Following his debut, Díaz sang as Figaro in *Le Nozze di Figaro,* the Grand Inquisitor in *Don Carlo,* Colline in *La Bohème,* and Mephistopheles in *Faust.* Then, in October, 1965, he made another debut, this time at Milan's famous La Scala Opera House, singing the title role in the premiere Italian performance of Menotti's *Death of the Bishop of Brindisi.*

Perhaps his greatest debut took place on September 16, 1966, when he was chosen to open New York's new Lincoln Center Metropolitan Opera House, singing the role of Antony, opposite Leontyne Price, in the world premiere of Samuel Barber's *Antony and Cleopatra.*

DAVID EGOZI

Manufacturer

A Cuban cobbler's son, David Egozi was in his mid-twenties and was the proprietor of a small but thriving leather business when, in 1959, the Cuban government confiscated his factory. Egozi and his family fled to the United States, where they found themselves almost penniless aliens in a strange land, crowded into a small unheated apartment that even in Miami Beach's climate was bleak and chill, especially compared with the spacious, comfortably furnished home they had left behind.

Father and son tried to make a go of it in the export-import business, but their limited capital and lack of experience in international sales, and the complications of customs laws and tariff regulations, kept them in constant difficulty. So, in 1961, Egozi plunged every cent he had and every cent he could borrow in small loans from relatives into the one business he and his father knew from the ground up: the shoe business.

Egozi's initial manufacturing enterprise involved just 20 men and an almost empty room. In 1971, just ten years later, the Suave Shoe Corporation, located in Hialeah, had grown to be the largest United States manufacturer of unbranded canvas shoes, supplying inventory to major brand manufacturers across the country and in South America. Estimated to be worth $40 million, Suave Shoes was set in 1971 to move its $4.5-million payroll and 1,500 employees to a new $3.3-million building in Miami Lakes Industrial Park.

Each year on January 6, to celebrate the Feast of the Epiphany, Egozi helps keep alive a gift-giving tradition that Cuba inherited from Spain, by joining with other business leaders and their companies in presenting children at Miami's Bayfront Park with presents that included 700 pairs of his shoes.

MARISOL ESCOBAR
Sculptor and Painter

Marisol (from the words for "sea and sun"—*mar y sol*) is a multi-media artist who was born in Paris, France, on May 22, 1930, of Venezuelan parents, and is now a naturalized United States citizen. Brought to Los Angeles by her father shortly after World War II, Marisol studied with Howard

Warshaw at the Jepson School there. Later she was encouraged to paint like Pierre Bonnard while at the Académie des Beaux Arts in Paris in 1949. Influenced by Yasuo Kuniyoshi at the Art Students League in New York the following year, she studied for the next three years with Hans Hofmann in New York and Provincetown.

Then, in the early 1950's, she saw a New York gallery exhibition of pre-Columbian sculpture, and, in a display of South American folk art at a friend's house, some small boxes with hand-carved painted figurines. The two forms delighted her, and she started, on her own, to make little figures in clay and wood.

"Something funny," she said, "so that I would be happier. It worked."

Indeed, it did work, and from 1957 on she was recognized as an inventive artist of genuine originality. At her first sculpture exhibit that year, *The New York Times* critic wrote that "if archeologists had found them in a South American jungle they would have aroused no surprise." *Life* magazine gave her national attention in 1958. And when the Museum of Modern Art in New York and the Albright-Knox Gallery of Buffalo both bought major pieces from a 1962 one-man exhibition at the Stable Gallery, she was effectively ensconced in her own special niche, somewhere between folk art and pop art. The Albright-Knox purchase, a piece called *The Generals*, epitomizes her work. It apparently depicts George Washington and Simón Bolívar tandem-riding a four-wheeled horse. The generals' legs are painted on its barrel-bodied sides, while the horse's legs, tail, and head are elaborately carved out of wood. A built-in transistorized phonograph supplies martial tunes, and the whole thing seems, as a *Time* art critic put it "designed to appeal to that part of the mind in which fantasy and reality seem identical."

Marisol, a friend and companion of pop art moviemaker Andy Warhol, was featured in Warhol's underground movie *The Kiss* and also in *13 Most Beautiful Girls*.

One of Marisol's most controversial episodes concerned her solicited design in an international competition to depict Father Joseph Damien, a Belgian leper missionary in Hawaii, for the United States' Capitol's Statuary Hall in Washington, D.C. The Art Commission approved her model, but it was rejected by the Hawaiian House of Representatives, "presumably because she gave the Hawaiian national hero features that showed a trace of leprosy, the disease that killed him," and a conventional, idealized depiction was selected, instead. When the Hawaiian Senate endorsed Marisol's model—after great public furor over the rejection—the House reversed its action, agreeing to "let Hawaii be judged by the 'maturity of its civilization,'" conveyed through Marisol's *Father Damien.*

JOSE ROLANDO ESPINOSA CARBALLO
Educator

Dedicated to Cuba, its culture, Cubans in exile, and their eventual return to their homeland, Dr. José Rolando Espinosa Carballo has written several books and many essays and articles in Spanish since his arrival in Miami, Florida, in 1962, all designed to increase knowledge and awareness of the Cuban heritage. Since 1964 he has also served as director and producer of programs over Radio America beamed at Cuba and bearing such messages as "The Voice of the Cuban Free Teacher" and the "Democratic School."

Born in Matanzas, Cuba, on September 20, 1925, young José went from San José de los Ramos elementary school to the Agricultural Teachers School at Matanzas and then, after a college preparatory school, to the University of Havana, where he studied Public Administration. From 1947 until 1962 he taught in elementary and secondary schools and at the university while continuing to study and achieving, by 1956, doctorates in both law and education. From 1959–61 he was president of the National Collegium of Doctors in Education and a member of the executive of

the National Collegium of Doctors in Law, both in Cuba.
Viewing communism as a destructive force to all of education in Cuba, Dr. Espinosa continued as president of the
National Collegium of Doctors in Education in Exile from
his new headquarters in Miami in 1962.

Widely traveled in Central and South America, Dr. Espinosa was a member of the Cuban delegation to the Interam-
erican Association of Education from 1965–71 and Secretary of Exterior Relations for the Cuban Teachers in Exile
from 1962–66. In addition to his Radio America Broadcasts,
Dr. Espinosa directed and produced a weekly "Cuban
School" in Miami from 1965–67, and in 1971 directed another weekly program, "History, Art and Culture."

Since 1966 he has been an interviewer at the Church
World Service Cuban Refugee Center in Miami and a pro-
fessor in the University of Miami's Division of Continuing
Education.

EULALIA de CALLIS FAGES
Governor's Lady

Born into a wealthy and aristocratic family in the northern
Spanish province of Catalonia, Eulalia de Callis succumbed
to the blandishments of the fiery and dashing Captain Pedro
Fages—another Catalonian of impeccable antecedents, who
had returned to Spain after being in command of the remote
Spanish outpost known as Alta California between 1770 and
1774—and became Doña Eulalia Fages.

But her husband had adventure in his blood.

As a lieutenant, Fages had been leader of the small but
remarkably sturdy detachment of Catalonian soldiers who
had been dispatched from mainland Mexico to the Baja Península in 1768 and then had struggled up the Baja. At Loreto, about one-third of the distance north along the Gulf of
California, they had joined the de Portolá party, which included Father Junípero Serra, as part of the first land expedition to Alta California. Arriving at San Diego on July 1,

1769, the expedition took part in the founding of that initial settlement in Alta California, then went on to found Monterey, 400 miles further up the coast. Subsequently put in charge, on the departure of de Portolá a year later, Fages was responsible for the territory from San Diego north, with a force of just 43 soldiers and the constant opposition of the clergy under Father Serra and the jealousy of his subordinate, Captain Fernando de Rivera y Moncada, who had led another detachment up the Baja Península and had also been at the founding of San Diego. Fages had given up his Alta California post and returned to Spain only when Serra succeeded in having him ousted and replaced by de Rivera, and he was not ready to settle down comfortably to spend the rest of his life in Catalonia squiring his wife to the social affairs she loved so much. So when, in 1782, he was offered the opportunity to return to Alta California—this time with the official title of "Governor"—there was dissension in the Fages household.

"I won't go to that forsaken, barbarous place on the other side of the world!" Doña Eulalia stormed. "Your place is with me and your son, Pedro, here."

"My place is where I can best serve my King and my Church," Don Pedro told her, "and your place and small Pedro's is with me!"

But Doña Eulalia would not leave Catalonia, and Don Pedro would not relinquish his post in Alta California, so she stayed and he left. And then when he was gone, she decided to follow him, but not until she had thoroughly rejected the pleas he made in several letters. In May 1782, she arrived in Loreto and was reunited with her husband. Then she began her royal progress northward to the capitol city of Monterey. The journey—which had only taken five months under the most difficult conditions on the original march by her husband and de Portolá a dozen years before—lasted from July 1782 until January 1783, with receptions in her honor at every cluster of missionaries, soldiers, settlers, and Indian huts. After all, Doña Eulalia was the wife of the Governor and the very first lady of rank and social standing ever to visit the province! And she played her role in regal fashion, relishing every gallant bow, every wondering stare, every lavish compliment.

But Doña Eulalia was shocked by the naked Indians and the ragged, undernourished Europeans. With sweeping largess she bestowed upon all various items of Spanish finery from her wardrobe and from her husband's.

"Go right ahead, my dear," Governor Fages encouraged her. "Give away all our clothes. But then we will be the naked ones, for there are no shops in Alta California!"

Governor Fages had been renowned for his verbal battles with Serra and de Rivera and others, but Doña Eulalia's renown soon surpassed his. During the year following the birth of their daughter on August 3, 1784, she constantly harassed her husband with demands to be sent back to New Spain with their children. When Fages refused, she refused to let him into her apartment. When three months of that treatment did not get her on her way from Monterey, she rushed out into the street in February 1785, and accused the Governor—at the top of her voice—of committing adultery with a servant girl.

"A divorce," she demanded. "I want a divorce!"

Told that there were no grounds for divorce, she still refused to make up with her husband.

"I would go to the *infierno* rather than go to that man again," she insisted.

Governor Fages, whose duties took him to distant posts, was concerned about the slight protection his soldiers could give his lady, and he asked the padres at Mission San Carlos to give her sanctuary. But she would not go with them, and, instead, locked herself and her children once again in her room. This time Don Pedro exploded. He broke down the door and threatened to tie her up and carry her off to the Mission, whereupon she meekly went along and waited until the Governor was out of sight before systematically breaking up the routine of the Mission and interrupting the services of the Church. Frustrated friars even tried threats of flogging and hinted of putting her in chains, but she disdainfully ignored them.

However, when the Governor returned in September, Doña Eulalia quietly returned also, and for five years assisted him as he brought Alta California from its frontier state to the beginning of the semi-stable romantic period of the great *ranchos* and *haciendas* before commerce and gold instigated the Anglo invasion.

Doña Eulalia ultimately succeeded in wooing Governor Fages away from Alta California, but not all the way back to Spain. In 1790, the Governor asked to be relieved of his post, and Doña Eulalia and the children preceded him to Mexico City, where she continued her role as the gracious Governor's lady until Fages's death in 1796.

JOSE VICENTE FERRER

Actor, Director, Producer

Oscar-winner José Ferrer was born in Santurce, Puerto Rico, on January 8, 1912. His father was a lawyer and was able to send Ferrer to Princeton University, from which he graduated in 1933. Conceded to be one of the outstanding stage, screen, and television actors of our time, Ferrer made his professional debut in *The Periwinkle*, a melodrama staged on a showboat that made one-night stopovers during the summer of 1934 on Long Island Sound.

Perhaps the most famous of José Ferrer's roles was that of Cyrano de Bergerac, for which he received the Tony Award for his 1947 stage performance and the Oscar for the 1950 movie of the same play, plus high critical acclaim for 1949 and 1953 television adaptations. Other memorable stage roles were Iago in the Paul Robeson production of *Othello*, and Jim Downs, the lead, in *The Shrike*, which he also produced and directed and for which he received a directorial Tony in 1952, as well as the Donaldson Award for acting and directing.

Ferrer's first professional directorial assignment was for Princeton University's Triangle Club. The show was *Fol-de-Rol*, the club's annual musical production, which was so successful that it went on tour. On Broadway, Ferrer directed *The Fourposter, My Three Angels*, and *The Andersonville Trial*, among a host of other lesser-known works. He produced and directed *Stalag 17, Strange Fruit*, and *Edwin Booth*, in which he played the title role. As general director of the New York City Theatre Company at New York City Center, he acted in a program of four one-act plays by Chekhov, starred in *Volpone*, directed and acted in four one-act Eugene O'Neill plays, portrayed *Richard III*, and romped through *Charley's Aunt*.

José Ferrer's contributions to the American theatre have been recognized not only by professional citations but also by the awarding of an honorary Master's degree from Princeton University, and honorary doctorates from Bradley University and the University of Puerto Rico.

ERNESTO GALARZA

Social Scientist

Born in Tepic, Nayarit, Mexico, in 1905, Ernesto Galarza, who became the United States' outstanding authority on migrant labor and Mexican immigration, started his career as an immigrant migrant farm worker.

Stooped over under the blazing sun, hot dust boiling up from the dry soil which had been wounded by the stab of his hoe as he chopped weeds along the endless rows of farm after farm, young Galarza endured dirt, discomfort, and deprivation so that he could go to school, study, and someday rise up out of the fields and lift others up with him. Between seasons in the vegetable fields, he attended Lincoln Elementary School in Sacramento, California, puzzling out the English language, geography, and Anglo history—with a little about Columbus and the conquistadores thrown in.

Later there were the fruit trees and the grape arbors as Galarza worked his way through Sacramento High School. And there were cannery jobs that paid better than field work while he attended Occidental College. Galarza had made it —he had risen up out of the fields. Now, as he started work on a master's degree at Stanford University, he could earn his living as a tutor in languages and history. And then there was Columbia University and a Ph.D., with an assignment as research assistant for the Foreign Policy Association to provide bread and board.

Galarza, having spent so many years trudging the weary traditional educational treadmill, experimented with new approaches to personal freedom for students as co-director of a private Long Island progressive elementary school. But his major work was seeking to identify and understand the problems of the immigrant worker and then to do something about them. In this role some of his principal assignments were as Chief of the Division of Labor and Social Information, Pan-American Union; Director of Research and Education for the National Agricultural Workers Union, AFL-CIO; and as consultant to the Bolivian Government, the National Farmers Union, and the Ford Foundation.

FABIOLA C. de BACA GILBERT

Home Economist

The Cabeza de Baca and Delgado families first entered New Mexico in the 17th century. As a girl in the 20th century, Fabiola C. de Baca absorbed the customs, culinary knowledge, and love of the land which her ancestors had brought with them and developed over the years. She also became fluent in two Pueblo Indian dialects as well as Spanish and English; and, as a college student, she enriched her background in Spanish culture during a year's study at Centro de Estudios Históricos in Madrid, Spain. She received her first teaching assignment in 1916, when she was just out of high school, and utilized all of her free time during the next five years to achieve her baccalaureate degree in pedagogy from Highlands University, Las Vegas, New Mexico, in 1921. Then, in 1927, after 11 years of teaching, Fabiola C. de Baca Gilbert returned to school as a student in the Home Economics Department of New Mexico A and M College, receiving her Bachelor of Science degree in 1927.

As Home Demonstration Agent-at-Large for the New Mexico Extension Service, Mrs. Gilbert put a pressure cooker in her car and penetrated remote rural areas to teach Spanish-speaking and Indian families basic principles of scientific food preparation. For 20 years she wrote a weekly homemakers' column in Spanish in *El Nuevo Mexicano*, a Spanish newspaper in Santa Fe, and she made a weekly broadcast in English and Spanish on Santa Fe radio station KVSF. From her personal contacts in the homes of people in every walk of life, Mrs. Gilbert compiled a booklet of food recipes from the past as well as the present—"an amalgamation of Indian, Spanish, Mexican, and American" dishes—published as a New Mexico A and M College Extension Service Circular which, over the next 15 years, went through six editions and more than 80,000 copies.

In 1952, Mrs. Gilbert wrote her first book, *The Good Life*, creating an imaginary New Mexico family and carrying them through a year's cycle of work, play, fiestas, and everyday living into which food entered three times a day. Her second book, published by the New Mexico Press in 1954, was a history of the settlement and taming of the *llano* country, titled, *We Fed Them Cactus*.

In Santa Fe, Mrs. Gilbert played a leading role in organizing a native products market to furnish an outlet for the canned food, rugs, baskets, pottery and other handicraft made by the native women of the area, and she directed the community kitchen in which she gave weekly demonstrations of correct food preparation and conservation.

A member of the New Mexico Folklore Society, she

served as president of the New Mexico Home Demonstration Agents Association in 1944–45 and was given the National Home Demonstration Agents Distinguished Award for Meritorious Service.

At the request of the United Nations, Mrs. Gilbert went to Mexico in 1950 and started 18 demonstration centers in Tarascan Indian villages around the lake at Patzcuaro in the State of Michoacán.

In 1957, in recognition of her many outstanding contributions to New Mexico home life, Fabiola C. de Baca Gilbert was given the Superior Service Award of the United States Department of Agriculture in Washington, D.C.

CHARLES C. GOMEZ
Public Official

Of Spanish, Apache, and Navajo descent, Charles Gómez was the eighth of nine children, and the Gómez family made up a big percentage of the population of the tiny town of Valdez in southern Colorado, where he was born. The Gómez children also made up a big percentage of the school population in nearby Sopris—a larger town whose some 800 inhabitants justified educational facilities—where Charles Gómez was bussed to both elementary school and high school.

But Charles Gómez made up a very small percentage of the population of the United States Marine Corps in which he enlisted and served for three years after he graduated from high school, and his education qualified him for little more than the farm work which friends of his who had dropped out of school were doing. So when he got out of the Marine Corps, Charles Gómez made the trip each day from Valdez through Sopris to Trinidad, a few miles farther east along state highway 12, to attend junior college in the large metropolis of almost 12,000 people.

And after he received his Associate in Arts degree from

Trinidad, he enrolled full-time in Adams State College at Alamosa, Colorado, just a little more than 50 miles away, straight over the mountains, but almost twice that far by blacktop highway. When he graduated from Adams State, Gómez got a job teaching elementary school in Colorado Springs, a hundred miles straight north of Trinidad along what was to become Interstate 25.

As a teacher, Gómez wanted to design effective innovative special educational programs to insure equal educational opportunity for all school children, no matter what their cultural background or initial scholastic ability. Among other activities, he helped start the Latin American Educational Foundation and the Latin American Research and Development Agency to provide scholarships and community services to the Spanish-surnamed population of southern Colorado. And he continued his own education, commuting part-time and summers to Adams State to secure his Masters degree in School Administration.

In 1968, Charles Gómez moved out of the public schools back to a military base—Fort Carson, on the edge of Colorado Springs, where he had been teaching—and became, a year later, Fort Carson's Equal Employment Opportunity Officer. He moved again in 1970, to Denver, another 50 miles north along Interstate 25, to take up the task of Regional Federal Equal Employment Opportunity Representative, which would involve extensive travel throughout a six-state region.

Constantly widening horizons characterized Charles Gómez's career, and he wanted to provide the same experience for others. In addition to his job and his personal educational endeavors, he was active in the American G.I. Forum, the League of United Latin American Citizens, the Latin American Educational Foundation, and served as Chairman of the Civil Rights Committee of the Denver Federal Executive Board. In his mid-thirties, Charles Gómez planned in 1971 to begin working toward a degree in law.

NAZARIO ANTONIO GONZALES, JR.

City Administrator

Tucson, Arizona, has provided a home, a career, and a family focal point for Nazario Antonio Gonzales, Jr., since his birth to Mr. and Mrs. Nazario A. Gonzales, Sr., in Tucson on September 17, 1912. In Tucson, young Nazario went to grade school and high school with his brothers and sisters. In Tucson, he attended the University of Arizona for two years. And in Tucson, in the midst of the depression of the 1930s, he was married to Aida López, a Tucson girl, and dropped out of college to start earning a living and raising a family.

There was a break in Nazario Gonzales's Tucson residence when, during the war years and for a short time afterward, he entered the Federal service and traveled as far as Washington, D.C., where he worked in the Rural Electrification Administration. Closer to home, he spent one period during the decade of the 1940s as an office manager at Fort Huachuca.

But Tucson was Gonzales's goal, and he left the Federal service to become an administrative assistant in the Tucson City Manager's office and to encourage his children to complete their education and build careers for themselves. Gonzales pursued his own education by enrolling in and completing a higher accountancy correspondence course and part of the certified public accountancy training offered by La Salle Extension University of Chicago, Illinois.

In the City of Tucson administration, Gonzales moved from the City Manager's office to the office of the Parks and Recreation Director, then to the office of the Library Director, and back to the City Manager's office, his work giving him an opportunity to assist in several aspects of the growth and direction of his home city.

His two oldest daughters, Norma and Olga, married and settled down to live close by in the city of Tucson. His two sons went on to college. Nazario A. Gonzales, III, completed law school, then served as an attorney for San Francisco's Housing and Urban Development Administration and as Deputy Public Defender in Santa Clara County before entering private practice in San Jose, California. Gonzales's second son, John, received his degree in education and also moved to California, filling his role as a teacher in the town of Elsinore. The youngest daughter, Sylvia, became the family activist. Her involvement with the concerns of the Spanish-speaking people of the United States took her to Washington, D.C., and to other major cities. She was a founder of Interstate Research Association, a national Mexican-American consulting firm, and co-author of a sociological study of the Mexican-American woman.

Since Tucson was the place where he was born and educated and the place where he worked and raised a family to achieve their own individual distinctions, it was appropriate that, in 1970–1971, Nazario Antonio Gonzales, Jr., was elected president of Los Tucsonenses, a Tucson cultural organization.

RICHARD "PANCHO" GONZALES
Tennis Champion

In the summer of 1948, Richard Gonzales was a resentful, pugnacious 20-year-old son of poor Mexican immigrants who had come to Los Angeles in 1918, a grade school dropout who had finished an undistinguished two-year hitch in the Navy just the year before, and who had no skills by which he could get a job. In the face of an ultimatum by his father that he either go back to school, get a job, or leave home, he chose to leave home. And so, in the summer of 1948, he found himself on the center court at Forest Hills, New York, competing in the finals of the National Men's Tennis Championships—and winning!

Gonzales' mother had given him a fifty-cent tennis racket for Christmas when he was 12 years old. Hanging around

tennis courts, he met a boy named Charley Pate who gave
him a better tennis racket and some balls for helping on
Charley's paper route. When he was 15, Gonzales—who
had been playing in every boys' tournament he could enter
and winning occasionally through sheer power rather than
skill—was offered coaching and major tournament chances
by Perry Jones, southern California's tennis czar. But Jones's
tournaments required scholastic eligibility attested to by a
school principal. Gonzales tried to follow Jones's advice to
go back to school and gain academic acceptability, but he
could not stay interested and finally, in his sophomore year,
left school for the last time to join the Navy.

Dissatisfied with the military, and having nothing else to
do once he left home in 1946, Gonzales used a friend's ap-
plication to get into a southern California invitational tournament. There he outblasted the other competitors and
landed in the final round across the net from Jack Kramer,
National Amateur Tennis Champion of the United States.
Before Kramer settled down to business and volleyed this
young upstart off the court, Gonzales had taken a set from
the champion and won himself an all-expenses-paid Eastern
tournament tour.

Dubbed "Pancho"—a derisive nickname for any Mexican—by the sportswriters and wealthy lily-white tennis followers, Gonzales felt totally out of place anywhere except
actually on the courts, where his blistering service and his
almost unbelievable reflexes allowed him to take out his ani-
mosity on the ball and on his opponent.

In 1948, Gonzales won the title Kramer had vacated the
year before by turning professional. And then Gonzales lost
six major matches in a row. "Pancho," the "cheese champion," was even more resentful in 1949 than he had been in
1948, but he came back against Ted Schroeder to win the
Nationals again, this time in five sets. But the fact that he
and his wife ate alone in the West Side Tennis Club after his
victory and were not invited to be guests of honor at the
championship dinner, as other winners had been, did not

make him any happier or more accepting of his society-conscious tennis associates.

However, Jack Kramer, now a professional tennis champion, had no false sense of propriety. He signed up Gonzales 15 days after the Forest Hills victory to a $60,000 one-year contract for a nation-wide tour.

Kramer beat Gonzales 94 matches to 29. Gonzales was not a graceful loser. Even when Kramer retired to become tour promoter, Gonzales sued him over his contract.

But with Kramer out of active playing, Gonzales ruled the courts. For eight years, from 1954 to 1962, Gonzales beat them all, and not until he retired to concentrate on coaching did others get any of the top tournament money.

As a coach, Gonzales was even more effective than as a player, because, as W. Harcourt "Hockey" Woods, chairman of the Davis Cup Committee, put it, "There is no better analyst in the game. But most important, our kids have tremendous respect for him."

SUSAN GONZALES

Accounting Technician

Polio and typhoid fever wracked the tiny body of three-year-old Susan Gonzales and left her paralyzed from the waist down. Not many years later both her parents died and left her responsible for the four other Gonzales children. Paralyzed and orphaned, she nonetheless graduated from high school second in her class and won first prize in a national essay contest, the award providing a scholarship for her to attend Western State College in Gunnison, Colorado, where, in addition to achieving her B.A. degree, she served on the student council and as an officer of several social and scholarship groups.

After graduation, Susan Gonzales went into Federal service and, over the next 18 years, worked at such a consistently high level that in 1969 she was given an Outstanding

Performance Award and in 1971 was named one of the top
ten Outstanding Handicapped Federal Employees in the
nation. She flew to Washington, D.C., for the presentation
of the award by Mrs. Richard M. Nixon.

In her spare time, Susan Gonzales worked with under-
privileged children and visited hospital patients, her own
career demonstrating more clearly than words that a handicap is whatever a person lets it be—an insurmountable ob-
stacle or a vitalizing challenge.

HENRY BARBOSA GONZALEZ

United States Representative

Henry Barbosa's father, mayor of a small Mexican village in
the State of Durango, decided during the violent political
trouble of 1911, to leave Mexico. Crossing the Rio Grande
to settle near San Antonio, the older Barbosa González
eventually became managing editor of the Spanish-language
newspaper, *La Prensa*.

But early times were hard for the Barbosa González family, and young Henry had to go to work at the age of 10,
putting in as much as 75 hours a week to take home less
than $12. Always working part-time, Barbosa González
completed grade school, junior high, high, and junior college, all in San Antonio. Then he went to Austin to work on
an engineering degree at the University of Texas, but had to
drop out during the depression because he could not get
even part-time work near school. At St. Mary's University in
San Antonio he finally achieved both a B.A. and an LL.B.
degree and then took a job in the juvenile probation office,
eventually working up to become chief probation officer of
Bexar County and then quitting when he was refused permission to employ a Negro on an equal basis with the rest of
the staff.

After a variety of jobs—teaching English to members of a

union, serving as executive secretary of the Pan-American Progressive Association, operating a Spanish-English translation bureau for radio and television, working on a slum clearance program for the San Antonio Housing Authority, and acting as public relations counselor for an insurance company—Barbosa González was elected to the San Antonio City Council in 1953, and from that time on politics was his business.

In the Council he sponsored an ordinance to end segregation in the city's recreational facilities. Elected to the Texas Senate three years later—the first Mexican-American in 110 years to win a Senate seat—Barbosa González participated in two filibusters—one for more than 36 hours, longest in Texas history—against ten "race" bills. In 1961, he won a special election to fill the one unexpired year of resigned United States Representative Kilday's term and thereby became the first Texan of Mexican ancestry ever to serve in the United States House of Representatives. In November 1962, Barbosa González was re-elected to the House of Representatives without opposition.

In the Congress of the United States, Henry Barbosa González sponsored bills supporting adult basic education, Puerto Rican rights, a Youth Conservation Corps, benefits for farm workers, adequate housing, manpower training and development, and a minimum wage; and he was instrumental in the 1964 defeat of the long-term "bracero bill," providing government protection and subsidies for temporary workers coming from Mexico to compete with citizen Mexican-Americans for subsistence farm jobs and factory labor.

JOSE GRECO
Dancer

He was born in France, his father was Italian, and he grew up in Brooklyn, but he became famous as one of the leading

Spanish dancers of the 20th century. José Greco, whose mother was Spanish, was born on December 23, 1918, and his family moved soon after to the United States, where young Greco grew up in a multi-lingual environment. He learned to speak and think in four languages. "I like to talk Italian," he once said, "when I make love; Spanish when I do business; English when I want to relax and be myself; and French when I lie. It is so easy to lie in French; I guess that's why the diplomats use it."

Young Greco also learned to use his body to add to the communicative effectiveness of his several languages, and in New York, one of the great culture centers of the world during the time he was growing up, he could find superb instruction in the dance. And in New York's nightclubs José developed a flashing, brilliant style of dancing that could capture attention of the jaded, gin-soaked "smart set," who crowded the smoke-filled rooms, and that could be performed on the postage-stamp floors most clubs provided for their entertainers. But Greco's dancing also captured the attention of La Argentinita, one of the great Spanish flamenco dancers, and she engaged José as her partner.

La Argentinita died in 1945, and Greco journeyed to Spain to attend her funeral, to reorganize her company, and to become, in addition to the troupe's lead dancer, one of the outstanding Spanish choreographers in the world. He has designed ballets—*Polo, Sentimiento, Cana y Farruca*— but more than anything else he is associated in the popular mind with clicking castanets and heels that tap the floor so rapidly and so fiercely that someone once said of the José Greco company, "They dance as if they're awfully angry at the floor."

RALPH GUZMAN
University Professor

At the age of five, Ralph Guzmán went with his family to the United States from Moroleón, Guanajuato, Mexico, to follow the crops from farm to farm across the vast acres of the Southwest just as the great depression hit in 1929. Through the lean years, Guzmán toiled in the fields and pursued an education, finally graduating from high school and then shipping out to sea in the merchant marine at the age of 19.

He served in the Navy during World War II from 1944 to 1946, and returned to school following the war, achieving an Associate of Arts Degree from East Los Angeles Junior College, and B.A. and M.A. degrees from the University of California at Los Angeles, all in political science. While working on his degrees, Guzmán, among other activities, taught bilingual classes in United States citizenship, sponsored by the Los Angeles Community Service Organization for elderly Mexican immigrants, and served as advisor to the Mexican-American Study of Occidental College.

In 1960, Guzmán became a Research Fellow at UCLA's Falk Foundation Center for Political Research, and then from 1962 to 1965 he was in South America, first as Associate Director of the United States Peace Corps in Venezuela, and then as Director of the Peace Corps' Northern Region in the Republic of Perú. Returning to the United States in 1965, Guzmán served as Assistant Professor of Political Science at California State College at Long Beach; as Commissioner of Compensatory Education, Department of Education, State of California; and he participated in the Conference on Problems of Mexican-Americans in American Society at the Center for the Study of Democratic Institutions, Santa Barbara, California.

Since 1965, Ralph Guzmán, while serving full-time as Assistant Director, Mexican-American Study Project, UCLA, has lectured on several campuses in California, becoming Associate Professor in Politics and Community Studies at Merrill College, University of California, Santa Cruz, in 1969. He has served on advisory committees for minority affairs and manpower training for HEW, the Office of Education, HUD, the Department of Labor, and the United States Information Agency, in Washington, D.C. He was a consultant to Office of Economic Opportunity, Educational Services, Inc., and Westinghouse Learning Corporation, on problems of migrant education and community development.

Professor Guzmán's important publications include: *Escape from Poverty: A Study of the Educational Problems of Migrant Farm Workers Living in Public Housing in California's Central Valley* and *The Mexican Americans: Our Second Minority*.

ANA HERNANDEZ
Teacher

Sigourney, Iowa's, population went up one from its 2,387 on a cold day in January, 1963, when Ana Hernández—who had left Miami, Florida, that morning in 80 degree weather —arrived—with just three dollars in the pocket of her light summer coat—to teach Spanish to the young men and women of the small farming community's high school. Met at the airport in Des Moines, she was whisked by car 85 miles southeast through flat, white, desert-looking country that would next summer produce some of America's finest corn, tasseling out six to ten feet tall with ears up to a foot long and three inches in diameter. It wasn't until she stepped out into two feet of snow and felt the blast of 20-degrees-below-zero wind that Ana knew overshoes and a thick winter coat would be necessities she would have to borrow—if she could make herself understood with the help of the Spanish-American dictionary she clutched in her hand—until her first payday, when she could start buying the kind of wardrobe that would insure survival in this grim, flat land of the north.

But even before winter was ended, Ana Hernández found something beautiful in Iowa: the warm friendliness and kindness of the people of Sigourney. Born near Havana, Cuba, in 1935, Ana Hernández had not wanted to leave her Cuban schoolroom, from which she could look out and see the shimmering waters of the blue Caribbean, but finally she had decided she could not go on teaching under a regime which she opposed, and so she had come to Miami and had applied and been accepted by mail for the teaching job in Sigourney, which she had seen advertised in a Des Moines paper that had come into her hands in Florida.

Although Ana had originally planned—as do most Cuban teachers and exiled Cuban people—to return to her beloved Cuba as soon as the political climate moderated, her sojourn in Sigourney moderated her resolve. Now she wanted to remain, but because she had entered under emergency conditions, she had to go even farther north—to Canada—and re-enter under the regular immigration laws with a permanent resident's visa, in order to become a legal resident of the United States. So Ana crossed the border into Canada and then returned to Sigourney.

"This is my hometown now," she announced, a slight Iowa twang touching the edges of her English-as-a-second-language enunciation. "English is my language for speaking," she added, "but Spanish is still my language for dreaming."

FATHER WALTER JANER
Priest

As a boy in the nineteen thirties, Walter Janer commuted with his family from Puerto Rico to New York and back again as economic conditions dictated, and he grew familiar with both the hard streets of Manhattan Island and the soft paths of his other island home in the Caribbean.

As an adult, Father Janer came to Nativity Parish in New York's Lower East Side in 1952, possessed of a master's degree in biology and a teaching background in physiology and genetics. At Nativity Parish he developed the skills of carpenter, electrician, legal counselor, social worker, administrator, and beggar. As a carpenter he learned to fasten blackboards to brick walls, as an electrician to repair pin ball machines; as a legal counselor, Father Janer spent a great deal of time in Children's Court attempting to clarify misunderstandings between Spanish-speaking children and the English-speaking Court Referees; as a social worker, he would find volunteers to take care of small children whose mother had been hospitalized, he would sign papers as a witness or a reference, and he would make "referrals" of people in need to potential employers or to other welfare agencies.

Father Janer's principal tasks, however, were as administrator and beggar. The total staff of one when he began, Father Janer achieved the assignment to his parish of three Spanish-speaking sisters from Puerto Rico, another Jesuit priest, a Puerto Rican social worker, and an Irish-American athletic coach. Providing a play place for children after school, club and discussion groups for youth and adults in the evening, and counsel and assistance for anyone anytime, involved scheduling and personnel skills. From outside the Center staff, Father Janer persuaded Catholic Charities to give him the part-time services of a Puerto Rican social worker; he talked another priest into being a part-time psychiatric caseworker; and he was able to solicit the part-time volunteer services of several doctors and lawyers. In addition, he wangled the part-time use of a gymnasium on Bleeker Street, and he secured camperships for thirty-two boys in the summertime. Money to pay for operating expenses and equipment, however, could come only through donations—an annual drive at a Catholic high school in Brooklyn, bingo and raffle parties, and simply passing the hat at likely places.

"The hardest thing," Father Janer said, "is to beg, but I am learning."

Father Janer's learning—not only to beg, but to be all the other things he learned to be—contributed to the learning and living of others throughout his pastorate in Nativity Parish on the Lower East Side, where to be a priest one had to be almost everything else but what a priest is usually thought to be.

ALFONSO RAMON LOPEZ
Baseball Manager

High school gave Al López a place to develop the basic skills and knowledge that carried him to the top of his profession.

Born in Tampa, Florida, on August 20, 1905, of Spanish-speaking immigrant parents, young Alfonso attended Catholic parochial schools and, in effect, "majored in baseball" at Tampa's Jesuit High School. From that experience, he started at the bottom in professional baseball, playing initially on the Tampa team in the Class D Florida league. Working up, he eventually made it to the majors and, as with most baseball players, traveled over the years with several teams: the Brooklyn Dodgers, the Boston Braves, the Pittsburgh Pirates, and the Cleveland Indians.

A catcher, Al López was much more than a large-gloved target for his battery mates' fast balls. As one pitcher with whom he worked put it: "He nursed you, led you, worried for you—and won for you." It was this skill in handling men—as well as his thorough knowledge of baseball strategy and his ability as a player—that led him to the managerial ranks after his active playing days were over.

Managing teams in the same league with the New York Yankees in their heyday as perennial pennant winners and World Series champions was usually the route to short tempers and even shorter tenure, but, throughout, Al López was able to remain easygoing and placid and even, a couple of times, the victor over the Yankees for the league championship. His basic rule was that his players should never let down, never stop trying, no matter how great the odds against them. "They can make errors," he said, "that's okay, it's part of the game. But there's no excuse for not hustling. These fans pay good money to see a game and the least the players can do is give them their money's worth."

TRINIDAD LOPEZ, III
Pop Singer

A one-room house in a Dallas *colonia* was the childhood home of Trinidad López, III, his mother, father, four sisters, and one brother. "My mother washed clothes on the rocks in the river," he said. "My mother and father plowed fields together, just to survive. You can't imagine how hard it was." Born in that one-room home on May 15, 1937, young Trini lived in a Spanish-speaking world except at school. But his father, though impoverished financially and perpetually fatigued from long hours of toil at common laboring jobs, never ceased striving for better, more remunerative employment and never failed to find time at home for getting out his guitar and singing songs of his Spanish heritage and popular songs of the day, picked up by ear from radio, records, and movies.

When "Trini" was 11, his father bought him a guitar of his own—for $12. "Trini," following his father's example, taught himself to play and sing by listening to Frank Sinatra and Ray Charles records. In his teens he organized a combo and played for pesos in a Mexican restaurant. But though the pay was poor, the group gained experience and finally began to play in Southwestern nightclubs with an engagement at the Ci Pango in Dallas. With visions of success in their minds, the combo packed up and went to Los Angeles in 1960. But they could not get any engagements, and "Trini" found himself on his own, alone, and without prospects—until he got a chance to do a fill-in single for two weeks at Ye Little Club. Although he had never before worked by himself, he caught on immediately, and the two weeks lasted for a full year.

Other nightclubs in the area were clamoring for him, and he performed at Ciro's and P.J.'s. In 1963 Reprise Records released an album, *Trini López at P.J.'s*, that sold more than a million copies; one cut was made into a single, reaching an international audience through more than 4,500,000 sales.

A European personal appearance tour followed, and in

June 1964, he opened in New York, backed by his own 11-piece band, one member of which was his brother Jesse on the tenor saxophone. To that point "Trini" López had amassed more than half a million dollars, and he was drawing $5,000 a week from his singing, which combined rock rhythms, Spanish words, old favorites, and a personality to generate foot tapping, hand clapping, and big box office receipts.

Investments in real estate, two shopping centers, "Trini" López Guitars, and a music company helped increase and diversify his income. His father, through his own unrelenting efforts to improve himself, had become Superintendent of Maintenance at Southern Methodist University, and "Trini" added to the comfort of his family's later years by buying them a spacious, attractive house and an expensive automobile. "Trini," himself, was given the "Dallas Man of the Year Award" in 1967.

NICK LUGO
Businessman

After just two months of formal schooling, Nick Lugo had to drop out to help on the family's small farm in Puerto Rico. But no amount of effort was great enough to wrest a satisfactory living from the meager land available, and so Nick, in the depths of depression, went to New York in 1930, an undernourished, undereducated youth who finally managed to get a job mopping floors at $8 a week. To get close to food he switched to dishwashing, and later he found a really good job folding shirts in a laundry.

Working long hours, living in cramped, crowded quarters, spending as little on food as possible and almost none on recreation, Nick Lugo managed, during ten depression years, to build up a small bank account. In 1940 he went into business for himself, the only kind of business he could find that did not require a big investment in inventory or equipment: selling real estate and making travel arrangements, both services demanding long hours, a concern for the customer, attention to detail, and a knowledge of the territory; but utilizing the capital investment of others as the commercial commodity.

The time was right. The depression was over and a war economy was building up, with Puerto Ricans clamoring for travel assistance to go to New York by plane, train, or boat and then clamoring for habitation of any kind while they worked at war jobs to build a stake so they could return to their permanent homes in Puerto Rico. Through the war years and into the boom years that followed, Nick Lugo prospered and expanded. In 1970, forty years after he had arrived in New York almost penniless and totally friendless and without resources, Lugo's agency, Cophresi Travel, had 35 offices on the mainland United States and in Puerto Rico. Lugo also owned extensive real estate properties; he operated a credit firm; and, as a leader in the Puerto Rican business community, was sought after by Senators and seated immediately by headwaiters.

ANTONIO JOSE MARTINEZ
Priest

The first school and the first printing press in New Mexico— these were two of the contributions of Father Antonio José Martínez, pioneer educator and socially conscious leader of the first half of the 19th century.

Born in 1793 at a place called Abiquiu in the uplands of New Mexico, now known as the Rio Arriba country, José Martínez was given his early education by tutors and by his parents, themselves well-educated landholders. Married at the age of 19, young José entered actively into the management of the family's properties until the death of his wife and infant daughter, events that caused him to withdraw from secular life and enter a monastery at Durango, Mexico, where he studied for the priesthood. He was ordained in 1822 at the age of 29.

Serving at first in parishes in Mexico, Father Martínez determined to return to the land where he had been born, and, through competitive examinations in Mexico, he succeeded in being charged with a parish at Taos, New Mexico. There,

shortly after his arrival in 1826, he established the first territorial public co-educational school (although attempts at
public education had been made earlier, in 1811, at Las
Vegas and Santa Fe.) Father Martínez's school prospered,
drawing students seeking a general education from all over
the territory and soon expanding to include studies preparatory to the priesthood as well as to contributing a foundation for prominent participation in civic life. He named
Congressmen and other leaders among former students, and
some 20 of his students later were ordained as priests.

As early as 1830, Father Martínez was preaching and
writing on the subjects of religious freedom, tolerance of
other sects, and the necessary separation of Church and
State, radical issues in the territory and in Mexico for another third of a century.

In 1835, Father Martínez brought the first printing press
to New Mexico, printing school books, which he distributed
free throughout the territory, and establishing a newspaper,
El Crespúsculo (*The Dawn*), in whose columns he advocated
equitable distribution of land to check the exploitation of
the small farmer by the large landholder. To set a clear
example, he gave his own lands to his servants and to his relatives and devoted all of his earnings to the enlightenment
of the people of New Mexico.

Under the Mexican regime, Father Martinez served as a
deputy in several sessions of the provincial assembly, and
after New Mexico had become part of the United States in
1848, he was a member of the Territorial Legislatures of
1851, 1852, and 1853. He urged education for all of the people, and a reduction of the civil powers of the church and
clergy. He died in 1867, a poor man financially but one rich
in the regard of his people, for his lifelong efforts to break
down the barriers of ignorance and bigotry.

FRANCISCO MEDINA
Grocer

Known to his friends as "Paquín," Francisco Medina was in
his early thirties and was getting nowhere in Cuba, where

his best job was that of usher at a motion picture theatre. Discouraged and disturbed by the political turmoil in his homeland, Medina fled, in 1959, to Honduras. There the only work available was hard labor in the mahogany forests, and Medina could see no future in depleting the ancient forests, with the only visible reward being a few *centavos* for the sweat that dripped from his chin and the blisters that covered his palms.

Late in 1960, Medina and his wife finally arrived in Miami, still somehow clinging to a small stake they had saved from his ushering job in Cuba and his woodcutting work in Honduras. They invested their savings in a tiny cubicle of a grocery store in southwest Miami and worked harder than they had ever worked before just to keep going; but at least they had a business of their own, and—with long hours, careful buying and pricing, and the continuing influx of Cuban refugees to the area—they began to show a small profit, which they re-invested in more space and a larger inventory. Soon they saw an opportunity to start up in another location and then to open a second store.

Calling their stores "Caribe," the Medinas, by 1971, had expanded to a chain of the four largest Latin American-style supermarkets in Miami, with assets in excess of a quarter of a million dollars and a constantly growing Cuban clientele.

PEDRO MENENDEZ de AVILES y ALONSO de la CAMPA

Governor of Florida

A descendant of an ancient family of the Asturias, Don Pedro Menéndez was born on February 15, 1519, in the Spanish seaport town of Avilés, one of 19 children. When he was just 14 years old he ran away to join a ship's crew, and, for two years, he brawled up and down the coast in the sea war that was going on at the time between Spain and France.

On the death of his father, Menéndez was able to use his

patrimony to buy a small vessel of his own, and by the time he was 30 he had distinguished himself in the capture of corsairs and their booty. In 1554 he was named by the King as Captain-General of the India fleet, in which discipline had grown so lax that ships—those which survived the ignorance and incompetence of their captains and crews in navigation and seamanship—were easy prey to pirates and French corsairs. In appointing Menéndez, the King bypassed the *Casa de Contratación* at Seville, which had always been the office of appointment. As a result, the powerful lords of the *Casa* hounded Menéndez for the rest of his career, trying to discredit him and regain their control over the India fleet.

Menéndez performed superbly but was put to such expense and embarrassment by charges brought by the *Casa,* that he requested a change in assignment and was given command of an armada to protect the coasts of Spain and Flanders. When the war with France was concluded, King Philip appointed Menéndez Captain-General of the *Carrera de las Indias.* His conduct of treasure fleets to and from the West Indies was effective, but the *Casa* continued to prefer charges against him, and at one point succeeded in imprisoning him for 20 months.

In 18 years in the King's service, Menéndez had been home only infrequently, and, at the age of 47 he planned to retire, but decided to take one last trip to seek his son, who, as commander of a fleet from New Spain, had been wrecked off the Bermudas and not heard from since. Since King Philip wanted to rid the Florida coasts of any French colonies—which were a continuing threat to Spain's West Indies shipping even though the two countries were at peace —he appointed Menéndez Adelantado of Florida, gave him complete control over commerce between Florida and the West Indies, and all the booty from pirates he captured. Menéndez set sail from Cádiz on July 28, 1565.

Menéndez did not find his son, but on his first Florida landing, he founded St. Augustine, now the oldest city in the United States. When the French fleet under Jean Ribaut sought to attack St. Augustine but were held off by a great storm, Menéndez attacked the virtually undefended French post of Fort Caroline (on present Parris Island, South Carolina), killing 132 of the 240 French in the battle, capturing 50 women and children, and a half dozen drummers and trumpeters, and letting the rest escape, many to die in the forests and swamps.

Menéndez has frequently been castigated for this bloody battle and the "massacre" a few days later of a contingent of survivors who surrendered to him, as well as the cold-blooded killing of Ribaut and his entire company, following their surrender. Frequently the only mention of Menéndez in history books is in connection with the bloody action at Fort Caroline. But Menéndez' service to Spain and his importance in the history of the Spanish-speaking people in the United States rests securely upon his extensive exploration of the coast and interior, and on the administrative acumen he displayed in setting up Florida as the first permanent Spanish foothold on the mainland of what was to become the United States.

Recalled to Spain to build and command a great armada by which Philip proposed once and for all to secure dominance over all of Western Europe, Menéndez died at Santander on September 17, 1574, before the armada—which eventually was completed in 1588—set sail to Spain's final disaster.

JORGE MESTER

Orchestra Conductor

At the age of 36, Jorge Mester, born in Mexico City, was appointed to three key classical music positions in the United States. Already Conductor of the Louisville (Kentucky) Orchestra and the Aspen (Colorado) Music Festival, Mester became Musical Advisor and Conductor of the Kansas City Philharmonic Orchestra in 1971.

Mester's musical training was at the Juilliard School in

serve the needs of 12 American colleges and universities in Bogotá, Colombia.

In the meantime, Dr. Nava was teaching regularly at San Fernando State College, where he was Professor of History. On his return from leave for the Colombia project, he was persuaded to run for the Los Angeles School Board and was elected, despite the "experts" who said it was impossible for a Mexican-American to win. By 1971 he was President of the Board, which administers an annual budget in excess of $700 million for 650,000 pupils.

In addition to his professional roles, Dr. Julián Nava has served—among other community activities—as Founding Chairman of Mayor Yorty's Committee to Preserve the History of Los Angeles; Co-Director, NDEA Institute on the "Role of Minority Groups in U.S. History"; Member of the Community Advisory Council, UCLA; and Member of the Mexican-American Statewide Advisory Committee to the Superintendent of Instruction.

ESTEBAN OCHOA

Merchant

As a young man in Independence, Missouri, where the wagon trains and settlers outfitted for the trek across the Great Plains and mountains to the lands and riches of the West, Esteban Ochoa learned the English language and conceived of a chain of stores that would serve the swiftly multiplying caravans and settlers along the route of their passage so that they would not have to drag the weight of all their needs across the endless, dusty miles, and so that they could make up on their journey for the omissions and losses that their inexperience and travel tribulation had caused.

Born in Chihuahua, Mexico, in 1831, Ochoa came from a long line of adventurers and merchants, the first of whom in the New World had marched with Cortés when he made the initial exploration and started the first exploitation of Mexico. At the age of 28, Esteban began the establishment of his line of mercantile establishments along the Santa Fe

Trail and the development of a wide-ranging pack-train system to keep them supplied.

During the Civil War, Confederate troops moved out into Arizona Territory, and, at Tucson, seized the town and its citizens, giving Ochoa the alternative of taking an oath of allegiance to the Confederacy or of losing his headquarters and stock. Ochoa mounted his horse and rode out alone into the Apache lands, arriving eventually in Mesilla. At war's end, he busily engaged in the expansion of his freighting firm, Tully and Ochoa, whose pack trains traveled the entire Southwest and deep into Mexican territory.

In the 1870s Don Esteban Ochoa was a member of the Arizona Territorial Legislature and Mayor of Tucson. One of his major political contributions was the establishment of the first public school system in the Territory.

Although he was probably the leading citizen of Tucson at the beginning of the 1880's, the coming of the railroads destroyed his wealth and influence. The end was sudden and unanticipated. On March 25, 1880, Don Esteban rode out to the dedication ceremonies of the rails' arrival at Tucson, and presented Charles Crocker with a silver spike to be used in commemoration of the event. As one author put it, "Don Esteban was, in effect, presenting his competitor with a spike to be driven into his own coffin." The pack trains could not compete with the railroads, and Ochoa died a few years later, a ruined man.

JUAN de OÑATE

Colonizer of New Mexico

Son of a conquistator—Don Cristóbal de Oñate—and married to Doña Isabel de Tolosa, granddaughter of Cortés—who was also great-granddaughter of Montezuma—Don Juan de Oñate, early 17th-century colonizer of New Mexico was almost literally born with a golden spoon in his mouth, since his conquistador father was owner of some of the richest mines in the world at Zacatecas, Mexico. Don Juan grew up in an environment of comfort and luxury and seemed destined to spend his life quietly and productively managing his family's mines, a task he took over following his father's death.

But Oñate was not satisfied merely to be known as a wealthy man of Zacatecas. In 1595, he proposed to the Viceroy of New Spain that he be made governor of the lands north of the settled Mexican provinces, lands known since they were so referred to by Francisco de Ibarra in 1565 as *otro* or *Nuevo Méjico.* Oñate also proposed that he be given 30 leagues of land "with all the vassals thereon," a salary of 8,000 ducats a year, exemption from the crown tax for working mines, and hereditary nobility for his family. In return, Oñate agreed to equip an expedition—at his own expense—of 200 men, livestock, implements and one year's provisions.

When the Viceroy agreed to most of the terms, a number of other wealthy and powerful citizens of Mexico decided Oñate was onto something good and, when a new Viceroy took over, tried to block Don Juan's trip and governorship. Although Oñate went ahead with his plans and even moved his expedition by easy stages up to Durango and the San Bartolomé Valley at the northern fringe of the Spanish settlements, his enemies were able to get one delay after another. It was not until January 1598—four years after he had first signed the contract to settle New Mexico—that Oñate was able to get rid of the last *visitador,* or official inspector, and move up across the Conchos to the Rio Bravo. The years of supporting the expedition had taken their toll, and Don Juan was no longer as wealthy as he had been when he started, but he was still as eager as ever to see what lay in the land beyond.

On April 20, 1598, the 83 wagons and 7,000 head of cattle, horses, and sheep reached the Rio Grande, and on May 4, Oñate located a ford and crossed over into what was to become the United States. The point of crossing has been known ever since as *El Paso del Norte.*

Oñate made the first permanent settlement in New Mexico—San Francisco de los Españoles—near the present site of Santa Fe. He established an irrigation system, provided the breed stock for the initial increments of the great herds of horses that later gave the native Indians the mobility to resist for many years the incursion of the Anglos, reexplored all of the territory covered by Vásquez de Coronado, and then journeyed west to the Gulf of California and back before his enemies finally prevailed and he was forced to resign in 1607.

His tour as governor was marred by dissension among settlers and soldiers, fierce battles with the natives—particularly those of the Acoma pueblo, largest and most formidable of all the New Mexico Indian strongholds, which he virtually destroyed in 1599—and starvation when the crops failed. Oñate was able to restore health, morale, and peace to the colony between his explorations, but his huge expenditures of energy and money reduced him to poverty and despair. He returned under pressure to Mexico, where he was charged with crimes varying from failure to obey royal decrees to disrespect for the Church, mistreating the Indians, and extreme cruelty.

Found guilty on May 13, 1614, he was perpetually banished from New Mexico and fined 6,000 Castilian ducats. Although he was later pardoned, he spent the rest of his life as the mine manager he had sought not to be, working in virtual obscurity to pay off his debts. But he did not die in obscurity, because before that time Captain Don Gaspar Pérez de Villagra—a member of the original expedition—celebrated to the world Oñate's conquest and colonization of New Mexico, in an epic poem of 34 cantos, first poem written about any section of the United States, published at Alcalá, Spain, in 1610 and entitled *Historia del Nuevo Méjico.*

LUIS QUERO CHIESA
Advertising Executive

In 1937 he was a charity patient in Bellevue Hospital, and the doctor told him, "There's no use filling my office with your germs. You've only got a few months to live, anyway. You Puerto Ricans are all riddled with tuberculosis."

Luis Quero Chiesa, his body wasted from the disease that had grown out of pneumonia contracted in the damp cold of New York, told the doctor, grimly, "I'll bury you."

And in 1971 the doctor had been long forgotten, but Luis Quero Chiesa, robust and vital at the age of 60, was vice president of an international advertising-public relations firm and had just been appointed Chairman of New York City's Board of Higher Education, policy-making body for the City's 200,000-student, 22-campus City University System. Yet Quero Chiesa's own traditional academic training had ended with his graduation from high school in Ponce, Puerto Rico, in 1922.

Quero Chiesa had not started life as a charity case. His father was a successful businessman in Puerto Rico, who encouraged his son's desire to be an artist by providing him with an account in the Bank of the United States and tuition at Parsons School of Design in New York City, from which he graduated in 1932. The next year Luis married a girl he had known in Puerto Rico who was living in the same building on 110th Street that he was. This was also the year his father lost his money and the Bank of the United States failed.

Destitute, Luis tramped Manhattan's streets looking for jobs that didn't exist and sought shelter in the Library on Fifth Avenue, where he immersed himself in Puerto Rican history and culture. His wife, a dressmaker, earned whatever money they had for room and food, except for work Luis got on a WPA Art Project and a short stint as an illustrator for the Board of Education, at $86.00 a month.

When given up by the doctors at Bellevue Hospital, Quero Chiesa spent a year at an upstate sanitarium and came back cured, but with one lung almost destroyed. Starting a graphics art company, he struggled without much success, and in World War II served as a translator, becoming, at the end of the war, art director for the National War

Fund, a relief agency representing 33 organizations raising and disbursing funds for international aid. His big break came when the Fund disbanded and the 33 organizations retained him as their free-lance art director. "I worked very hard," he said, "but I did very well." Roy Blumenthal International Associates, Inc., the company which he now serves as vice president, was the outgrowth of his free-lance activity.

With success in advertising and public relations, Luis Quero Chiesa was able to expand his knowledge and concern for Puerto Rican culture developed during his depression sessions in the New York Public Library. He became President of the Institute of Puerto Rico, which sponsors lectures, exhibits, concerts, and poetry readings. He began to write short stories, many of which were used in schools in Puerto Rico. He chose Puerto Rican motifs in his paintings, shown in New York, in San Juan, Puerto Rico, and as part of a traveling exhibit of American art. He became Chairman of the Coalition of Hispanic American Peoples (CHAP), a civil rights group, and of the Puerto Rican division of the Americans-All Council of the Democratic Party.

As the first Puerto Rican member of the New York City Board of Higher Education since 1964, he helped to sponsor the City University of New York's open admissions policy. Quero Chiesa says he is dedicated to providing "the best possible education for *all* students."

ANTHONY RUDOLPH OAXACA QUINN

Motion Picture Actor

His father was Irish, his mother an Aztec, and, during the "Pancho" Villa revolution, to avoid involvement with either belligerent faction, he was smuggled out of Chihuahua, Mexico (where he had been born on April 21, 1916), in a wagonload of coal, almost choking to death on coal dust before his family reached El Paso, Texas. When Anthony was four years old, the Quinns moved to Los Angeles, and his father got a job as a cameraman in the infant Hollywood movie industry. Tony's film debut was as a juvenile Tarzan in a very early jungle film.

Anthony's father was killed in an automobile accident in 1925, when such accidents still were unusual, and nine-year-old Anthony worked at odd jobs to stay in school. A speech impediment kept him out of school plays, but he played lead saxophone in an orchestra he founded while he was still in his teens.

During the depression he bummed around the country, working as a ditch digger, cement mixer, fruit picker, cab driver, boxer, and at one point he was promoted to foreman in a mattress company. Preaching during the late 1920s at Aimee Semple McPherson's Four-Square Gospel Temple in Los Angeles had helped him overcome his speech handicap, and when he got in with the Federal Theatre Project, in the 1930s, he knew acting was his forte.

1936 launched his career on stage and screen. He burlesqued John Barrymore in Mae West's play, *Clean Beds*, and then went to a bit part as a convict in the movie, *Parole*, followed by the role of a Cheyenne Indian in Cecil B. DeMille's *The Plainsman*. Ethnic parts continued: Arab in *The Road to Morocco*; Chinese warlord in *China Sky*; Mexican-American in *Guadalcanal Diary*; Filipino guerrilla in *Back to Bataan*. Then came his great roles: *Viva Zapata*; Paul Gauguin, in *Lust for Life*; *La Strada*; *Requiem for a Heavyweight*; *Zorba the Greek*. Now he had Academy Award Oscars to use for book ends! He had an apartment in Paris, a farm in Connecticut, and a home in Pacific Palisades, California. He had a Renoir, a Degas, and a Rouault in his art collection and had one-man shows of his own paintings in national galleries. His career had demonstrated a constant drive toward self-improvement. "I don't demand security," he said. "That's the way to dissipate strength, and I'm like a guy playing a horn: there's a note I hear inside me, but I can't play it yet—someday, though, I'm going to hit that note!"

HORACIO RIVERO, JR.
Admiral, U.S. Navy

Third in a class of 441 at the U.S. Naval Academy at Annapolis, Maryland, Puerto Rican Horacio Rivero, Jr., was commissioned Ensign in the U.S. Navy on June 4, 1931. Born in Ponce, Puerto Rico, he had early in life set his sights on a Naval career, and achieved his first goal by securing one of the Puerto Rican appointments to Annapolis.

Promoted to Lieutenant, j.g., on the staff of Admiral J. M. Reeves, Commander-in-Chief of the U.S. Fleet, Rivero was made full Lieutenant in 1938 and, after study at the Naval Postgraduate School in Annapolis, went on to receive the degree of Master of Science in Engineering from the Massachusetts Institute of Technology in June, 1940. Just before World War II, Lieutenant Commander Rivero was assigned as Radar Fire Control Officer in the Bureau of Ordnance, the first person to be responsible at that level for the Navy's secret new target-finding system, which proved to be one of the crucial elements in the nation's ultimate victory at sea.

Assigned as part of the original complement of the USS *San Juan*, named after the Puerto Rican city where he had gone to high school, Lieutenant Commander Rivero controlled the after batteries of that ship in support of the landings at Guadalcanal-Tulagi, in a lone raid on the Gilbert Islands. In the battle of the Santa Cruz Islands, he shot down both land- and carrier-based Japanese aircraft, sank two Japanese patrol boats, and captured sixteen prisoners.

Reassigned as Executive Officer of the USS *Pittsburgh*, Commander Rivero was at Iwo Jima and Okinawa, in support of the first carrier raids on Tokyo. Then, on June 5, 1945, a typhoon caught the Third Fleet at sea. Torrential rains and gigantic waves pounded the ships. The *Pittsburgh* began to take water. Commander Rivero rushed below to move personnel from the damaged areas, sealing bulkheads behind them. When the bow section was wrenched from her, the *Pittsburgh* stayed afloat and, with the calming of the waters, struggled into port under its own power with the loss of not a single life. With a makeshift bow she put to sea again and crossed the entire Pacific to the United States for permanent repairs. Even the battered bow section, its compartments securely sealed, was recovered afloat and towed into Guam for salvage. For his actions in this emergency, Commander Rivero was awarded the Legion of Merit.

The war over, Captain Rivero participated in the atomic weapons tests in Eniwetock in 1948 and, after graduating from the National War College in 1953, became Assistant Chief of Staff for Operations of the Pacific Fleet. Promoted to Rear Admiral in 1956, he commanded Destroyer Flotilla One, and in 1960 became Deputy Chief of Staff for the Atlantic Fleet.

When, in October 1962, the nation found itself confronting the Russian threat of atomic missiles sighted offshore in Cuba, the Navy turned to Puerto Rican Vice Admiral Horacio Rivero, Jr., who assumed command of the Atlantic Fleet Amphibious Forces, positioning them to react swiftly and decisively, providing a powerful deterrent which, because of its very existence, was never used. For his actions in the Cuban missile crisis, Vice Admiral Rivero was awarded a Gold Star in lieu of a second Legion of Merit.

Promoted to full Admiral on July 31, 1964, he served first as Vice Chief of Naval Operations and was then detached for duty as Commander-in-Chief of the Allied Forces, Southern Europe, wearing in addition to his Legion of Merit with Gold Star and lesser combat awards and campaign ribbons, the Distinguished Service Medal, the Order of Abdon Calderón from the Republic of Ecuador, and the United Nations Service Medal.

ARMANDO M. RODRIGUEZ

Public Administrator

Highest ranking Mexican-American in the United States Office of Education, Washington, D.C., Armando Rodríguez was born in Mexico. A naturalized citizen, he served in the Army in World War II and then, with other G.I.'s, used his veteran's benefits to go to college, supplementing this income during his last two years at San Diego State with his first stipend from teaching, as a physical education instructor at the college.

On graduation, Rodríguez taught in San Diego's junior high schools while working on his Master's degree at the college. Then he was, successively, a guidance consultant, a junior high vice-principal, a junior-senior high principal, and consultant to the California State Department of Education. In 1966, Rodríguez became Chief of the Bureau of Intergroup Relations in California, and the next year he moved to Washington, D.C., to open the Mexican-American Affairs unit of the Office of Education, a unit later called the Office for Spanish-Speaking American Affairs. In December 1971, he was appointed Assistant Commissioner of Education for Regional Office Coordination.

Throughout his career in education, Rodríguez maintained active interest in a broad range of concerns, from the mentally handicapped—he was president of the San Diego Council of Exceptional Children—to athletics—he also served as A.A.U. Commissioner for Wrestling, Pacific Southwest Association, and on the National Committee for the Amateur Athletic Union. But his principal involvement in community affairs has been in such organizations as the San Diego Urban League, for which he served as Vice President; the American G.I. Forum, of which he was California State Vice Chairman; and the Bi-Cultural Council of San Diego and Tijuana. Among his publications are: "Speak Up, Chicano," "The Necessity for Bilingual Education," and "The Mexican American—Disadvantaged—Ya Basta."

ISIDORO RODRIGUEZ

Food Manufacturer

Cuban trucking magnate Isidoro Rodríguez was grossing more than $3 million a year from his transportation enterprise, and he and his wife had leisure time to enjoy the fruits of their early labors, which had resulted in what was obviously a stable, secure business with a sound future. But when, in 1960, Rodríguez decided to leave Cuba, he found he could not take his wealth and security with him; the trucking business was totally insular; both capital equipment and customers had to be left behind, and Rodríguez arrived in Miami with no money and no salable skills. The once-wealthy Rodríguez family had to subsist on $100 a month relief money: charity.

However, Rodríguez did not sit at home bemoaning his fate. Daily he trudged from factory employment office to factory employment office, seeking any kind of a job, just to get a start. But without a trade, jobs were scarce, and Rodríguez spent most of his time sitting or standing in line waiting for fruitless interviews. With the other job seekers, he patronized the mobile lunch wagons that toured the factory areas, munching dry ham sandwiches choked down with pallid Miami coffee and yearning for some familiar Latin foods.

And suddenly he realized he had a salable idea. Converting into cash the small bundle of heirloom jewelry they had managed to bring from Cuba, Rodríguez and his wife bought some secondhand pots and pans and some basic food ingredients. While Mrs. Rodríguez cooked, Isidoro talked to the operators of the lunch wagons and convinced them that since most of their clientele were Cubans, some good Cuban food would sell better than the items they were carrying. Even more convincing were the actual sales. Soon the volume had surpassed Mrs. Rodríguez's production capacity, and they had to expand.

But the idea was good enough that others got into the game, so Rodríguez took his profits and put them into a totally new enterprise: the manufacture and packaging of banana and plantain chips, a Cuban food that did not have to be sold just from mobile canteens but could be warehoused and trucked to lunch counters and grocery stores all over the country.

Starting with a small family-operated factory in 1962, Rodríguez's National Food Industries had grown by 1971 to a half-million-dollar-a-year business, with more than 50 distributors making the trade name "Mariquitas" a household word in Anglo as well as Cuban households across the entire United States.

EDWARD R. ROYBAL

United States Representative

In 1947, Los Angeles was still smoldering from the aftereffects of the racial "zoot-suit" riots of the war years and the cultural dislocations of a city suddenly become a metropolis in a country plunged abruptly from war into peace. In this environment, a group of concerned Mexican-Americans and Anglos formed a committee to try to get a Mexican-American elected to the Los Angeles City Council. Their candidate was Edward R. Roybal. He was not elected. The committee had failed.

But instead of giving up and disbanding, the committee became more firm in its purpose. As the Community Service Organization, it broadened its goals and, through voter registration drives, citizenship classes, legal rights actions, and other activities, it became a vital force in insuring representation through the democratic process of people who otherwise would not be represented.

And instead of giving up politics and dropping back into his already important role as Director of Health Education for the Los Angeles County Tuberculosis and Health Association, Edward Roybal ran again for a seat on the City Council in 1949—and this time he was elected!

Edward R. Roybal was born on February 10, 1916, in Albuquerque, New Mexico. Graduating from high school in the midst of the depression of the 1930's, he joined the Civilian Conservation Corps (CCC)—an organization created to provide food, jobs, and education for unemployed youth and to involve them in work for the public good in the process.

As a result of his CCC experience, Edward Roybal determined on a career in public service. He studied business administration at the University of California at Los Angeles and at Southwestern University, and then entered social work and health education, activities interrupted by service in the Army in World War II and changed to service through public office by his election to the Los Angeles City Council in 1949.

Re-elected to four terms, Roybal was Council President, protem, in 1961–1962. Then he became a candidate for the United States House of Representatives and was elected, taking office in January, 1963. In Congress, his major concerns have been Veterans Affairs and Foreign Relations.

GEORGE I. SANCHEZ
Professor

From a New Mexican Spanish-American heritage dating back to colonial days on both sides of his family, Jorge Isidoro Sánchez y Sánchez was born in Albuquerque on October 4, 1906. His father was a hard-rock miner who moonlighted running a poker game in a saloon. From the time Jorge was seven until he was fifteen, his family lived in the booming copper community—now a ghost town—of Jerome, Arizona. The Sánchez children scavenged copper and brass from trash dumps and abandoned mines for spending money, and spent Sunday mornings using a yardstick tipped with gum to fish money from the boardwalk cracks where it had been spilled from the pockets of drunks. They sorted rotten potatoes, eggs, fruit, and vegetables at a grocery store. Jorge used his wealth to buy a cornet, and took advantage of free music lessons at school.

"We lived the good life," Dr. Sánchez wrote later, "until the depression of the 1920s." Then the cornet came in handy as Jorge and his older brother "kept the family in beans and tortillas" playing at dances, weddings, and fiestas. Jorge added to his income as "Kid Feliz," boxing at 112 pounds—until, in a demonstration at the University of New Mexico, he zigged when he should have zagged and got knocked halfway across the gym by the 220-pound coach.

By 1934, however, George I. Sánchez had achieved his degree in Education from the University of California at Berkeley, after teaching in rural New Mexico schools while working on his B.A. at the University of New Mexico and his M.S. at the University of Texas. Only 16 when he started his first teaching assignment at Yrrisarri, a *ranchería* some 50 miles east of Albuquerque, he made the round trip once a week on horseback "across the mesa to Tijeras Canyon, up the canyon to Cedro Canyon, and up that one to the divide in the Sandia Mountains called Tiroteo (Shootout)," leaving Albuquerque at midnight and now and then building a tumbleweed or pine-needle fire "to thaw out the icicles on my horse's nostrils." A year later at San Ignacio, "better known as El Ojo Hediondo (Stinking Springs), the traveling hazards were sand, desert mesas, sand, the Rio Puerco, and more sand."

Director of the *Instituto Pedagógico Nacional* in Caracas, Venezuela, from 1937–38, Dr. Sánchez returned to teach at the University of New Mexico from 1938–40, and then moved to the University of Texas, where he has remained as Professor and Consultant in Latin-American Education. Taking time off for work in Washington, D.C., during World War II he returned as Chairman of the University of Texas' Department of the History and Philosophy of Education from 1951–59, also lecturing, consulting, and directing studies on education, language, and minority problems for colleges, universities, foundations, and state, Federal and foreign governments.

Author and editor of hundreds of articles, many books, films and reports, Dr. Sánchez has also served as a director or chairman of numerous councils and committees devoted to the problems of migrants and minorities. One of his most personally rewarding assignments was to prepare the brief for the United States Supreme Court appeal in the case of *Pete Hernández v. Texas*, in which the Texas courts had held that since Mexican-Americans were white, and whites (Anglos) served on the jury which tried and found Hernández guilty of murder, there had been no discrimination against Mexican-Americans. Dr. Sánchez had long asserted in his "class apart" theory that, in Texas, Mexican-Americans were recognized as a separate class—by the U.S. Bureau of the Census, by the public schools, by the state government, and others. The unanimous and far-reaching judgment of the Supreme Court, based on a study of Sánchez's brief and the legal brief of Carlos Cadena, a post-graduate student, held that when a sector of the community is recognized as a class apart and given differential (inferior) treatment, that class comes under the protection of the Fourteenth Amendment. Hernández was given a new trial resulting in a short sentence, most of which he had already served.

MIGUEL JOSE—JUNIPERO—SERRA

Missionary

Miguel José Serra was born on November 24, 1713, in the village of Petra, on the island of Majorca, off the east coast of Spain. At the age of 16 he entered the Franciscan order and took the name of Junípero. For the next 20 years he led the sheltered, routine life of student, teacher, and preacher, becoming a doctor of theology and a professor at the University of Palma. Then, at the age of 36, he felt the call to become a missionary and sailed from Cádiz in 1749 for New Spain. Landing first at San Juan, Puerto Rico, the ship finally made harbor at Veracruz on December 10, more than three months out of Cádiz.

For the next ten years, Serra was Father-President of the Sierra Gorda missions in northeastern Mexico, living in comparative peace and comfort at the mission of Santiago de Jalpan. At one point—in 1758—he received orders to move to the San Saba area at the northern tip of Spanish penetration in Texas, but an Indian uprising wiped out the mission before he left Santiago, so instead he found himself in the even more secure surroundings of the Franciscan College of San Fernando in Mexico City for almost another ten years.

Then, in 1768, he was appointed Father-President of the

Fernandine missions of Baja California, and in 1769—at the age of 56, after 40 years in the priesthood—Father Junípero Serra began the journey that made him probably the most famous of all of the Spanish missionaries: he joined the de Portolá party as part of the first land expedition into Alta California, and, in his role as Father-President of all the missions in the territory, he founded the mission at San Diego and the Mission of San Carlos at Monterey.

On de Portolá's departure, Serra found himself at odds with the new commander, Captain Pedro Fages, about the division of their authority, and, in 1774, he succeeded in having Fages replaced by Captain Fernando de Rivera. The new secular commander was more trouble than Fages had been, so Serra determined to have him transferred to be succeeded by Filipe de Neve in 1777. By that time, Father Serra had established missions at San Gabriel, San Fernando, San Luis Obispo, San Francisco, San Juan Capistrano, and Santa Clara; and, despite conflicts with Governor Neve that waxed even hotter than those with his predecessors—Neve wanted to found a chain of inland missions but with the authority of the friars severely limited; Serra refused to do so, and again prevailed—he went on to found two more, San José and San Buenaventura, leaving ten established missions, strong church authority, and an indelible impress of his personality as his legacy to Alta California at the time of his death at San Carlos on August 28, 1784, at the age of 71.

FELIX TIJERINA

Businessman

Founder of a successful restaurant chain and co-creator of an innovative bilingual educational program, Félix Tijerina was born in Sugar Land, Texas, of field hand Mexican immigrant parents and had only six months of formal schooling. Tijerina's father died when Félix was nine years old, and from that time until he was 13, Félix spent long days and months with his mother and four sisters chopping and picking cotton in the vast Texas fields. Then he left home for Houston, 20 miles away, and got a full-time job as a busboy in a Mexican restaurant. Because he could not read or speak English, young Tijerina was stuck in the busboy job, and so he enrolled in a six-month night course in English at the Hawthorne School in Houston. After that he studied on his own, puzzling out the basics of grammar, spelling, and vocabulary from textbooks and "menus and the labels on catchup bottles." He got a job as a waiter, and then saved, planned, and borrowed until he was able to open his first restaurant. By 1961, he had three Félix Mexican Restaurants in Houston and one in Beaumont, employing some seventy people and grossing a half million dollars a year.

Active in community affairs, Tijerina served on the board of directors of the Downtown Rotary Club, the Montrose National Bank, and the Houston Housing Authority. For four years he was president of the League of United Latin American Citizens (LULAC).

In 1956, during his first term as president of LULAC, Tijerina met with the Texas State Board of Education in Austin to try to get them to initiate a special program to teach English to Spanish-speaking children. He got nothing from the Board, but he did get one volunteer, a 17-year-old high school junior, Isabel Verver of Ganado, Texas. Tijerina agreed to pay her $25 a week if she would teach the preschool children of Ganado enough English during summer vacation so they could understand their teachers when they started first grade in September. He visited her school every two weeks, paid her, and passed out candy and fruit as rewards to the children who answered his questions in English. When Isabel's children did better in school than those who had not had their head start in English, Tijerina started nine more schools. They were now called the Little Schools of the Four Hundred, because they taught a basic vocabulary list of 400 words devised by Mrs. Elizabeth Burrus of Baytown, Texas, a friend of Tijerina's restaurant executive assistant, Tony Campos, who had been an elementary teacher in Baytown before Félix hired him.

Tijerina spent some $25,000 of his own money and cajoled $15,000 from the Gulf Oil Company, $9,000 from LULAC, and another $15,000 from businessmen and Rotarians to develop the Little Schools. He then persuaded the Texas legislature to pass a bill providing for preschool training in English, so that by 1961 the Little Schools of the Four Hundred had fulfilled their purpose and could close their doors. The State Education Agency hired more than 600 public schoolteachers to work with some 15,500 Spanish-speaking youngsters in special English classes in 136 school districts, largely because Félix Tijerina remembered how his inability to speak English had held him back in his youth and felt that it was the same lack that was holding back other Spanish-speaking youngsters and causing very high school dropout rates among Latin children.

SABINE R. ULIBARRI

University Professor

Poet, short story writer, and literary critic, Sabine Ulibarri is a native United States citizen whose creative work appears mostly in the Spanish language. Born in Tierra Amarilla, New Mexico, in 1919, Ulibarri attended public schools in that tiny town of fewer than 400 people in the high country of northern New Mexico, close to the Continental Divide. At the age of 19, Ulibarri started his teaching career in the county schools of that same upland Rio Arriba territory, and at 21 he became a teacher of teachers at El Rito Normal School, in El Rito, a Rio Arriba hamlet so small its population was not recorded in most atlases.

Thrust into World War II, Ulibarri joined the Air Force, flew 35 combat missions, and was awarded the Distinguished Flying Cross and the Air Medal with three Oak Leaf Clusters. Returning to New Mexico, Ulibarri took two degrees, B.A. and M.A., from the University, journeyed to the Coast to achieve his Ph.D. from the University of California at Los Angeles, and then came home again to the

University of New Mexico, where he eventually became a full professor of Spanish and the Spanish-American Language, Literatures and Civilization.

Though thoroughly rooted in New Mexico, Ulibarri has, during his career, toured widely in the United States and abroad, having also taught at the University of California and Colorado Western University and having lived and studied both in Mexico and in Spain. Ulibarri's home away from home, however, has been Quito, Ecuador, where he was Director of an N.D.E.A. Language Institute during the summers of 1963 and 1964 and Director of the University of New Mexico's Andean Center in 1968–69. So close did the people of Ecuador feel to Ulibarri that they named him "Distinguished Citizen of Quito" in 1964.

Two volumes of Sabine Ulibarri's poems and one volume of his literary criticism were published in Madrid, Spain. A volume of his short stories was published in Quito, Ecuador. And a volume of both poetry and short stories were published by the San Marcos Press at Cerrillos, New Mexico, in 1971. Also in 1971, Ulibarri was invited to make a lecture tour throughout Mexico by the United States Embassy.

ATILANO A. VALENCIA

Educator

With family roots reaching back to the early Hispanic-Mexican settlements in New Mexico, Atilano Valencia, as a boy in the 1930's helped his parents farm the remnants of land that his parents and grandparents had inherited from the continually diminishing holdings of their parents and grandparents. The language and cultural practices of the community and the Valencia family were very little changed from the Hispanic-Mexican language and cultural practices of their ancestors. Yet in the Albuquerque Public Schools, which Atilano attended, the language and the cultural practices were Anglo. Despite the educational difficulties presented by the English-oriented curriculum, Atilano re-

mained in school. He graduated from high school at the age
of 16 and immediately enlisted in the United States Navy,
getting in on the last years of World War II and heading the
aviation radio component on the *U.S.S. Portland*, earning 12
battle stars for his participation in naval and aerial engage-
ments in the Pacific.

Under the G.I. Bill, Valencia entered New Mexico Highlands University, where he achieved his Master's degree in
history and education. And then he went back to the public
schools, this time as a teacher and administrator determined
to do something about bilingual and bicultural education.
Valencia taught in schools in New Mexico, California, and
Colorado, and he was Director of Related Programs for
Mexican-Americans for the Southwestern Cooperative Educational Laboratory in Albuquerque. With all of his teaching and administrative activities, however, he continued his
own education. Pursuing an interest developed in the Navy,
Valencia enrolled in the Capitol Radio Engineering Institute in Washington, D.C., and, over a three-year period,
conscientiously completed the series of correspondence lessons that led to a diploma in electronics engineering technology.

Awarded a Research Associate scholarship and a Ketter-
ing Foundation scholarship, Valencia returned to the classroom as a student at Stanford University and, 17 years after
receiving his Master's degree, he was awarded a Ph.D. in
education. He had an extensive knowledge of the principles
of flexible modular scheduling, micro-teaching, and other
innovative educational strategies which he used in research
and development of educational programs for Mexican-
Americans and Indians.

Valencia, a member of the National Education Task
Force de La Raza, was appointed Assistant Dean in Mexican-American Research Programs at the University of Colorado; he has served as an advisor for the Colombian Minis-
try of Education and, at the invitation of the United States
Embassy in Mexico, as a lecturer on educational innovations

for a group of Mexican professors and administrators in Mexico City.

Education, Valencia feels, must be given top priority by American cultural groups not equally represented in the economic, political, and social areas.

VINCENTE T. XIMENES

Economist

Son of a small Texas farmer, Vincente T. Ximenes began his career as a part-time clerk in a small grocery store while he attended the Floresville (Texas) High School. Then he graduated to be a full-time clerk in the Texas Civilian Conservation Corps, the depression-born, New Deal organization designed to provide constructive work opportunities for unemployed youth. His next job was as an untrained elementary schoolteacher—Ximenes was still just a high school graduate—in Picosa, Texas, for one year, and then on to the United States Air Force, emergency-born organization designed to provide effective support to World War II ground forces by making skilled combat aviators out of untrained young men in the shortest possible time. Ximenes went through flying school, flew 50 missions in North Africa, was awarded the Distinguished Flying Cross and Air Medal, and returned to train new air cadets at San Angelo Air Base in his home state of Texas, completing his military career, in seven years, as a Major.

Ximenes had managed to get in two undergraduate semesters at the University of Texas before the war, and afterward he entered the University of New Mexico, full time, and from 1948 to 1951, managed to garner two degrees, a B.A. and M.A. in economics, becoming an economics instructor and a research economist at the University in the process, the latter being a profession he pursued for ten years until he accepted a position as Program Officer and Economist for the Agency for International Development (A.I.D.) in Quito, Ecuador, from 1961 to 1964.

In 1965, Ximenes returned to the United States to serve as Assistant to the Inspector General of the Office of Economic Opportunity, and then the next year he was Deputy Director, and chief operations officer, for the A.I.D. Mission to Panamá, after which President Lyndon B. Johnson called him back to Washington, D.C., to be Chairman of the President's Committee on Mexican-American Affairs, in which capacity he reported directly to President Johnson, conferring regularly with the President and six members of his Cabinet to determine policy on social and economic development issues in the United States. In 1967, Ximenes was nominated by the President and confirmed by the Senate for a four-year term as a member of the U.S. Equal Employment Opportunity Commission.

While in New Mexico, Ximenes founded that state's American G.I. Forum, and he served two years as National Chairman of the organization, receiving the Forum's National Leadership Award. He also was the recipient of the United Nations Human Rights Award and a Fellowship at the Race Relations Institute, Fisk University. He was Director for the Viva Johnson-Humphrey campaign, and is a Board Member of the "Reading is FUNdamental" National Advisory Board.

Following his term of service on the Equal Employment Opportunity Commission, Vincente Ximenes became Vice President of Field Operations for the National Urban Coalition.

Selected Bibliography

Following are a few of the most useful books relating to specific aspects of the history of *The Proud People*:

Early History: The West

Blackmar, Frank W. *Spanish Institutions of the Southwest*. Baltimore: John Hopkins Press, 1891.

Bolton, Herbert E. *Pageant in the Wilderness*. Salt Lake City: Utah State Historical Society, 1950.

Bolton, Herbert E. *The Spanish Borderlands*. New Haven: Yale University Press, 1921.

Bolton, Herbert E. *Wider Horizons of American History*. Notre Dame: University of Notre Dame Press, 1939.

Calvin, Ross *Sky Determines*. Albuquerque: University of New Mexico Press, 1934.

Chapman, Charles E. *A History of California: The Spanish Period*. New York: The MacMillan Company, 1936.

Farish, Thomas Edwin *History of Arizona, Vol. I*. Phoenix: Filmer Brothers Electrotype Company, 1915.

Forrest, Earle R. *Missions and Pueblos of the Old Southwest*. Cleveland: Arthur H. Clark Company, 1929.

Ghent, W. J. *The Early Far West, 1540–1850.* New York: Tudor Publishing Company, 1936.

Holmes, Maurice *From New Spain by Sea to the Californias, 1519–1668.* Glendale: The Arthur H. Clark Company, 1963.

Jameson, J. Franklin (ed.) *Original Narratives of Early American History:* Spanish Exploration in the Southwest, 1542.

Lowery, Woodbury *The Spanish Settlements within the Present Limits of the United States.* New York: Russell & Russell, Inc., 1959.

Lummis, Charles F. *The Spanish Pioneers.* Chicago: A. C. McClurg & Co., 1893.

Pitt, Leonard *The Decline of the Californios, 1846–1890.* Berkeley: University of California Press, 1966.

Priestley, Herbert Ingram *Franciscan Explorations in California.* Glendale: The Arthur H. Clark Company, 1946.

Thomas, Alfred Barnaby (Trans. & ed.) *After Coronado.* Norman: University of Oklahoma Press, 1935.

Early History: The East

Craven, Wesley Frank *The Southern Colonies in the Seventeenth Century, 1607–1689.*

Fritz, Florence *Unknown Florida.* Coral Gables: University of Miami Press, 1963.

Lanning, John Tate *The Spanish Missions of Georgia.* Chapel Hill: University of North Carolina Press, 1935.

Lockey, Joseph Byrne *East Florida, 1783–1785.* Berkeley: University of California Press, 1949.

TePaske, John Jay *The Governorship of Spanish Florida, 1700–1763.* Durham: Duke University Press, 1964.

Agricultural Contributions

Carrier, Lyman *The Beginnings of Agriculture in America.* New York: McGraw-Hill Book Company, Inc., 1923.

Kupper, Winifred *Golden Hoof.* New York: A. A. Knopf Company, 1945.

Salmon, D. E. and Ezra Carman *Sheep Industry of the United*

States. Washington: U.S.D.A., Government Printing Office, 1892.

Sandoz, Mari *The Cattlemen*. New York: Hastings House, Publishers, 1958.

Stong, Phil *Horses and Americans*. New York: Frederick A. Stokes Company, 1939.

Towne, Charles Wayland and Edward N. Wentworth *Shepherd's Empire*. Norman: University of Oklahoma Press, 1945.

Wyman, Walker D. *The Wild Horse of the West*. Lincoln: University of Nebraska Press, 1945.

Mexican-Americans

Gamio, Manuel *Mexican Immigration to the United States*. New York: Arno Press, 1930.

Grebler, Leo, Joan Moore and Ralph Guzmán *The Mexican American People*. New York: Free Press, 1970.

Madsen, William *Mexican-Americans of South Texas*. New York: Holt, Rinehart and Winston, 1964.

Manuel, Hershel T. *Spanish-speaking Children of the Southwest*. Austin: University of Texas Press, 1965.

McWilliams, Carey *North From Mexico: The Spanish-speaking People of the United States*. Philadelphia: J. B. Lippincott Company, 1949.

Nabokov, Peter *Tijerina and the Courthouse Raid*. Albuquerque: University of New Mexico Press, 1969.

Nava, Julián *Mexican Americans, Past, Present, and Future*. New York: American Book Company, 1969.

Rubel, Arthur J. *Across the Tracks in a Texas City*. Austin: University of Texas Press, 1966.

Samora, Julián (ed.) *La Raza: Forgotten Americans*. Notre Dame: University of Notre Dame Press, 1966.

Sánchez, George I. *Forgotten People, A Study of New Mexicans*. Albuquerque: University of New Mexico Press, 1940.

Servin, Manuel P. *The Mexican-Americans: An Awakening Minority*. Beverly Hills: Glencoe Press, 1970.

Steiner, Stanley *La Raza, The Mexican Americans*. New York: Harper Bros., 1970.

Tuck, Ruth *Not With The Fist.* New York: Harcourt, Brace & Co., 1946.

Vogt, Evon Z. and Ethel M. Albert (eds.) *People of Rimrock.* Cambridge: Harvard University Press, 1966.

Puerto Ricans

Chenault, Lawrence R. *The Puerto Rican Migrant in New York City.* New York: Russell & Russell, 1970.

Handlin, Oscar *The Newcomers.* Cambridge: Harvard University Press, 1959.

Mills, C. Wright, Clarence Senior and Rose Goldsen *The Puerto Rican Journey.* New York: Russell & Russell, 1967.

Padilla, Elena *Up From Puerto Rico.* New York: Columbia University Press, 1958.

Rand, Christopher *The Puerto Ricans.* New York: Oxford University Press, 1958.

Senior, Clarence *The Puerto Ricans, Strangers—Then Neighbors.* Chicago: Quadrangle Books, 1965.

General

Barron, Milton L. (ed.) *Minorities in a Changing World.* New York: Alfred A. Knopf, 1967.

Helm, June (ed.) *Spanish Speaking People in the United States.* Proceedings of the 1968 Meeting of the American Ethnological Society. Seattle: University of Washington Press, 1968.

Huthmacher, J. Joseph *A Nation of Newcomers: Ethnic Minorities in American History.* New York: Dell Publishing Co., Inc., 1967.

Kramer, Judith R. *The American Minority Community.* New York: Thomas Y. Crowell Company, 1970.

Marden, Charles F. and Gladys Meyer *Minorities in American Society.* New York: American Book Company, 1968.

Index

321